ONE YOU
ONE YEAR

365 FOR GIRLS

ONE YOU ONE YEAR

LIVE. LOVE. LEAP.

CWR

Published 2019 by CWR, Waverley Abbey House, Waverley Lane, Farnham, Surrey GU9 8EP, UK. CWR is a Registered Charity – Number 294387 and a Limited Company registered in England – Registration Number 1990308.
For a list of National Distributors, visit cwr.org.uk/distributors
Reading curriculum adapted from various issues of YP's, daily Bible reading notes for ages 11–14, a four-year rolling programme published by CWR.
Concept development, editing, design and production by CWR.
Cover image: Unsplash/Jesse Bowser
Printed in the UK by Linney.
ISBN: 978-1-78259-993-7

CONTENTS

HOW TO USE ONE YOU, ONE YEAR

1 Each day, grab your Bible and your copy of **One You, One Year** and find somewhere where you won't get distracted. Talk to God and ask Him to help you understand what He wants to show you that day.

2 Turn to the right day in **One You, One Year** and find the Bible reference. If it says John 3:16 then go to the book of John (use your Bible contents to help with this), go to chapter 3 (look for a big '3') and finally find verse 16 (shown as a tiny 16).

3 When you've read from the Bible, read everything else on the page in **One You, One Year**. Pay attention to the 'Think' points, which help you consider how what you've read affects your life, and the 'Pray' points, which help you talk with God.

BEFORE WE GET GOING...

Hello! We're so glad you're here. If you're looking to explore more of life and faith, you're in the right place.

There's not one person in the world who is the same as you. That makes you both unique and really important! You're an original – there is only One You. So take some time out of this One Year to get to know your maker. Get closer to Him and you'll see yourself grow more and more, every day.

The Bible has got so much to say to us girls about who God is and who we are. This is the stuff we really need to hear. To help you out, we've picked some great topics that we think you'll love. You can look forward to hearing all about some of the leading ladies of the Bible, the different names of God, knowing who you are, prayer and more – all with a look at some great psalms in between. It's going to be incredible!

There is only One You and here is One Year that will change your life, bring you closer to Jesus, and help you grow as a girl of faith.

MAKER OF ALL THINGS

Read: Genesis 1:1–13,31; 2:1

KEY VERSE: 'In the beginning God created the heavens and the earth.' (1:1)

Some of us have a name that seems perfect for us; for others of us, our name is nothing like us. For example, someone called Joy might be a right misery! But God is always true to His names – and He has lots of them! Let's take a closer look at the very first one...

Just four words into the Bible, we are introduced to God for the first time as 'El' (the singular of God) or 'Elohim' (the plural for God – as in God the Father, Son and Holy Spirit). 'Elohim' means 'creator'. God is the mighty powerhouse of *all* life and matter. He made the universe and everything in it – it didn't exist before He got to work on it, designing it and bringing it to life. He is the ultimate power. No one can destroy Him. By nature, God is a stunningly brilliant creator. From show-stopper sunsets to beautiful flowers, God's artwork is always out on show.

THINK Think about how much God has created. The world, the solar system, the entire universe – everything. But do you know what part of His creation He's most proud of? You!

NAMES OF GOD

ACTIVELY INVOLVED

Read: Genesis 2:1-7,18-22; 3:8-9

KEY VERSE: 'But the Lord God called to the man,
"Where are you?"' (3:9)

When God created humans, He introduced Himself as
'the Lord God'. When you see LORD all in capitals, it is
translated from the Hebrew word 'Yahweh' or 'Jehovah',
which means 'active presence' or 'life-giving one'.

God wants to create, to give life, and to be actively
involved in the lives of the people He has created. The
Lord spent time with Adam and Eve, showing them His
creation. Just imagine the fun they had! Unfortunately
their rebellion then brought death into God's creation
and destroyed their close relationship with God. But the
Lord doesn't change – even when humans messed up,
Jesus gave up His own life so that we could live and be in
relationship with Him once again. When we know Jesus,
we experience life like never before.

God is not far away; He wants to be involved in our
lives. But like Adam and Eve, sometimes we can push Him
away. To know God's presence in our lives, we need to
make Him Lord of our lives.

PRAY Lord, thank You that You want to
be close to me and give me life. I am sorry for
when I've ignored You. Thank You for sending
Jesus to die for me, so that I could have a
relationship with You. Amen.

COMPLETELY CAPABLE

Read: Genesis 17:1-22

KEY VERSE: 'I am God Almighty' (v1)

Why is a 99-year-old man rolling on the ground with laughter? Well, God told him what he'll get for his 100th birthday. And it's not a letter from the Queen.

When you and your wife are in your nineties, you hardly expect to have a baby. Abraham and Sarah were at the age for pushing zimmer frames, not prams! Years ago, God had promised Abraham and Sarah a son. But Sarah couldn't get pregnant. It's a little embarrassing being called the 'father of many' when you're childless. And it's just plain weird when you're at retirement age and God announces you'll have a baby within a year.

Abraham might not have laughed so hard if he had listened carefully to the way God introduced Himself (v1). He says He's 'El Shaddai', meaning 'God – the Enough'. One year later it's Sarah who gets the giggles (Gen. 21:6–7) when she gives birth to the son God had promised them. God is enough for the impossible to happen. God is enough for any situation. Nothing is too difficult for Him to handle.

THINK Do you ever doubt that God can do something? Are there things that you haven't talked to Him about because you think He can't help with them?

EVERLASTING ARMS

Read: Deuteronomy 33:26-27

KEY VERSE: 'The eternal God is your refuge, and underneath are the everlasting arms.' (v27)

Have you grown up with a friend who you've seen change over the years? Everything around us can be constantly shifting but God is the same yesterday, today and forever.

Here God is introduced as our 'Eternal God'. (For you keen ones, the Hebrew words for Eternal God are 'El Olam'.) It's amazing to know that God will always be around and will always be the same. Our Eternal God is pictured with 'everlasting arms'. Why? Well, God knows we need some help and so He scoops us up in His loving arms.

When God promises to forgive us and look after us, it's not just for today. It's FOREVER, because He is the 'Forever God' – it's in His nature! If you have any doubts that God loves you or cares for you, talk with Him about your fears. Let God show you that He is your Eternal God. Our moods, feelings and situations might change, but God stays the same. He'll never change His mind about loving you.

PRAY Father God, thank You for always being the same. I'm so glad that You'll always be with me and never change. Help me to know how much You love me. Amen.

EVERYTHING WE NEED

Read: Genesis 22:1–14

KEY VERSE: 'So Abraham called that place The LORD Will Provide.' (v14)

Remember Abraham, the 99-year-old laughing man we met two days ago? Well, he's not laughing this time. Because, after all that, God has now told him to sacrifice his son, Isaac.

God tested Abraham's faith in a very strange way, but He never intended that Isaac should actually be barbecued. God's not like that, and Abraham knew this. God had even promised Abraham that Isaac's family line would become a great nation. Abraham knew from experience that God always kept His promises, no matter how impossible they seemed. So he knew that God could be trusted.

When Isaac pointed out that they had brought the barbecue set but not the meat, Abraham replied that the Lord would provide. It was at the last moment that God provided a different sacrifice, sparing Isaac's life. 'Jehovah Jireh' means 'God who provides'. Abraham knew that God could be trusted to live up to His name. While God doesn't ask us to do anything like what He asked Abraham, He provides for us in every way, even providing His own Son (Jesus) as our Saviour.

THINK Think about how much God has provided for you. You might want to write a list and then praise Him for all those things.

PERFECT HEALER

Read: Exodus 15:22-27

KEY VERSE: 'for I am the LORD, who heals you.' (v26)

Have you ever been on a treasure hunt where you go from clue to clue, each one just telling you the next step? Moses and the Israelites were basically living in a treasure hunt, trusting God each step of the way.

Moses has led the Israelites out of slavery; he's guided them across the Red Sea and now they have been travelling for three days without finding drinkable water, and are about to collapse from thirst.

Interestingly, thirst was the first plague God brought on the Egyptians, turning their water source – the Nile – into blood. For the Israelites, He does the opposite, turning the bitter spring into drinkable water. God uses the moment to introduce Himself as the Lord who heals ('Jehovah Rophe' in the original Hebrew), and says that if the Israelites listen to Him and obey Him, He will not bring on them the diseases He brought on the Egyptians. He quenches their thirst, and now wants to make them completely healthy. God has power over sickness and that's why it's so important to pray when people who we know are ill.

PRAY Father, You are the great healer. I bring before You anyone that I know who is sick and ask for You to heal them and show Yourself to them. Amen.

COMMANDER-IN-CHIEF

Read: Exodus 17:8–16

KEY VERSE: 'Moses built an altar and called it The
LORD is my Banner.' (v15)

Armies in ancient times carried a banner into battle, and
during the battle the banner served as a base for the troops.

Moses' staff symbolised the authority of God. It was
used to bring plagues to Egypt and open a path through
the Red Sea. So, when the Amalekites launched their
desert attack on the Israelites in the wilderness, Moses
reached for his staff. Using his staff as a banner, Moses
held it high on a hilltop while the battle raged. While
he held the banner high (which took a little help after a
while!), the Israelites pushed back their enemies; as soon
as he dropped his hands, the Israelites were the ones
being pushed back.

Because of this, a new name for God is introduced:
'Jehovah Nissi' – the Lord is my banner. God is our base.
When we lift God up in our lives we walk in His power
and are winners. When we try to do life without God, not
only do we become tired and weak, we miss out on all the
great stuff He has planned for us!

THINK What parts of your life would
you say that God is in, and what parts would
you say that He is out of? How can you change
this so that He is in all parts?

NAMES OF GOD

HE'S GOT YOU COVERED

Read: Jeremiah 23:1-8

KEY VERSE: 'This is the name by which he will be called: The LORD Our Righteous Saviour.' (v6)

Have you ever had a big problem that you just could not fix on your own? Maybe it was something you'd done wrong, something someone else had done to you, or just a really tricky situation that you needed help with.

In Jeremiah's time, God's people were in BIG trouble. They had become as bad as they could get. Into this mess steps God, announcing Himself by a surprising new name, 'Jehovah Tsidkenu' – the Lord Our Righteousness.

God sees that people are destroying themselves and each other, and He knows that they need His help – He alone has the power to save them from their evil ways. So God tells Jeremiah that He's sending a holy King to earth – the Lord Jesus Christ – who would swap all our 'wrongness' for His complete 'rightness'. 'Being right' – as in a God-kind-of-right, completely right and good – is something that no person in the history of the world has ever been able to be, except Jesus.

Jesus is the answer to life's biggest problem: our mistakes. Because of Him, we can be forgiven and made right.

PRAY Lord Jesus, thank You for making me right. I praise You for the amazing gift that You have given me. Amen.

KEEP CALM AND TRUST GOD

Read: Judges 6:1,11–14,19–24

> **KEY VERSE:** 'So Gideon built an altar to the LORD there and called it The LORD Is Peace.' (v24)

Feeling confused, frightened or annoyed? Gideon was. His life was going in circles. Like everyone else, he kept disobeying God, then saying sorry, then returning to his old habits again. Making things worse, the Midianites raided after every harvest, stealing crops and setting fields on fire. Like the rest of the Israelites, Gideon was fed up.

It was into this situation of chaos that God revealed His name 'Jehovah Shalom' – the Lord is our Peace. Now Shalom-peace is not a nice little 'I feel relaxed' kind of peace. This kind of peace is packed with power! Shalom means safety, wellbeing and completeness. Now that's what Gideon needed. But he wasn't sure that God could deliver it. It took a staff, meat, bread and fire (work that one out! vv20–22) to convince Gideon that God was serious. But God didn't just convince Gideon what His name was – Jehovah Shalom. He also showed Gideon His name for him – 'mighty warrior' (v12). Having peace in life is all about knowing God, and knowing who we are in His eyes.

THINK What are you confused or frightened about? Do you want God to give you His 'shalom' in these situations? Ask Him!

COMPLETE CARE PACKAGE

Read: Psalm 23:1-6

KEY VERSE: 'The LORD is my shepherd' (v1)

In Bible times sheep were easy targets for wild animals and thieves. Shepherds could fight off attackers or do a runner. The good shepherds were those who protected their flocks at all costs. David spent his early years as a shepherd – caring for his sheep, even getting into combat with lions and bears to protect them. So when God introduced Himself as his shepherd, David was over the moon. What more could he want? If the Lord was caring for him, he had everything he needed. Just as he had searched for good fields for his sheep, so God would look after his needs.

David knew how freaked out sheep get by rushing water and so was relieved to know that God would lead him by still water and bring peace to his life. David had used his staff to reach out for stray sheep and keep others away from danger. So it must have been comforting to know that God would keep him on the right paths and rescue him from danger. When the Lord is your shepherd, you have everything you need.

PRAY Father, thank You for being my shepherd and always looking to do what is best for me. That's just amazing and I am so thankful to have You in my life! Amen.

LORD OF ALL

Read: Isaiah 6:1-8

KEY VERSE: 'I saw the Lord... seated on a throne' (v1)

At the time when God gave Isaiah this vision, there was a growing crisis in Israel. The people were worshipping false gods, and eventually this would bring disaster to the nation. The bloodthirsty Assyrian army were a constant threat, and God warned Isaiah that the people were about to become slaves of the Babylonians. To say the future looked grim was an understatement.

It's right here that we find another name for God. The word 'Lord' in verses 1 and 8 comes from the Hebrew word 'Adonai', meaning Lord and Master – the one who rules all things with royal majesty and power. God's encouragement to Isaiah was that while kingdoms come and go, His power is strong and everlasting.

Isaiah was completely gobsmacked by his vision. As he took in the awesome holy power of God, he realised how unholy he was in comparison. God used this understanding not to scare Isaiah silly, but to help Isaiah recognise his own sinfulness, to forgive him and get him ready to serve his Lord and Master.

THINK Sometimes we can take God's kindness for granted and forget that He is actually Lord and Master. We need to respect Him as well as be friends with Him.

UNSHAKABLE

Read: Psalm 18:1–3

KEY VERSE: 'The LORD is my rock, my fortress and my deliverer' (v2)

Have you ever heard the expression 'rock solid'? It's used to describe someone or something strong, dependable and secure. That's quite a good way to describe God, don't you think?

God is our eternal rock – unshakable, unmovable, reliable and safe. No one can take Him by surprise or defeat Him by force.

In Old Testament times a city or fortress built on a high rock was easy to defend. A man who built his house on rocky foundations instead of on sand was safe when the floods came. David, the psalm writer, described God as his rock, and he wasn't the only one that saw God that way. Joseph knew God as his rock – the one who kept him strong and steady through many trials. The prophets Samuel, Isaiah and Habakkuk all spoke of God as the rock of His people. And Christ is described as the rock that our spiritual water comes from.

Hopefully by now you can see just how much God wants to let us know that He's our rock! It's very important to Him that you know you can depend on Him.

PRAY Lord, thank You for being strong, secure and dependable. It's so comforting to know this. I want to base my life on You, my rock. Amen.

INTO HIS IMAGE

Read: Leviticus 20:6–8,22–26

KEY VERSE: 'I am the LORD, who makes you holy' (v8)

A few days ago, we looked at how Jesus makes us righteous, but what do we do with that? Once you're made righteous, should you just live as you like with a few 'forgive me' prayers thrown in? No way! God wants His people to lead lives that are amazing because they are holy — lives that show people what He is like.

'Holy' simply means 'set apart for God'. It's our way of saying, 'Lord, I want to spend my life thanking You, living for You and serving You.' It's choosing to live God's way, not our way.

But again, we can't do that by ourselves. God's ways are just too perfect for us to achieve. But don't despair! Right after giving the Jews His long list of instructions on 'how to be holy', God introduced Himself as 'Jehovah M'Kaddesh' — 'the Lord who makes you holy'. So not only did God make a way for us to be forgiven, He's now able to make us holy!

THINK God makes us into the people He wants us to be, and He never asks us to do something without helping us to do it. What do you think He is asking you to do today?

NAMES OF GOD

STUCK ON YOU

Read: Ezekiel 48:35; Revelation 21:1-4

KEY VERSE: 'THE LORD IS THERE' (Ezek. 48:35)

Have you ever seen somebody really, really upset? It's hard to know what to say when someone is feeling that way, but most of the time they just value someone being there for them.

God gave both Ezekiel and John glimpses of His future plans for us. And He introduced Himself by a new name, 'Jehovah Shammah' – the Lord is there. What a difference God makes to a place when He is there! John literally fell to the floor when he saw a vision of the place God had been preparing for those who love Him to end up in – it was beyond incredible! There was genuine, over-the-top joy – no sadness or pain, no sickness or frustration, no death. Why? Because God is there, and God's presence makes all the difference. One psalmist wrote: 'Better is one day in your courts than a thousand elsewhere' (Psa. 84:10).

The most amazing thing? God is with us, all the time! From the moment we ask Jesus to be in our hearts and to be our Lord, He never leaves us. He is always with us, protecting us, guiding us and throwing blessings our way with His awesome power.

PRAY God, Jehovah Shammah – thank You for always being there for me through thick and thin. Amen.

WHAT A NAME

Read: Matthew 1:18-21; Philippians 2:10

KEY VERSE: 'give him the name Jesus, because he will save his people from their sins.' (Matt. 1:21)

God's names are very special, each one describing what He is like. So when He introduces His Son, it's with the most precious name of all. Jesus means 'Jehovah saves'. God came to earth to save us from the separation humans caused when we first ignored Him, way back in the Garden of Eden.

We've been ignoring Him, living by our own rules ever since. But Jesus willingly chose to sacrifice Himself to rescue us, so that we could come back to our loving God and spend forever with Him. 'Jesus' is the most powerful name in existence. It's a name you can count on – a name you can call on, and you will be saved. What an incredible thing! No other world religion worships a Saviour like Jesus. If there's one thing about Him that stands out to you, let it be this: He has saved you. You've done nothing to deserve it, but He loves you that much. What an amazing God He is!

THINK Have you ever thought about what your friends believe about Jesus? Why not ask them what they think about Him? It could be a chance to tell them what He's really like.

LIGHT IT UP

Read: John 8:12

KEY VERSE: 'Jesus... said, "I am the light of the world."' (v12)

When God spoke to Moses He called Himself 'I AM' – the one who has always existed and always will exist. So when Jesus came to earth it should be no surprise to hear that He introduced Himself as 'I AM...'

Yes, only one verse to read today, but it's worth reading several times. The New Testament was written in Greek, and the Greek word for light is 'phos'. The word 'phos' is where we get words like photograph (meaning writing with light), and phosphorous (meaning glowing in the dark) from. Have you ever seen phosphorous glowing? Perhaps one day you could talk your science teacher into setting some alight. But get your goggles on – this stuff gives off such a fierce, intense light that you will probably need to shield your eyes. Jesus called Himself 'I AM' because He IS God. He described Himself as the light of the world because He is holy. His holiness is like a fierce, intense light that overpowers the darkness of our unholy world.

PRAY Lord Jesus, empty me of all darkness, cleanse me with Your forgiveness, fill me with Your Holy Spirit and help me live like a fierce light for You. Amen.

THE ONLY WAY

Read: John 10:1-10

> **KEY VERSE:** 'I am the gate. Those who come in through me will be saved.' (v9, NLT)

Jesus often referred to Himself as the good shepherd to us beloved sheep who are often making baa-d, baa-d choices. Now He explains more about what a good shepherd does and introduces Himself by a new name – our gate.

In ye good olde Bible days, shepherds herded their flocks to fields during the day and back to a sheepfold at night. The sheepfold had strong stone walls covered with thorns to put off those wanting to sneak over for a cheap leg of lamb for their Sunday roast. It also had just one entrance. But the gate was not a big iron one with padlocks – the shepherd was the gate. He would lie across the entrance to keep the sheep in and the thieves out.

Jesus introduced Himself as our gateway to safety and security for eternity. He is the one entrance by which we can know God. It's through putting our trust in Jesus that we are forgiven and become God's children. And Jesus, the good shepherd, knows us by name, cares for us and protects us.

THINK The Bible tells us that once we've entered through the gate, nothing can steal us away from God. Do you truly believe that?

NAMES OF GOD

HE REIGNS SUPREME

Read: Psalm 8:1-9

KEY VERSE: 'LORD, our Lord, how majestic is your name in all the earth!' (v1)

As we have seen, one word cannot begin to cover the awesomeness of who God is, what He is like and what He has done. When David says 'majestic' in this psalm it can also mean glorious, magnificent, mighty, powerful – words are not enough!

As David looked up at the night sky he was absolutely amazed by the power and majesty of God. The universe that God made was so big! And David felt so small and tiny compared to it. Why did God bother with human beings? That someone as big as God, who flung the stars into space, should do so much for someone as small as him really impressed David. He was star-struck by the awesome greatness and love of God.

David the king had to take his crown off to God the King of kings. The wonder of the universe made his royal title seem rather small in comparison. In absolute awe, the king praised the Lord and told Him He was majestic! Beyond-the-universe majestic! How can we respond to the glory and power and majesty of God? By PRAISING Him!

PRAY Lord, You are wonderful and absolutely incredible. I'm so impressed with all that You've made! Thank You for also choosing to make me. Amen.

ON THE GUEST LIST

Read: Psalm 98:1-9

KEY VERSE: 'Shout for joy to the LORD, all the earth' (v4)

Have you ever not been invited to something and been really upset about it? Today's worship psalm is about the whole earth being invited to something and saying, 'Yes'. It's about the whole of creation having a party, and it's not going to be a nice little polite tea-and-biscuits thing – it's going to be a MASSIVE celebration praising God.

The people who sang this song were God's people from the titchy little nation of Israel. He is their God and you might think they wouldn't want anyone else to know about Him. But here they are telling the whole world to praise God and saying that all nations are going to know Him.

Do you ever feel like Christianity is just for a few people? Maybe the people you get on with? Well, we can all feel like that sometimes, but it's a good job for us that God doesn't feel that way! He wants *everyone* to come to Him. He is preparing a party and the whole world is invited.

PRAY Lord Jesus, thank You that anyone can be a part of Your party. Please be close to my friends, and give me a chance to tell them about You. Amen.

 PSALM

ROYALTY

Read: Psalm 97:1-12

KEY VERSE: 'he guards the lives of his faithful ones and delivers them from the hand of the wicked' (v10)

When you've been for an activity — perhaps a game, performance or even some work — have you ever been really glad that you've had a certain person on your side? Having someone on our team who is really good at what they do is the biggest confidence boost.

Throughout everything, we've got God on our side. And He's really good at what He does. Whatever challenges we face, we do so with the King who is totally in charge. Just look at how powerful this psalm says He is! He has a red carpet of fire, he has a light-switch for lightning, and He's even stronger than the mountains. If there's anyone we know we're safe with, it's Him.

But sometimes it's hard to believe that God is really the King. When people in school give you a hard time for being a Christian, it's easy to feel like God's losing. Although we can't always see it with our eyes, this psalm gives us a picture of just how powerful God really is.

THINK We are on God's team but we also have other team members — other Christians. Do you meet up with your team regularly?

PSALM

THE FIRST LADY

Read: Genesis 3:1–13

> **KEY VERSE:** 'The woman said, "The snake deceived me, and I ate."' (v13)

Imagine being the very first woman ever to be created by God. Your name literally means 'the mother of all living'. You get to live in Eden – the most perfect place ever. You walk side by side with God and enjoy perfect perfection all day, every day.

But just because Eve was made for a perfect world, it doesn't mean she was perfect. God made us all human. He gave us *choice*. Eve chose to listen to the sweet-talking slitherer who convinced her to doubt God. And if we're honest, most of us probably would have done the same thing.

But here's the best thing about Eve's story – she and Adam were the first to experience God's forgiveness. Sure, the consequences of their sin meant being kicked out of paradise. But God *never* stopped loving them. Even though their relationship had changed, He never let them out of His sight. And He had a plan to win them – and us – back.

THINK Most of us find it hard to resist temptation, and the last person we would want to talk to about this is God. But He's the best person to chat with. Jesus Himself was tempted, so He is able to help us when we are tempted to go against God.

 **LEADING LADIES**

BABY TALK

Read: Genesis 18:1–15

KEY VERSE: 'Is anything too hard for the LORD? I will return... next year, and Sarah will have a son.' (v14)

Have you ever felt like other people have looked down on you and made you feel really upset because you haven't got what they've got? Here's someone who felt just like that. Sarah was too old to have children – it was a scientific fact. It just wasn't going to happen. In that culture, not being able to have children was seen as shameful – people thought it meant God didn't like you. So Sarah felt like a complete failure. But God had promised that she would be a mother, and He *always* keeps His promises.

What did Sarah make of this? Her hopes had been raised and crashed to the ground before – and now she was far too old to have children. It's no surprise that she laughs with disbelief when God says she will have a boy, is it? But God reminded her to ask herself this: 'Is anything too hard for God?' A year later Sarah was holding her newborn son, Isaac. God kept His promise and took away her doubts.

PRAY God, You are bigger than my doubts and my hurts. Please help me to let go of these things and trust in You. Amen.

DON'T LOOK BACK

Read: Genesis 19:1–3,12–17,26

KEY VERSE: 'But Lot's wife looked back, and she became a pillar of salt.' (v26)

Mrs Lot enjoyed the finer things in life. Her husband had given her a luxury lifestyle, and one she wanted to hang onto. Back in the day, Mr and Mrs Lot had thought about following God with their uncle Abraham – but they moved to Sodom instead, preferring the bright lights of the city of sin.

Sodom was full of people you wouldn't introduce to your grandparents, but there were lots of opportunities to make money there. So when the two angels warned the Lots to get out of the city fast – without even glancing back over their shoulders – Mrs Lot hadn't taken it seriously. She didn't want to leave it all, and it ended up costing her life. Money, glamour, luxury – her chase for it all meant she lost the lot.

THINK So what can we learn from Mrs Lot? A lot. Her story shows us lots about not caring so much about stuff. Yes, it's nice to have things that are precious to us. But at the end of the day, it's just *stuff*. Whatever we have, wherever we live, let's be prepared to stuff the lot of it when God asks us to leave it all behind.

LEADING LADIES

WORSHIP LEADER

Read: Exodus 15:1-6,19-21

KEY VERSE: 'Then Miriam the prophet, Aaron's sister, took a tambourine in her hand, and all the women followed her, with tambourines and dancing.' (v20)

Meet Miriam, the big sister of Moses and Aaron. She got a front row seat to see the events that led up to her people being freed from slavery. As a young girl, Miriam saved her baby brother Moses from being killed by floating him in a basket down a crocodile-infested river. It sounds bonkers — but she trusted God to save her brother's life, and He did!

Just like the rest of us, she wasn't perfect. She had doubts, and made mistakes. But today we hear about her being a worship leader.

God had just parted the seas to save the Israelites, and then sent them crashing back again to destroy their enemies. With her own eyes, Miriam had seen God do incredible and awesome things to save her. What was her reaction? To get the tambourine out and start a party!

How do you react when God does something good for you? Start your own praise party today, whenever you see God doing something great!

PRAY Lord God, thank You for saving me. You are amazing, and I love You. Help me to remember to praise You every day. Amen.

YOUNG, FREE, SINGLE...
AND RICH

Read: Numbers 27:1-7; 36:5-12

KEY VERSE: 'So Zelophehad's daughters did as the LORD commanded Moses.' (36:10)

Today we meet Noah — but no, it's not *that* Noah with the big boat and all the animals — meet a *lady* called Noah! She and her four sisters had just inherited money and the freedom to choose their own husbands. The family money usually went to the eldest son, but they didn't have a brother. So what then?

They asked Moses to find out what God wanted them to do, and he did. God said that the five girls should have their father's money. But God also said that the girls should marry within their own tribe. This would mean there would be no chance of gold-diggers trying to flirt with them for their money. Noah and her sisters knew that God knew best and so decided to trust Him. God wasn't out to ruin their fun — just to protect them from people who might hurt them. So they did what He said.

God really does have our best interests at heart. He's always the best person to get advice from.

THINK Do you ever talk to God about the money you have or the person you might like? He's the best advice-giver, so have a chat with Him about these things!

LEADING LADIES

WOMAN IN A MAN'S WORLD

Read: Judges 4:4-10,14-22; 5:1-3

KEY VERSE: 'Now Deborah, a prophet, the wife of Lappidoth, was leading Israel at that time.' (4:4)

Today we meet a no-messing woman in charge: Deborah. She makes her appearance as the top decision maker in the land and leads the Israelites into battle. This lady wasn't at all the kind of person who wanted to sit at home while the Israelites were being bullied by Sisera and his boys.

Deborah was a married woman, working in a man's world – and she gained their respect. She didn't shy away from telling the men to trust God. Deborah loved God and didn't fear speaking up for Him. She wasn't bossy, she just knew that God could help them. And when one of her men, Barak, didn't want to go into battle alone, she led the troops with him.

Attacking a well-armed group of 900 chariots with only wooden farming tools took some serious guts and a whole lot of faith. But Debs had a secret weapon – prayer. God brought the chariots to a stop so the Israelites were able to take the enemy. After all that, what did Deborah do? She led the troops in praising God.

PRAY Lord God, help me to always pray when I feel like I'm up against something. I know it's You that has the power. Amen.

FROM BITTER TO SWEET

Read: Ruth 1:1–22

KEY VERSE: '"Don't call me Naomi," she told them. "Call me Mara, because the Almighty has made my life very bitter."' (v20)

Ever felt like everything's going wrong? Naomi and Ruth were a mother and daughter in-law duo who'd been through some terrible times. Both had been widowed – so for Naomi, that meant losing her husband *and* both her sons. And she had a big question on her mind: why had God allowed her to suffer like this?

Tragedy, pain and suffering might cause us to question God's love and care for us – but He always has a plan. In Naomi's case, God was about to turn things around, big time, though her loyal daughter-in-law Ruth. Ruth stayed with Naomi and in doing so she met Boaz, the kind, generous, wealthy (and let's face it, probably rather dashing) gentleman who fell head over heels for her. A happy ending indeed!

Ruth made Naomi a grandmother as she had a son called Obed. He was the grandfather of King David. But not only that, Jesus' mother was born of this line. Ruth had stepped into Jesus' family tree!

THINK Do you feel like life has been treating you unfairly? Talk with God about this. He's in the business of turning things around!

LEADING LADIES

RELATIONSHIP GOALS

Read: Ruth 2:1–13; 3:9–13; 4:13

KEY VERSE: 'I've been told all about what you have done for your mother-in-law since the death of your husband' (2:11)

If they were a modern-day celebrity couple, they'd have been known as 'Roaz'. But what was it that brought Ruth and Boaz together?

There was obviously something about Ruth that caught Boaz's eye (2:5), but it was her character that made her the woman for him. He'd heard about her loyalty and he could see that she was working doubly hard to support Naomi – a mother-in-law she was no longer bound to, now that her first husband was dead. Boaz was impressed that Ruth wasn't flirtatious or a gold-digger. He was touched by her kindness to Naomi. And when he saw her decked out in her best dress, he was really wowed. Soon they were an item – and the rest is history!

Sometimes we miss out on what God has for us because we're trying to do things our way instead. The best place to be is right where God wants us to be. And if we're keeping our character in check and living for Him, we'll see His plans unfold in our lives.

PRAY Father God, thank You for choosing ordinary people like Ruth and Boaz to be part of Your family tree. Help me to worship You through my life. Amen.

BREAKTHROUGH

Read: 1 Samuel 1:1-28

KEY VERSE: 'So now I give him to the Lord. For his whole life he shall be given over to the LORD.' (v28)

As we discovered in the story of Sarah, being a woman in Bible times and not being able to have children was seen as the worst-case scenario – and here we are again. Meet Hannah.

Hannah was heartbroken at the sight of the empty nursery in her house, but she took her heartache straight to God. Day after day she prayed at the temple, trusting God and asking Him to give her a child.

God answered Hannah's prayers, and she soon became pregnant. Hannah's son, Samuel, became a great prophet and prayer warrior throughout his entire life.

So how did Hannah respond when she finally became a mother? Well, she knew that it was God who had answered her prayers, and to show her worship to Him, she gave Samuel over to the Lord (v28). She knew that God could be trusted to take care of Samuel.

Do you see a pattern developing with some of the women we've been looking at? Whenever they see breakthrough in their lives, they give all the glory to God.

THINK When God answers your prayers, do you remember to thank Him? Why not keep a prayer journal so you can write it down when you see a breakthrough?

SPIES

Read: Joshua 2:1-21

KEY VERSE: 'But the woman had taken the two men and hidden them.' (v4)

The Bible is full of ordinary – often very flawed – people that were used by God in amazing ways. Today, meet Rahab – the last woman on earth you'd expect to do something nice for men. Rahab's job meant she wasn't a particularly valued member of society. But in today's passage, she's nothing short of a hero.

In this case, the 'spies' were on the side of the good guys, and had been sent on their covert mission by their leader, Joshua. And when the authorities were hot on their heels, it's Rahab who saved the day by hiding them in her house.

Rahab knew that the spies were men of God, and here to fulfil God's purposes. She knew that in helping them, she was stepping into God's big plan. And by saving the spies' lives, Rahab encountered God and was saved from death.

God is in the business of using even the outcasts of society to show Himself to the world. Let's be looking for ways to show God's love to others – and keep our eyes peeled for when God is using others to speak to us!

THINK Have you ever been treated kindly by someone and been surprised by it? Could it have been God trying to tell you something?

SKINT

Read: 2 Kings 4:1-7

KEY VERSE: 'Elisha said, "Go round and ask all your neighbours for empty jars."' (v3)

What do you do when your husband has given up everything to work full-time for God, and then he dies... leaving you with two sons to bring up, no money and the debt collectors on their way to take your sons and sell them as slaves?

This poor widow didn't run away from her problems but took them to a wise and godly person who she knew would listen and give good advice – Elisha the prophet.

She didn't expect Elisha to be able to dip into his pocket and help – he was just as skint as she was – but she needed advice on how to handle her difficulties God's way. Her problems hadn't dented her faith in God.

Elisha's plan might have seemed a little bonkers, but she and her son still did just as he said. By the end of the day they had what they needed to pay off their debts. God has some incredibly inventive ways of meeting our needs when we trust Him!

When we face difficulty, talking to a trusted Christian can help us figure out what God's way out is. Try it!

PRAY Father God, I know that You have good plans for me. Thank You that You've always got my back. Amen.

LEADING LADIES

HOSPITALITY LIKE A BOSS

Read: 2 Kings 4:8–17

KEY VERSE: 'Let's make a small room on the roof and put in it a bed and a table, a chair and a lamp for him.' (v10)

Today's woman of God is doing pretty well for herself, financially speaking – and she had a heart of solid gold. (Not literally, obviously...)

This woman most likely had a nice house, but instead of throwing fancy dinner parties for Shunem's high-rollers, she and her husband served meals for cheaply dressed prophets like Elisha. Here we have a generous lady who does hospitality like an absolute boss.

In today's verses, she actually talks about building a loft extension onto her house so that Elisha has a place to stay whenever he needs one. And she's not holding back, either – she's already talking furniture!

This woman had something missing from her life: 'She has no son, and her husband is old' (v14). But God blessed her generosity, and a year later she was a mum.

Are you a welcoming person? Someone who makes others feel wanted and loved? A friend who's out to give not get? Someone who goes out of their way to help those in need?

THINK How can you show hospitality to someone today? You don't need a fancy house – think outside the box!

BIG FORGIVENESS

Read: 2 Kings 5:1-15

KEY VERSE: 'If only my master would see the prophet who is in Samaria! He would cure him of his leprosy.' (v3)

This girl seemed so insignificant that she isn't even named. She only has one line, but let's take a look at her story...

So, imagine you are this girl:

1. Naaman and his thugs have been raiding your neighbourhood for years, stealing and killing.
2. On one of their raids they kidnap you, making you work as a slave for Naaman's wife.
3. Your parents are probably dead and there is no hope of being rescued.
4. You have been brought up to love God but everyone around you worships idols.
5. You have to speak Naaman's language, Aramaic.

To cut a long story short, you have every reason to hate your boss. So when you find out he's diseased up to the eyeballs, you're smug as can be – right?

Naa-man, not this girl! She was willing to help Naaman and had faith that God would heal him. Her forgiving attitude meant Naaman the hard-man discovered who God really is. Incredible!

PRAY Lord Jesus, I don't want any of my own feelings to get in the way of reaching others with Your love. Help me to let go of my past hurts. Amen.

LEADING LADIES

BEAUTIFULLY BRAVE

Read: Esther 7:1-7

KEY VERSE: 'If I have found favour with you... spare my people — this is my request.' (v3)

Queen Esther was an absolute stunner — in fact, she'd won the king's beauty contest. But she was also secretly Jewish, at a time when it was not safe to be Jewish.

Smarmy Haman was the criminal mastermind trying to wipe all the Jews off the face of the earth. But God had a plan to save His people. He'd placed Esther in the palace just at the right time. With her uncle Mordecai operating on the outside of the palace walls, together they would prevent the Jews being killed.

But it took immense courage from Esther to pluck up the nerve to even speak to the king. He was her husband, but to approach him without being invited could be punishable by death! Out of love for her God and love for her people, Esther took the risk — and it paid off.

God puts us in situations where we can do good things for Him, but often that means being brave. If you need some courage you can always ask Him. With His help, you can handle anything!

THINK Do you find the idea of talking to your friends about Jesus scary? God might have put you in their lives to do just that! Ask Him for some courage.

A SUPER MODEL

Read: Proverbs 31:10–31

> **KEY VERSE:** 'Charm is deceptive, and beauty is fleeting; but a woman who fears the LORD is to be praised.' (v30)

As girls, we're often swamped with ideas of what we need to look like. We're told that certain things are 'must haves'. But God doesn't see things that way. He isn't interested in what you appear to be, but in who you *are*. So what really is the 'ideal woman'?

Well, this proverb says quite a lot: she's a hard worker, she provides for those around her, she gives to those in need, she is strong, she is wise and she has good relationships with her family. But most of all, the thing that *really* makes her stand out, and what makes her all these things, is her relationship with God. He comes before anything.

It's not wrong for us to want to look good, but looks fade. So make sure you're putting way more effort into loving God, building on your relationship with Him, and living out your faith – because that's what's so fabulous about this woman!

None of us are perfect. But God is most interested in our hearts. So, what are your priorities in life? Is God the top one?

PRAY Lord God, teach me to live for You. I want to put You first – I know that's best. Amen.

LEADING LADIES

NO MATTER WHAT

Read: Psalm 43:1-5

KEY VERSE: 'I will yet praise him' (v5)

If all music was lively and happy then it would not tell the whole story of what life is like (and Adele wouldn't have sold any albums). This psalm was written at a time when things had gone pear-shaped. The people had let God down big time and were now paying the price – they were frightened refugees.

The worst thing about being not-yet-perfect people is that when we make a mess of things, it's God who we feel we've let down. It's bad enough getting into trouble, but it's worse letting down someone you love!

Often when we have times like this, the last thing we want to do is pray or believe that God is doing amazing things in the world, let alone that He has incredible plans for us. All we want to do is hide.

Even so, the psalmist grabs hold of the last bit of faith he has and asks God to bring great things out of a miserable situation. God is good to us – all the time – no matter what!

THINK How are you today? If you're a bit down, ask God to help – don't try and solve everything on your own. And whether you're feeling great or rubbish, praise God today!

PSALM

THE MEANING OF LIFE

Read: 1 John 1:1–5

KEY VERSE: 'And our fellowship is with the Father and with his Son, Jesus Christ.' (v3)

We were born to know God and enjoy His friendship. Fellowship is Bible speak for friendship – close friendship. It's far more than knowing about God, it's knowing God as a person – as a friend.

So why isn't everyone enjoying God's friendship? Well, God is holy (living in light) and people are far from holy (living in darkness). Living lives that are selfish, confused or misdirected is like living in the dark: you can't clearly see the way ahead.

So how do we become friends with God? When darkness comes close to the light, it is changed into light. And to get closer to God, we need to become holy.

Only Jesus can make us holy and help us to live a life with purpose, free from sin. He died to rescue us from darkness so we could enjoy friendship with God in the light. When you make a mistake, a good friend doesn't rub it in – they rub it out. That's what God is like – He's the ultimate friend.

PRAY Lord God, it's amazing that You created me just so that I could be friends with You. Help me to have a close friendship with You for the rest of my life. Amen.

A FRIEND AT THE TOP

FRIENDS FIRST

Read: Genesis 2:15–22

KEY VERSE: 'The LORD God said, "It is not good for the man to be alone."' (v18)

Did you know that God created you so that you could be His friend? That's why He created Adam and Eve. God's original plan was for the three of them to hang out as friends in paradise.

God didn't just create Adam and then stop there – He knew that Adam would enjoy having a human friend too, and that's why He made Eve. God gives us each other as friends. None of us were created to be alone. We need friendships so that we can support and care for each other. We need each other in good times and bad. Most of all, we need God's friendship and He passionately wants to be our friend.

God, Adam and Eve were close friends until they epically failed and had to leave paradise. Ever since, it has been God's plan to restore that perfect relationship. God wants to walk with us through every area of our lives just as He did with Adam and Eve. He is the best friend you could ever have.

THINK Do you see God as your closest friend? Think about how you could share more of your day-to-day life with Him.

DARKNESS AND LIGHT

Read: 1 John 1:5-10

KEY VERSE: 'if we walk in the light, as he is in the light, we have fellowship with one another' (v7)

God says that if we keep Him out of an area of our lives, then that area is in darkness. We are not letting His light shine in that part of our lives. But why don't we want to involve God in everything we do? Is there something we want to hide because we know that it's not His way? It might be our attitudes to friends, how we spend our spare time, or how we behave towards our parents or carers.

Friendship with God means inviting His loving presence to every part of our lives. We might think that going to church is God's space and everything else is our space. But we can't enjoy a close friendship with God if we divide our lives into different compartments, like rooms in a house. These rooms could be school, home, church, friends and spare time. We might decide to let God in one room but not another. If we do that, we miss out on so much.

THINK Is God invited into all the areas of your life? Take a moment to talk to Him about this now, and remember that He loves you.

FOR REAL

Read: Matthew 11:25-30

KEY VERSE: 'Come to me, all you who are weary and burdened, and I will give you rest.' (v28)

Do you sometimes hear the words, 'Jesus loves you' but find it difficult to really believe? You might feel that you have let God down so often that He couldn't possibly still want to be friends with you. Or you might think, 'God is far too busy sorting out big world problems such as famine and wars. He's not interested in how I am finding it hard to make friends at school.'

But Jesus is really interested in you – massively! There's no one else like you. And even if you keeping making the same mistakes, you can always talk to Jesus about it and He will keep helping you to put it right. Jesus will never give up on you. He is a friend we can trust – someone we can talk to about our problems, and someone who carries them for us.

When we make a new friend, someone usually has to make the first move. But Jesus has already made that first move and all we have to do is accept His offer.

THINK Do you think that God doesn't have time for you? Well, think again! He's always interested in us. The question is, do you make time for Him?

HE'LL NEVER LET YOU DOWN

Read: 1 John 4:4-16

KEY VERSE: 'And so we know and rely on the love God has for us.' (v16)

It isn't planned but it sometimes happens — we let our friends down or they let us down. This might lead to sadness and feeling like we can't trust that friend. But God's friendship is for life and He will *never* let us down.

Some friends might not be interested in everything we do, but God really wants to get involved! He wants to give purpose and meaning to every part of our lives. Things we enjoy doing like singing, dancing, art and sports become a lot more enjoyable when we bring God into them.

God is not a spoil-sport, waiting for us to make mistakes so He can punish us. His name is love and He loves us too much to abandon us. When we get things messed up, He will put us right because He cares about us so much. He is a friend who will never — repeat, never — let you down. How do we know this? Because He gave us Jesus.

God is really interested in all our activities. How can you involve Him in what you love to do?

PRAY Dear Lord, thank You that You want what is best for me. Please help me to involve You in all areas of my life. Amen.

A FRIEND AT THE TOP

BRAND NEW

Read: 2 Corinthians 5:14–21

KEY VERSE: 'if anyone is in Christ, the new creation has come: the old has gone, the new is here!' (v17)

Have you ever seen an old photo and felt so glad that you now dress with a new, different style?

Well, when you become friends with God, your life gets completely changed and you become a new person – a new, God-filled you! God begins to give you new hope, purpose and direction for your future. Everything is different.

Think of it like clothing – Jesus gives you a brand-new, perfectly-fitting and unique outfit specially made for you. God wants us to look good – on the inside. He wants us to get kitted out and get ready to carry out a special job: showing others how much He loves them. When we feel distant from God, it might be because we're trying to put our smelly old clothes back on, forgetting what Jesus has actually put in our wardrobe for us to wear.

So do others notice the changes God has brought to your life? Or do you hide behind the old look so that you don't draw attention to Him in your life? God wants you to power-dress!

THINK Write a list of some of the great things about being in Christ, and then praise Him for it all!

PATCHWORK

Read: Mark 2:21-28

> **KEY VERSE:** 'No one sews a patch of unshrunk cloth on an old garment. Otherwise, the new piece will pull away from the old, making the tear worse.' (v21)

The change that Jesus brings to our lives is not just like changing paths – it is going in a whole new direction. If we don't try and change our ways completely then it is a bit like patching up an old pair of shrunk jeans with a piece of new unshrunk denim. The new fabric won't hold on to the old denim and the jeans will soon have holes again. It's the same with Jesus in our lives – we can't just add Him on to our existing life and hope for the best. We need to make a fresh start and put our old ways behind us.

Today's Bible reading also talks about Jesus as being the Lord of the Sabbath. God created us to take at least one day off a week to rest and spend time with Him. So try and make it a priority to put some time aside each week to get to know God better. Remember – He likes being involved in every area of your life.

PRAY Jesus, thank You for giving me a fresh start with You. Help me to let go of all the old things. Amen.

COUNTING THE COST

Read: Luke 14:25–33

KEY VERSE: 'those of you who do not give up
everything you have cannot be my disciples' (v33)

Friendship with God means that we gain eternal life, love,
joy and peace – pretty much everything we need. But
what do we give to Him? Well, actually everything.

Giving God everything doesn't mean you have to hand
over everything you own, it means that nothing in your
life should be more important than your relationship with
God. That might mean making some tough choices. Do
you have some friends that have a bad influence on you?
Are there some habits you need to stop doing? If there
are things you need to change, it might be difficult and
costly to do but it will be worthwhile.

Jesus encourages us to see the huge benefit of
friendship with God. We will have an amazing relationship
with our heavenly Father who looks after us and gives
us everything we need. We might need to make some
changes but it will definitely be worth it in the end.
Remember God has given us His Son, His Spirit and His
love. That's how much He thinks of you and me. How
much do you think of Him?

THINK What would be the hardest
thing to change or give up in your life because
you know it is not helpful to your friendship
with God?

DAUGHTERS OF GOD

Read: Galatians 4:1-7

KEY VERSE: 'God sent the Spirit of his Son into our hearts, the Spirit who calls out, "*Abba*, Father."' (v6)

Today's reading describes God as *Abba*. This is an Aramaic word which means 'Dear Father'. Friendship with God means you are welcomed into His family. God becomes your heavenly Father who loves His children just as they are. He always has time for them and never lets them down.

Sometimes people think that God is a harsh person who wants His children to work very hard in order to be a 'good' Christian. But that is not true. God wants us to see Him as a 'Dear Dad'.

All human Fathers make mistakes but God never lets us down. He wants us to talk to Him every day, about anything. He is always ready to listen, understand and help. Talk to your heavenly Father today because He is waiting to hear from you. And if you find it difficult thinking about God as a Father figure, then talk to Him about that as well. He will help you see what a loving Dad He really is.

PRAY Heavenly Father, thank You that I am Your child. Help me to get used to the idea of you being the best Father. Amen.

THE FORGIVING FATHER

Read: Luke 15:11-24

> **KEY VERSE:** 'he ran to his son, threw his arms round him and kissed him' (v2)

Do you sometimes feel as though your parents don't understand your problems? Do you think you'd be better off running away and enjoying some freedom? You might even feel like running away from God.

Today's reading is a story of a loving father who was desperate for his son to come home. The father never gave up on his son and as soon as he saw his son walking back up the path, he ran to meet him. He didn't have a go at him, instead he was prepared to forgive his son even before the son had said sorry, and welcomed him home.

If you were the son (or daughter) in this story, what stage are you at now? Having a great time doing what you want? Feeling sorry for yourself because you realise that you have seriously messed up? Or are you slowly making your way back to God, because you know that actually being with Him is the best place for you? Whichever stage you are at, it's important to realise that God sees you, loves you and is running towards you.

THINK How does this story make you feel about forgiveness? Do you find it easy or hard to ask for, and receive, forgiveness?

ENJOYING GOD'S COMPANY

Read: John 1:35-40

KEY VERSE: 'So they went and saw where he was staying, and they spent that day with him.' (v39)

Andrew and his friend wanted to speak to Jesus, and just look how He responded. Jesus spent the day with the two of them – answering their questions and getting to know them. He gave them all the time they needed.

To get to know someone, it's really important to spend time with them – talking, listening, having fun and sharing. Getting to know God is the same. He's available for you to spend time with Him all day, every day. We might think that spending time with God means praying and reading the Bible. Well, that is part of it, but it is also about doing life with Him.

We can whisper a quick prayer when we are nervous about something, or tell God about how great He is for the beautiful sunset. God can talk to us as well and often reminds us of a helpful verse from the Bible just when we need it. Real friendship develops when we enjoy just being around someone, and the same is true about our friendship with God.

PRAY Lord, thank You for always being there for me and enjoying my company. Help me to be aware of You being with me. Amen.

A FRIEND AT THE TOP

THE GOD OF ALL COMFORT

Read: 2 Corinthians 1:3–7

KEY VERSE: 'the Father of compassion and the God of all comfort' (v3)

At times, we might wonder why there is so much suffering in the world. Why doesn't God do something to end wars, prevent sickness and put an end to famine? Doesn't He care? The Bible tells us that God *does* care and it makes Him sad when bad things happen. God doesn't cause suffering, He loves us very much. However, we live in an imperfect world full of imperfect people who do not always make good decisions. One day, He will put an end to suffering, tears and sadness when He comes again and puts everything right once and for all.

Most of us go through sad times, but if we love Jesus, we can talk to Him about our troubles. God promises to help us, be with us and comfort us. Whatever problems we face at home, at school, with friendships or with our health, it's comforting to talk to God about our worries. He is a true friend who is always there when we need Him.

THINK Is there something troubling you at the moment? Talk to God about it. He completely adores you and He can give you peace and courage in your saddest times.

GETTING TO KNOW YOU

Read: Exodus 33:7–14

> **KEY VERSE:** 'teach me your ways so I may know you' (v13)

The more time Moses spent with God, the more he wanted to know God. No matter how old we get, there's always more we can learn about God. As we read the Bible and learn more about Jesus, we see more of what God is like. When we talk to God, we can share our lives with Him and listen to what He is saying to us.

Even though we might not hear God out loud or see Him performing an amazing miracle in front of us like Moses did, we can still have a real relationship with Him. Do you remember getting to know your closest friends? Sometimes it takes a while to get to know them really well. As we take time to talk to God and make time for Him, we will realise that we have the ultimate friend who is interested in everything we do!

So why not read your Bible and ask God to teach you more about Himself? The more time you spend with Him, the more you will get to know Him.

PRAY Lord Jesus, I want to know You better. Help me to find the time each day to learn more about what You're really like. Amen.

A FRIEND AT THE TOP

A SIMPLE INSTRUCTION

Read: John 15:9–17

KEY VERSE: 'You are my friends if you do what I command.' (v14)

What Jesus is saying here might sound strict, but what He is actually asking us to do is love each other. When we do this, the world will know that we follow Him. By loving each other, we accept, value and show friendship for one another.

Jesus wants us to be welcoming and loving to everyone. Sadly, some people might think that Christians are unfriendly and quick to judge people. They might have gone to church and not received a particularly warm welcome. Christians aren't perfect and it can be hard to love people who annoy us or who are different to us – but we have to learn to all get along.

When we remember that we are God's friends, we find it easier to show friendship. We can ask Him how to live the right way, and how to interact with others. He will always help us. Remember, we are examples of what being a Christian means to the world, so let's be good at loving each other.

THINK Is there someone at your church who you find it hard to get along with? Have a think about why that is and ask God to help you to make an extra effort to be a good friend to that person.

A LIFE TRANSFORMED

Read: Luke 8:26-39

KEY VERSE: 'Return home and tell how much God has done for you.' (v39)

None of the locals here wanted anything to do with the man who was possessed by demons. They had tried to control him by tying him up with chains and keeping him under guard, but he had broken free and mostly lived in a graveyard. Because of his strange and violent behaviour, the people in the town were scared of him and kept their distance.

But all that changed when the man met Jesus. The evil spirits inside him were commanded to come out of the man. When these spirits left, he became calm and sat at Jesus' feet. The man was so grateful to Jesus and wanted to stay with Him, but Jesus told him to go and tell the town what He had done for him.

Telling our friends and family what Jesus has done for us is never easy because they know us so well. But Jesus wants us to introduce Him to the people we know. So don't be afraid to show your faith to those around you. It might be difficult at first, but ask God to help you to keep going.

PRAY Lord God, thank You for my friends and family. Help me to stand up for my faith and to show love to those around me. Amen.

A FRIEND AT THE TOP

KEEPING IT IN THE FAMILY

Read: Ephesians 6:1–3

KEY VERSE: 'obey your parents in the Lord' (v1)

Whether our parents or the people who look after us are Christians or not, God wants us to respect them – even when it seems like they're just out to spoil our fun! That's not just about making sure we don't get into trouble, it's about valuing them. It can be tempting to ignore our parents, but let's not forget that as well as caring for our physical needs, parents can also give us some great advice about life – they've got a lot of experience! And it's good to remember that it is not easy being a parent but we can help them too.

Have you heard the phrase, 'actions speak louder than words'? When we love and respect our parents, then they will see that our friendship with Jesus is impacting the way we live. It can be really hard to shine for Jesus in your family if you are the only Christian, however, if you ask God to help you then He will show up in one way or another.

THINK What's your relationship like with your parents, or whoever looks after you? Is there anything that you would like to improve or change? Talk to God about it now.

WHAT DO YOU PUT FIRST?

Read: 1 John 2:12–17

> **KEY VERSE:** 'The world and its desires pass away, but whoever does the will of God lives forever.' (v17)

It's OK to admit that putting Jesus first in everything and following His ways is not easy. But it is something we need to work at because our friendship with God is going to last forever.

Have you noticed how other people's habits and values tend to rub off on us the more we spend time with them? If we want to be liked by people, then we might start copying what they think and say and how they act. The same is true the more time we spend with Jesus. His attitudes of kindness and love will rub off on us. And because of this, maybe Jesus' ways will start to change your friends who don't know Him yet!

Think about your actions and what you say this week. Do they show that you have a friendship with God? Are they kind and loving actions and words? Spend time with God and make Him your ultimate friend and influence. He will always be there for you and will never stop loving you.

PRAY Lord Jesus, I want to reflect Your love to those around me by being more like You. Please be my best friend and influence what I say and do. Amen.

A FRIEND AT THE TOP

THE BEST THING
IN THE WORLD

Read: Philippians 3:8-14

KEY VERSE: 'I consider everything a loss because of the surpassing worth of knowing Christ Jesus' (v8)

In today's Bible reading, Paul is saying that knowing Jesus is the best thing in the world — and it really is! Everything else seems unimportant when compared to having Jesus as a best friend. Paul reminds us that God has done everything possible to win our friendship, including sending His Son to earth to tell us about Him.

Paul introduced a lot of people to Jesus but it wasn't always easy. Paul suffered and was bullied for what he believed. He could easily have decided to stop spreading the good news about Jesus, but he knew that friendship with God which lasts forever was worth any temporary troubles.

Your friendship with God is the most important friendship of all, so make an effort with it. Read the Bible, get to know Him and talk to Him every day. Try to avoid anything that will spoil your relationship with God, like acting selfishly and ignoring Him. And remember that God loves you deeply and wants to have a close relationship with you. He is the best friend you will ever have!

THINK Do you want a closer friendship with God? What can you do to make that happen?

TAKING CARE

Read: Psalm 104:10–30

KEY VERSE: 'All creatures look to you to give them their food at the proper time.' (v27)

Do you have any pets? If so, how good are you at looking after them? Does God look after the world in a similar way to how we look after our pets?

The people of God understood that He had not only created the universe but that He is fully alive and at work in it all the time. That is why we are able to see God all around us in the world. He's holding the whole thing together and making it work.

It's good to know this. It means that God is very, very close to us. When we pray for a miracle, we're not asking God to step into the world from way out in space somewhere – He's already here! When we see that God is at work in everything, it's easier to believe that He can do anything. He's doing a lot of behind the scenes work that keeps this world running. This psalm tells us some of the things that God has done and still does. He is brilliant at taking care of us and this world.

PRAY Lord, I believe that You do care about me and about this world. When I feel like You don't care, please help me to remember the truth. Amen.

PSALM

NUMBER ONE FAN

Read: Psalm 139:1–18,23–24

KEY VERSE: 'you know me' (v1)

Who do you like hanging out with best? Probably people you can relax with – people who know you well and accept you for who you are. Well this song is about how great it is to be close to God because He knows *everything* about us!

God knows us even better than we know ourselves. He made us unique! He knows our good side, our bad side, our interesting, boring, fun, dull, strong, weak, nasty and kind sides – and He still wants to be close to us. He knows absolutely everything about us and He still loves us. Now that's something worth singing about!

The way that the psalm ends is important too. The songwriter knows he's not perfect, and he asks God to give him a check over. God is totally for us, not against us. He wants to help us improve in any and every way we can – so that we can be more like His Son, Jesus. He's not like a mean or uncaring teacher – He's more like our number one fan, always there and ready cheer us on!

PRAY Father, it's amazing that You see every part of me and are still my number one fan. Please help me to become more like Jesus in the ways that You know I need to. Amen.

PSALM

JESUS!

Read: Matthew 1:18-25

> **KEY VERSE:** 'give him the name Jesus, because he will save his people from their sins' (v21)

Joseph and Mary didn't have to Google baby names when they found out Mary was pregnant. They knew the baby was a boy and they had been given the name for Him already. In Jewish tradition, the father names the child. And here we get a clue why Joseph didn't name the baby. He wasn't the father – God was. So it was God who named His Son, and what a great name He chose – Jesus!

Everyone knew what that name meant. It was a popular name already. Jesus meant 'Saviour'. More than that, God spelt out what His Son had come to save people from – sin!

Jesus wasn't the only name God came up with in heaven. He also chose the name Immanuel. Six hundred years before Jesus was born, God let Isaiah in on His big plan (Isa. 7:14). Immanuel means 'God with us'. God's Son had come to live with us!

Jesus is God with you – yes, you! He promises that He will always be with you (Matt. 28:20). You are never alone.

THINK Jesus is with you in your neighbourhood, your school, your home, your life! What sort of welcome do you think He deserves?

HE'S CALLED...

MAN

Read: 1 Timothy 2:1-6

KEY VERSE: 'the man Christ Jesus' (v5)

Jesus is God. He is holy, loving, kind — all that God is. But Jesus was also human — flesh and blood — just as we are. So Jesus is unique, both God and man. But why did God bother to become like us?

Jesus restricted Himself to living in a human body for just over 30 years. He experienced growing up and being a young person, with all the stresses that come with it. So when you face hard times in your teenage years, know that you can talk to Him about it because He's been there too! Then, as a man, Jesus experienced hunger, thirst, tiredness and stress. Also, famously, He faced temptation and was victorious over it! Jesus went through a lot of the same stuff we go through, and He gives us a great example to follow in dealing with these things.

In 1 Timothy 2:5, Jesus is described as 'the man' — not just a man but *the* man. The greatest, gentlest and most holy man ever. That makes Him the best role model ever, but also the best friend that we could ever want.

PRAY Lord Jesus, I am so thankful that you came to earth. Help me to always try and be like You and remember that You understand what life is like. Amen.

LIGHT

Read: John 8:12-19

KEY VERSE: 'I am the light of the world.' (v12)

Here's a five-letter word you could use instead of the word 'Jesus' that shows us what He's like and what He's done for us: light. It's used 33 times in John's Gospel alone!

In the days of Moses, God lit up the way to the Promised Land with a pillar of fire. This was celebrated at the Feast of Tabernacles when four large bowls in the Temple courtyard were filled with oil and the priest's uniform from the last year, and then were lit for everyone in Jerusalem to see. Light was also associated with freedom. It was in this culture that Jesus announced He was the light of the world. He was the pillar of fire leading people of all backgrounds to God.

To celebrate their victory over Antiochus IV (a Syrian dictator who tried to stop them worshipping God), the Jews held an annual festival of lights. Candles and torches were lit in every home and kept burning for eight days. In the evenings they sang and danced to music. Jesus, our light, came to win our freedom from the darkness of living without God.

PRAY Thank You, Jesus for lighting up my life, showing me the way and giving me freedom. Help me to always choose to follow Your light. Amen.

HE'S CALLED...

THE WAY

Read: John 14:1-9

KEY VERSE: 'I am the way' (v6)

In Moses' day God used a cloud by day and a fire at night to show the Israelites 'the way' (Deut. 1:33). From then on people spoke about following God's 'way'. Psalmists sang songs asking God to show them His 'way'. And then Jesus arrived, giving Himself another title... 'the way'.

Sat-navs can show us different routes to get to the destination we have entered, but in Jesus' day there was only one safe route between places – 'the way'. So when Jesus called Himself 'the way' He was stating He was the only way – to God. It's only through Him that we can be saved.

There was also another meaning to this name. Jesus often referred to the first five books of the Bible, the law, as 'the way' because it told them the way to live their lives. So in saying that He was 'the way', Jesus was announcing that the old way of becoming right with God through sacrifices was over. Instead He was about to become the sacrifice to open up a new way.

THINK Some people live their lives not knowing what God thinks of them and if He accepts them. When we trust in Jesus, no matter what we've done, we are saved and forgiven! Do you believe that?

FIRST AND LAST

Read: Revelation 1:8–18

'I am the Alpha and the Omega' (v8)

Before sat-navs, most people used an 'A-Z' map book to find their way around. When John was shown a vision of heaven, he saw an A *and* Z. No, not a guidebook of heaven, but the most awesome person.

The New Testament was written in the Greek language and while our alphabet starts with 'A' and ends with 'Z', the Greek alphabet starts with 'Alpha' and ends with 'Omega'. Jesus used this to show that He is the first and the last.

He is the first because He was there at the beginning of everything, creating our world and everything in it. He is the last because He is in control of all events in the future and will reign with God the Father over a new heaven and earth (Rev. 21–22).

He is our 'A' because Jesus is with us from the beginning of our lives, knowing us before we were born (Psa. 139:14–16). He is our 'Z' because, if we believe in Him, when we die we'll be with Him forever.

THINK With Jesus as our A-Z we never need to feel lost, because He can show us the right way ahead. Got a situation where you need someone to point you in the right direction? Ask Jesus.

HE'S CALLED...

THE TRUTH

Read: John 14:6; 18:33–38

KEY VERSE: 'I am... the truth' (14:6)

When people exaggerate we ask them to 'get real'. People who are honest and tell it like it is are 'real' with themselves and others. Was Jesus real with people?

Pilate asked Jesus an interesting question: 'What is truth?' Truth means nothing hidden. It is possible to say something that is true without telling the truth — you can reveal some facts but not others to mislead people. This is why in a court of law you are required to tell 'the truth, the whole truth and nothing but the truth'.

When Jesus said, 'I am the truth', He could equally have said, 'I am real'. Jesus didn't tell lies or try to con people. He didn't make Himself out to be anything He wasn't. He could easily have denied being a king to Pilate and avoided crucifixion, but Jesus was real. Jesus didn't just tell the truth, He *is* the truth. It is not in His character to mislead, deceive or lie. He is 100% genuine, trustworthy and reliable — a friend who cannot and will not let you down.

PRAY Jesus, thank You for being so trustworthy and for being my friend. I want to be true and real — please help me with this! Amen.

THE GATE

Read: John 10:1-9

KEY VERSE: 'Very truly I tell you, I am the gate for the sheep.' (v7)

Many of those who listened to Jesus owned sheep or were hired to look after flocks. So, Jesus used an example based on their experience to help them understand who He is.

There was one way in or out of a sheepfold. A shepherd stood by the gate to count his sheep in the fold. Sick or wounded sheep would be singled out for treatment and those not belonging to him turned away.

We've mentioned before about how many shepherds slept across the entrance, acting as a 'living door' to protect their sheep. Jesus didn't say He was one of many ways to God, but 'the gate': the only entrance to the kingdom of heaven. You cannot be forgiven and enter the security of God's family without meeting Him first! It is Jesus who opens up our access to the Father.

Also, once we've entered through the gate (been saved by Jesus) we don't need to feel trapped into only being around Christians. The sheep could go in and out, and we can get to know all sorts of people too.

THINK Do you have more friends who are Christians, or who aren't? It's great to have a mix of both! Ask God who He might be guiding you to today.

HE'S CALLED...

RESURRECTION

Read: John 11:17–27,38–44

KEY VERSE: 'I am the resurrection' (v25)

One of Jesus' best friends was dead. To make matters worse, Jesus had arrived late for the funeral. The dead man's relatives were distraught. Was this the best time for Jesus to announce a new name? It was, as it happens. Jesus' sense of timing is always perfect.

Poor Martha was overcome with grief when her brother Lazarus died. When Jesus arrived He introduced Himself as 'the resurrection and the life'. Resurrection means 'to stand up again'. Was Jesus claiming He could bring Lazarus to life and up on his feet again? Yes! Jesus has power over death. And He demonstrated it by commanding Lazarus to walk out of the tomb. Lazarus, his feet still wrapped together with burial cloths, came out like a bandaged pogo stick!

Jesus' promise is that all who believe in Him will live even though they die. In other words, when Christians die, that is not the end. Jesus is there to see us 'standing up again' in heaven with a new body and eternal life!

PRAY Lord Jesus, thank You for having power over death and for promising that everyone who trusts You will be with You forever. I trust You and want to live my life for You. Amen.

BREAD OF LIFE

Read: John 6:30-51

KEY VERSE: 'I am the bread of life.' (v35)

After providing bread for the 5,000+ people, Jesus announced that He was the 'bread of life'. He expected those listening to be able to work out what He meant.

Back in the time of Moses, six days a week for 40 years, God delivered 'bread from heaven' – wafers that tasted like honey. This 'bread', called manna, gave hundreds of thousands of Jews the protein, vitamins and energy they needed to survive in the desert. Seven times as He was speaking, Jesus said He came down from heaven (vv33–58) – not to fill stomachs but to fill lives. Jesus was the new manna God had sent to bring new life to the world.

But what does that mean? Well, Jesus provides us with what we need in life. He is where we can draw our energy from. More than that, He is able to satisfy us. Lots of us can feel 'spiritually hungry' without realising it. Some people describe this as having a 'God-shaped hole'. Jesus fills us so that we don't feel that hunger anymore – He is what we've been craving.

THINK Do you value the 'bread of life' in this way? Do you thank God for Jesus? Tell Jesus how much you appreciate Him, and tell others as well!

HE'S CALLED...

THE VINE

Read: John 15:1-8

KEY VERSE: 'I am the true vine' (v1)

In the Old Testament, the Jews were pictured as a grape vine that God had planted. And vines were carved on the outside of synagogues to remind people that God cared for them. Jesus' announcement that He was the true vine was a bit of a shell-shocker. God was still the gardener, but Jesus was the vine and those who believe in Him were the branches.

If a grape is removed from the life supply of the vine, it dries up. If we remove ourselves from Jesus, we shrivel up too! But if we stay close to Him, we grow. To take this further, a vine branch can produce lots of grapes or it can grow wild, with all wood and little fruit. We can also show spiritual fruit, or become a tangled mess. Pruning (getting rid of the unwanted bits) is what makes the difference.

The Greek word for 'prune' also means 'to clean'. God wants to clean up our lives. The result, the spiritual fruit — a big, awesome mix of love, joy, peace, patience, kindness, goodness, faithfulness, gentleness and self-control in our lives.

PRAY Father, thank You for being my provider and for cleaning up my life. Help me to stay connected to You so that I can continue to grow and produce good fruit. Amen.

GOOD SHEPHERD

Read: John 10:1-29

KEY VERSE: 'I am the good shepherd.' (v11)

In the Old Testament, God described Himself as a good shepherd caring for His flock. The flock was not of the woolly four-legged variety, but the two-legged species – His people. Jesus introduced Himself to the world as the shepherd – the good shepherd with the emphasis on *good*.

Let's look at the difference between a regular ol' shepherd and Jesus...

A HIRED SHEPHERD – Doesn't own the sheep. He doesn't bother to remember their names. If thieves or wild animals arrive he shouts, 'Abandon sheep!' and runs for his life. The sheep are captured, killed or scattered.

THE GOOD SHEPHERD – He knows each of His sheep by name. His sheep recognise His voice and follow Him when He calls to them. They are absolutely safe – 100% secure. He protects them at all costs – even to the ultimate cost of dying for them.

With Jesus as your good shepherd there is nothing to be scared of. He always cares for you. Nothing you do can ever remove you from God's family.

THINK Do you find it easy or difficult to see Jesus as your protector when you can't physically see Him? Even though we can't see Him right now, we can know His presence by praying to Him.

HE'S CALLED...

FOUNDATION

Read: 1 Corinthians 3:10-23

KEY VERSE: 'For no one can lay any foundation other than the one already laid, which is Jesus Christ.' (v11)

What do you base your life upon? What makes you do the things you do?

Jesus once told a story about two builders. One was foolish and built on sand. The other was a wise guy who built on rock-solid ground. The building on sandy foundations collapsed in the first storm. The one with solid foundations didn't rock. Paul continues the theme of this story by asking about the foundations of our lives. Some people build their lives on their future hopes, desires and dreams. Others build their lives around people or belongings. Paul learnt that Jesus is the only foundation worth building your life on. He is totally secure, reliable and strong.

You see, while having dreams is great, what happens if the dream doesn't work out? It's not safe to build our lives on things that can crumble. Jesus is the only foundation that won't ever let us down. So let's base our lives on Him!

PRAY Lord Jesus, I am so thankful that You are strong and invite me to base my life upon You. Help me to always see You as my foundation, not anything or anyone else. Amen.

CHRIST

Read: John 1:35-42

KEY VERSE: '"We have found the Messiah"' (that is, the Christ).' (v41)

Andrew introduced Jesus to his brother as 'the Christ'. To most of us, Christ is simply another name for the Lord Jesus. But to Andrew, Peter and the people of that day, the word 'Christ' was *really* meaningful. Christ meant 'the anointed one'. People chosen to be kings or priests were anointed.

From the earliest times, God promised to choose, anoint and send someone to save the world. His choice was His Son, Jesus. When Andrew met Jesus, he realised he hadn't been speaking to an ordinary man, or even a special man – but God's 'anointed one'. That's why he was so keen for Peter to meet Jesus.

Some time later, Jesus asked His disciples who they thought He was. Peter answered, 'You are the Messiah [Christ], the Son of the living God' (Matt 16:16). It wasn't a lucky guess. God had let Peter in on His secret – Jesus is the one anointed by God to be our Saviour.

THINK The New Testament talks about us belonging to Christ (see 1 Cor. 15:22–23). We belong to the one and only anointed Saviour; we belong to the King of kings. What might some privileges of this be?

HE'S CALLED...

BAPTIST

Read: Luke 3:1–17

KEY VERSE: 'He will baptise you with the Holy Spirit and fire.' (v16)

Have you heard of John the Baptist? He was Jesus' relative who went around preaching before Jesus got started. He preached that people should do a U-turn away from wrong and follow God. Many turned to God and were baptised in water by John. It wasn't long till he was nicknamed 'John the Baptist'. But have you heard about '*Jesus* the Baptist'?

John the Baptist prepared people for the arrival of 'Jesus the Baptist'. He made a point of telling his disciples that Jesus would do more for them than he could. John baptised people in water to show they had turned to God for forgiveness. But Jesus would baptise people with the Holy Spirit – God living in them! The English word 'baptise' comes from the Greek word *baptizo*. It means to soak, drench or sink. So Jesus would send the Holy Spirit to live within them and it wouldn't just be a trickle, but a complete drenching. They would be absolutely soaked with God's power so that they could show the world their new life in Jesus.

PRAY Holy Spirit, I want to see more of You in my life – not just a little bit, but a complete drenching! Please show Your mighty power in my life. Amen.

PEACE

Read: Isaiah 9:6; John 14:27–31; 16:33

KEY VERSE: 'Prince of Peace' (Isa. 9:6)

Have you ever feel stressed as if everywhere you go seems to be filled with noise, distractions and confusion? Well, take time now to find out about another of Jesus' names.

What a title this is – 'Prince of Peace'. That's Jesus! He is not just a peaceful person, or someone who makes us feel at ease. Jesus *is* peace – it's in His nature. Peace is not something you find by acting laid-back and cool. Real peace begins and ends with Jesus. We cannot have peace with God without Him. Music, games or watching a movie can help us to escape our worries and problems for a short time, but only Jesus can give us lasting peace.

Jesus warned His disciples that they would face trouble. But before they had the chance to get all worked up and freaked out about it, He told them not to worry because He would give them His peace. Christianity is not a ticket to an easy life, but even in the toughest times, we can turn to Jesus and He can make us calm and confident.

THINK If we want peace, it's important to take time out to spend with Jesus, reading the Bible and talking with Him. He is the way to peace with God, others and ourselves.

HE'S CALLED...

SLAVE

Read: Mark 10:35-45

KEY VERSE: 'slave of all' (v44)

James and John hoped that being followers of Jesus would give them the chance to sit back and give the orders. They'd got it totally wrong. Jesus reminded them that He hadn't come to boss them around. Neither did He expect them to run around after Him doing His chores. He had come to serve them. Not just some of them — all of them... everybody! Jesus put Himself at the bottom of the pile.

So, when there were smelly feet that needed a wash and scrub down, Jesus was on His knees with a bowl of water. When people with diseases, criminals, traitors and other not-liked people needed help, He met them, forgave them and healed them.

But the ultimate act of putting others first was Jesus' willingness to die on the cross. He gave up the number one spot and all the perks of heaven to become the lowest of the low — hated, rejected and hurt — all so we could be forgiven by God. Jesus is our servant King. He deserves to be praised!

PRAY God, I know You want me to serve the people I know, but it isn't easy. Please help me to find ways to do this, and the confidence to go ahead with it. Amen.

DEFENDER

Read: 1 John 2:1-14

> **KEY VERSE:** 'we have an advocate with the Father – Jesus Christ' (v1)

Those facing trial need lawyers to plead their case in court. They are the ones wearing black gowns and white curly wigs. Did you realise you have a case pending? Yes, one day all of us will have to face up to God. On our own? No, we have someone to defend us.

Jesus is our defence. He is willing to talk to God on our behalf. Although we are guilty of breaking God's laws, Jesus is there to argue that we are 'not guilty'. Why? Simply because He died to take the punishment for our sin. Our sentence has been paid. The evidence for this? His blood poured out on the cross.

Jesus cares about us so much that He prays for us. Yes, you are on His prayer list! Sometimes problems or mistakes can make us feel so low that we wonder if anyone really cares or understands. Jesus knows what we are going through, prays for us and brings our situation to God the Father.

PRAY Lord Jesus, thank You so much for being my defender. I'm amazed that You would be punished in my place. You deserve all the praise and fame. Amen.

HE'S CALLED...

PIONEER

Read: Hebrews 2:1-11

KEY VERSE: 'the pioneer of their salvation' (v10)

Can you think of any famous pioneers? Here's one you might have heard of: Christopher Columbus. He's the guy who set out to pioneer a route to India going west from Europe, and discovered North America! And there are lots of other people who have pioneered new routes, new ways of doing things, new inventions, and made new discoveries.

Who is the greatest pioneer ever? Jesus is! You might be thinking it's quite strange to think of Jesus as a pioneer. What is He the pioneer of? He's the pioneer of our salvation. He left heaven, came to earth, suffered, died and rose again to open a new route for us to join God's family. No one else could have done that. God wanted us to be saved and Jesus made it a reality by dying on the cross and rising again.

What is the greatest achievement of all time? Saving the world – and that's all down to Jesus. Because of Him, we are forgiven. He deserves all the praise!

THINK Do you think your friends understand what Jesus was doing when He died and rose again? How can you help them to understand this more?

TEACHER

Read: John 13:3–17

KEY VERSE: 'I, your Lord and Teacher' (v14)

Teachers have lots of practice telling their pupils what to do. 'Do this... do that... be quiet... I won't tell you again... QUIET!' Teachers in Jesus' day were no different. Rabbis (the Jewish name for teachers) expected their pupils to do as they said.

Jesus was a great teacher – the greatest ever. He spoke with great power and people travelled miles to hear Him. But Jesus taught with more than words and interesting parables. He taught by example. So when He wanted to teach His disciples to serve each other, He showed them how He wanted them to do it. He grabbed a bowl and a towel, and started washing the disciples' manky feet!

Jesus showed His followers His attitude, and what He wanted them to be like. And if Jesus, their 'Lord' and 'teacher', treated others better than Himself, His pupils didn't have an excuse not to do the same. Jesus is our teacher in the big lesson of life. He doesn't expect us to go it alone and know what to do, He says, 'Follow my lead'.

PRAY Lord Jesus, I want to be like You and follow Your example. Help me to value others like You do, and to always treat people the way that You teach me to. Amen.

HE'S CALLED...

FRIEND

Read: Luke 7:34-48

KEY VERSE: 'a friend of tax collectors and sinners' (v34)

We can't choose our family but we can choose our friends. When Jesus came to earth He was free to choose His friends. Who do you think God's Son, fresh out of heaven, would want to mix with?

Jews hated tax collectors. They were traitors who worked with the Romans and cheated people out of their money. So the Jews refused to speak to them. They also kept away from people who were thought of as 'sinners', like the woman with the bad past who visited Jesus.

Jesus saw things differently, though. He was friends with these people – not telling them that what they had been doing was OK, but telling them that God hadn't rejected them.

Stuck-up Simon the Pharisee was shocked that Jesus didn't tell this woman to clear off. Jesus then reminded Simon that we all sin. Yes, some sin much more than others. But that means that they've got more to thank God for when He forgives them. Jesus then forgave the woman.

THINK What is Jesus when you mess up? Your enemy? No! He's still your friend. Have you got any bad habits that keep you away from Jesus? Talk to Him about them and ask for His forgiveness.

KING OF KINGS

Read: Revelation 19:11–16

KEY VERSE: 'KING OF KINGS' (v16)

Jews believed a mighty king, greater than King David or King Solomon, would come to defeat their enemies and make them into the greatest nation. There was good news, bad news and excellent news.

The good news: Jesus arrived as king to deliver people from the big enemy – not the Romans, sin!

The bad news: Jesus was crucified with a sign mocking Him as the 'King of the Jews' nailed to His cross.

The excellent news: Jesus rose from the dead and returned to heaven to be crowned as the greatest king, the King of kings!

When John wrote Revelation, Caesar ruled the world. Christians obeyed Caesar, but they worshipped Jesus as the King of kings. Jesus was much more important to them than anyone else. When Caesar ordered Christians to worship him and turn their backs on Jesus, they refused. Thousands of Christians were put in prison or fed to the lions for refusing to say that anyone other than Jesus was the King of kings.

THINK Have you ever been treated badly for worshipping Jesus? While we don't get thrown to the lions, we do sometimes face insults. Try talking to a Christian friend or youth leader about this.

HE'S CALLED...

LORD OF LORDS

Read: Revelation 19:16

KEY VERSE: 'LORD OF LORDS.' (v16)

It's the same key verse today as yesterday. It's not that we don't think you read it carefully enough yesterday, but that there is another revelation about Jesus in the book of Revelation.

In Bible times, many kings were known as 'lord'. The title meant 'one who is in control'. The word 'Lord' is used thousands of times in the Old Testament to describe God. Moses reminded God's people that 'the LORD your God is God of gods and Lord of lords' (Deut. 10:17). There were hundreds of gods that people worshipped, but they were all fakes and God was more powerful than any of them!

In the New Testament, Jesus is called 'Lord' hundreds of times. But even better – Jesus is the 'Lord of lords'. He's not just another lord. He is greater than Caesar, Herod or any other power. The first Christians openly said that Jesus was the 'Lord' and completely believed that.

Jesus is above every other power. Yet, He still thinks it is important to be close to us. How great is that?!

PRAY Jesus, You are Lord of everything. You're higher up than anyone in power in the whole world. Please be Lord of my life, too. Amen.

LORD JESUS CHRIST

Read: Acts 2:22–36

KEY VERSE: 'Jesus... both Lord and Christ' (v36, NKJV)

The title 'the Lord Jesus Christ' does not appear in any of the Gospels, but when the Holy Spirit came at Pentecost, He started to be known by this great title more. The first Christians called Jesus 'the Lord Jesus' or the 'Lord Jesus Christ'. We have already discovered what these words mean on their own, but look at their power when they're thrown together:

Lord – the ultimate authority, Lord of lords.

Jesus – Saviour, saving us from sin.

Christ – anointed by God to be King – King of kings.

Looking at that, we can start to understand why the first Christians were so dedicated to telling others about Jesus.

Christians do not follow a brilliant man, or a hyped-up superhero, but the Lord Jesus Christ. He is Lord of all creation! He is our King, our master, our everything. Even those in heaven who have power fall down to worship Him, respecting and admiring Him (Rev. 5:8–13).

THINK Unfortunately, many people in the world don't see the name of Jesus as important, and even use His name as a swear word. Let's make a choice to always do our best to respect the name of Jesus.

HE'S CALLED...

ABOVE ALL OTHER NAMES

Read: Philippians 2:5-11

KEY VERSE: 'the name that is above every name, that at the name of Jesus every knee should bow... and every tongue acknowledge that Jesus Christ is Lord' (vv9–11)

Who's your favourite famous person? Maybe they're an actress or actor, a YouTuber, a singer... whatever! Have you ever wondered what their life is like? Here's a secret: you know something about their future that they might not know.

One day everyone, absolutely *everyone* will kneel with respect in front of the Lord Jesus. That means every celebrity, all the world's rulers, all the sporting heroes, every school bully, anyone and everyone. There's not a person alive who won't meet Jesus one day. Many will face Him as their judge. Those who have believed in Him will face Him as their Saviour. And there's a big difference in what those experiences will be like.

Never forget that there is only one name in the whole of heaven and earth with the authority to save us from our sin – the name of the Lord Jesus Christ (Acts 4:12)!

PRAY Lord Jesus Christ, Your name is above every other name. I worship You right now and want to tell You that I believe You are Lord of everything. Amen.

'I HATE YOU!'

Read: Psalm 109:1–15

KEY VERSE: 'They repay me evil for good, and hatred for my friendship.' (v5)

Today's reading is a seriously angry one! 'Argggh! I hate you!' is the feeling behind this psalm. The songwriter has an enemy and he *really* wishes bad things would happen to him. Do you ever feel like this? Has someone got you really, really angry? It can be so tempting to repay their wrong with another wrong, can't it?

Well, in the New Testament, Jesus explained that God wants us to forgive our enemies, because, after all, we have been forgiven by God. Jesus taught us how to love those who are mean or rude to us. Even on the cross, He asked God to forgive those who had so hatefully put Him in that awful place.

It's by no means easy. Everything within us may want to lash out. But let's think about why we should forgive. God is patient, forgiving and kind. And with the Holy Spirit living in us, we can be these things too. When we forgive others, we show them what God is like.

THINK If you need some help dealing with your anger towards someone, instead of blowing your top, talk to God about it. Let Him help you stop hating and start forgiving.

PSALM

RUN TO YOU

Read: Ephesians 6:18-20

KEY VERSE: 'And pray in the Spirit on all occasions with all kinds of prayers and requests' (v18)

Have you ever felt pulled in different directions? Sometimes life can be a bit confusing, but there's one place you can take all your questions...

Did you know that God *loves* to listen to you? It doesn't matter that He knows everything already, He just loves to sit and listen to everything you have to say, down to the tiniest detail. He also has *the* most brilliant answers, but sometimes He helps you figure it out for yourself too.

Talking through things can really help us to sort out our jumbled thoughts and feelings, and God has all the time in the world to spend with you. He's never too busy; with Him there are no silly questions. Your needs and wishes are important to Him. Sometimes we don't get the exact answers we want, but the answers God gives are always the best thing for us in the long run. And like in any relationship, the more you speak to Him, the more you know Him.

PRAY Father God, I come to You now with everything going on in my life. Please help me with _____. I'm so thankful that You listen to me. Amen.

TALKING WITH GOD

SHAKEDOWN!

Read: Acts 4:23-31

> **KEY VERSE:** 'After they prayed, the place where they were meeting was shaken. And they were all filled with the Holy Spirit and spoke the word of God boldly.' (v31)

Peter and John had been ordered by the Jewish authorities to stop talking about Jesus or there would be serious, and we mean *serious*, consequences. But they weren't shaken by their experience. Instead, they met with other Christians to plug in to the ultimate power source: God. And what did they say? 'Sovereign Lord...' That was a good start. It was the same as saying, 'Lord, you are the real boss, You are In control of the situation...' They had the creator of the universe on their side, so why worry about a few trumped-up men in fancy robes?

The group of believers didn't ask for an opt-out option on sharing about Jesus, or for God to zap their enemies. They asked God for the power to obey Him and fearlessly tell the world about Jesus. God heard them, answered their request and dispatched the power supply they needed – so much of it that it nearly brought the house down!

THINK Is there something you need to pray for today? Strength? Courage? Wisdom? Asking another Christian to pray with you can be really helpful.

THE INTERPRETER

Read: ROMANS 8:22-27

> **KEY VERSE:** 'We do not know what we ought to pray for, but the Spirit himself intercedes for us through wordless groans.' (v26)

Fumbling for words? Don't know what to say? Still learning 'prayer' language? Even if you're shy, overwhelmed or new to the ways of prayer, you don't need to worry. Help is near!

One of the names Jesus' followers called Him was Rabbi, meaning 'teacher'. He taught a completely new, wonderful way of approaching life. But in learning something new, we need constant practice. Often we have a tutor, and that's where the Holy Spirit comes in.

Prayer is an absolutely essential skill for every Christian to have. It is the key to everything else because prayer is how we communicate with God. And if we can't communicate with God, we're not going to be able to live *for* God. That's why He sent His Spirit to coach us on how to pray. He's even there in those times of frustration when we just don't know how we feel – let alone what to pray – stepping in to translate the feelings that we can't put words to.

PRAY Lord, I don't always find it easy to pray. Thank You for sending Your Holy Spirit who puts the power into my prayers. Help me to listen to Him. Amen.

IN IT TOGETHER

Read: Genesis 1:26–30

KEY VERSE: 'Then God said, "Let us make mankind in our image, in our likeness, so that they may rule over...all the creatures that move"' (v26)

When you create something as a group — for school or just for fun at home with a friend — what's the very first thing you do? You talk about it, don't you? Without communication it would be chaos and a waste of effort! Besides, half the fun is in the talking about it. Right back at the beginning of time, God made a stunning world for His children, then said, 'It's over to you... Go explore, create and rule!' We are co-workers or partners with God, joint guardians of this earth!

But God lets us choose how we live. We can live only for ourselves, doing our own thing and ignoring Him (look where that got Adam and Eve!) — or we can accept the offer to join with Him, live a meaningful life, and be on talking terms with the creator of the universe.

THINK Do you consider yourself to be on God's team? He wants us to be — it's the best team to be a part of! How often do you talk to your God, your team leader?

TALKING WITH GOD

MIRROR IMAGE

Read: Psalm 8:1-9; 115:16

KEY VERSE: 'The highest heavens belong to the LORD, but the earth he has given to the human race.' (115:16)

Ever been told you look like someone else? Maybe a relative, or maybe just someone from TV? Well, we really *were* made to remind people of someone else. But who?

You guessed it – people are made in the image of God, crowned with glory! When the rest of creation saw Adam, they saw a reflection of God. Just as the moon has no light of its own but reflects the light from the sun, Adam was simply reflecting God. And (at first, anyway) he kept in close contact with God so he could rule the earth under God's guidance.

So what went wrong? Basically, Adam and Eve believed a lie from the devil, stopped trusting in God and disobeyed Him, destroying their relationship with God. BUT when Jesus defeated Satan on the cross, He took us back into God's family. Being in God's family means we have His Spirit at work in us, and the more time we spend with God, the more we'll be like Him.

PRAY Father, thank You for creating me in Your image and sending Jesus to die for me. Help me to keep talking with You so that I can live under Your guidance. Amen.

USE YOUR SWORD!

Read: Luke 4:1-13

KEY VERSE: 'Jesus answered, "It is written: 'Worship the Lord your God and serve him only.'"' (v8)

Ugh! Don't you read today's passage and think what a massive liar the devil is?! He'd never do anything nice for anyone, especially Jesus!

Everything that comes from Satan's mouth is dripping with lies (he's even known as the father of lies.). If Adam and Eve had realised this back in Eden, the world would not be in the mess it is today – so let's make sure we learn from their mistake.

The brilliant thing here is Jesus' responses to Satan's temptations. Every lie of an offer is met and defeated... with Scripture. Jesus used God's Word as His weapon against enemy attack, and the devil was disarmed. When we know and speak the truth of God's Word, we will win hands down, every time.

This is really important for us to remember as we pray. If any lies about God pop into our head and tempt us to stop talking with Him, we can slam them down with a good bit of Bible!

THINK Do you think the Bible is important? Jesus showed us just how important it really is! Your Bible is a letter from God to you, so open it up, read it out loud and speak His truth into your life.

TALKING WITH GOD

RAIN, RAIN... HURRY UP!

Read: 1 Kings 18:1–4,41–44

KEY VERSE: 'the word of the LORD came to Elijah: "'Go and present yourself to Ahab, and I will send rain on the land'"'

Things start out promisingly for Elijah, chosen by God to pull Israel back from the edge of self-destruction. To punish some evil behaviour, Elijah prays for a stop to all rain. Sure enough, three and a half years pass without a drop. His point made, he now prays for the rain to start again, and God tells Elijah to get ready.

But first there's a showdown on Mount Carmel: 450 bad guys lined up against Elijah and God (vv22–24). The bad guys rave around their altar but their false god doesn't respond. Elijah prays, God barbecues his offering and the bad guys get wiped out. But still no rain... So Elijah gives a faith-filled forecast of thunderstorms, then gets his prayer on!

Drumroll... nothing, even six prayers later. Time to quit? Never! The seventh prayer leads to a single cloud starting a huge downpour. God *always* listens to our prayers – but sometimes He doesn't answer them when or how we expect Him to.

PRAY God, I know that You always hear me. Help me to not give up when my prayers don't seem to get answered. Keep me talking with You. Amen.

MAKING A WAY

Read: Daniel 9:1-6

KEY VERSE: 'So I turned to the LORD God and pleaded with him in prayer and petition, in fasting, and in sackcloth and ashes.' (v3)

If God has the future all mapped out and has the power to do anything He wants, is there any point in praying?

Daniel certainly thought so. Today's Bible reading finds Daniel, erm, reading his Bible! He's been a prisoner of war in Babylon for 70 years when suddenly, in the middle of his daily quiet time he notices something in the book (well, scroll at that point) of Jeremiah. As Daniel reads he realises that God has limited the time of the Jews being kicked out of their land to 70 years. He does some quick maths... 'That's it, time's up!'

So what's his next move? He enters into serious prayer talks with God, pleading for the Jews' freedom. Prayer opens doors for the power of God to move through, and Daniel knew that. When we decide to trust God and partner with Him, that's when things get really exciting.

THINK Is there a certain person or situation that you need to pray about? Write the name/issue on a piece of paper and stick it in your Bible or on your mirror, to remind you daily.

TALKING WITH GOD

YOUR TIME IS YOUR TREASURE

Read: Psalm 86:8-13

> **KEY VERSE:** 'Teach me your way, LORD, that I may rely on your faithfulness; give me an undivided heart, that I may fear your name.' (v11)

David asked God for an undivided heart. What do you think that means? We have a divided heart when our love of other things, even other people, takes away our dedication to God. Have you ever felt torn between spending time with God and watching TV or doing something else?

Don't feel bad — we've all felt that way. And there's nothing wrong with those things in themselves. God wants us to enjoy different activities in life. But how we spend our time shows who is most important in our lives. When we love God with all our hearts, when He is number one in our life, we don't allow anything to stop us from knowing Him better.

Are you managing to find time to chat to God each day? Do you see prayer as essential or optional? If you don't feel like you've got an undivided heart for God, here's the good news — you can ask Him to help!

PRAY Father, I want to spend time with You and I know You want to spend time with me. Please give me an undivided heart for You. Amen.

SET YOUR SIGHTS HIGH

Read: John 17:1-12

KEY VERSE: 'Now this is eternal life: that they know you, the only true God, and Jesus Christ, whom you have sent.' (v3)

When Jesus faced a terrifying situation, He knew who to look to and what to say.

Jesus was under huge stress. He knew He was soon to be brutally crucified as a sacrifice for us. Yes, Jesus and the Father had planned it together – the only way to save the world – but that just meant that Jesus was even more aware of how much He would suffer. In that moment, when He felt more human than ever, Jesus looked to God to give Him the desire and strength to see things through. He prayed to His Father about it.

Prayer helps us to approach situations from a place of God's power and goodness, rather than from a place of human weakness – sometimes showing us His viewpoint, but sometimes just helping us to trust Him. Prayer isn't begging God to go along with our plans, but asking Him to help us go along with His.

THINK Do you find it easy or hard to live life God's way? If you need a big dose of His power and strength, He is right there waiting to help you. Chat to Him!

TALKING WITH GOD

POSITION YOUR HEART

Read: Philippians 4:4-9

KEY VERSE: 'Do not be anxious about anything, but in every situation, by prayer and petition, with thanksgiving, present your requests to God.' (v6)

So far we've looked at the main reasons why we pray. Now let's get down to discovering *how* we should pray.

How does God want us to talk to Him? Is there a particular set of words to use? Do we need to include 'thou' to make it more holy? Or will God be OK with us using our everyday language? And do we need to stand up, or sit down?

The Bible shows us a whole load of different ways people prayed. Lying face down, standing with hands lifted up, loudly, silently, as a group, alone, in the Temple and in a field. It's safe to say that if we're going to look to the Bible for examples of how to pray, we've got a lot of choice!

Really, the only 'how' God cares about is how real and honest you're being with Him — the attitude of your heart. If you've got that right, the rest is up to you!

THINK Think about how you normally pray. Are there certain things you always do? Do these things help you talk to God, or are they just what you thought you had to do?

I WANT WHAT YOU WANT

Read: 1 John 5:1–5,13–15

> **KEY VERSE:** 'And if we know that he hears us –
> whatever we ask – we know that we have what we
> asked of him.' (v15)

Wow! So prayer is basically a fast-track ticket to anything
we want, the way we want it and when we want it? Well,
not quite. If we want a successful prayer life, we need to
learn to pray in line with what God wants.

OK... so how do we know what God wants? Ask Him! If
you wanted to know what your best friend wanted or was
thinking about, you'd ask and listen to the reply.

We also have the Bible to guide us. We may not always
get specific answers to our questions (eg who should I sit
with at lunch?) but we learn God's guidelines for living (eg
Galatians 5:22–23 has a handy list of good things to look
for in a friend). So, by knowing what the Bible says and
talking to God about the situations we face, we can work
out what He wants us to do.

PRAY God, You're such a good Father.
Thank You for always looking out for me and
knowing what's best. Help me to listen to You
and know what You want. Amen.

PSST!

Read: 1 Kings 19:9-13

KEY VERSE: 'After the earthquake came a fire, but the LORD was not in the fire. And after the fire came a gentle whisper.' (v12)

Since we're on the topic of learning to listen to God, it would be really helpful to know what God's voice sounds like, wouldn't it? Lucky for us, Elijah's got that covered.

God wants us to be able to hear Him as He guides us down good paths, as He speaks loving words over us, as He inspires, strengthens and comforts us. So He shows Elijah how to hear His voice, and because God wrote the Bible, this is also His way of telling us how to hear Him. But why would God whisper? Well, think about it, when you're lonely, sad or frightened like Elijah was, do you want someone shouting at you – or do you want someone to sit down with you, listen and speak gently to you?

That's generally what prayer is like – not so much an out-loud voice (although God does occasionally speak to people like that), more an inner voice like the way you talk to yourself without anyone being able to hear.

THINK Have you ever heard God speaking to you? What did He say? Writing down your prayers and thoughts can be helpful if you want to see how God speaks to you.

I KNOW THAT VOICE

Read: Revelation 22:12–21

> **KEY VERSE:** 'I warn everyone who hears the words of the prophecy of this scroll: if anyone adds anything to them, God will add to that person the plagues described in this scroll.' (v18)

'How can I know whether God is speaking to me?' That's a common question. One thing to remember is that God will never contradict Himself. If you think God is telling you to do something that goes against what the Bible says, think again.

The Holy Spirit is gentle. When He speaks to you, He might warn you off something that you are doing, but He will never condemn you (make you feel guilty and give you negative labels) – any words like that come from the devil.

God loves you. He *is* love, and love is the language He speaks to His children. What He says to you will never be unloving.

The more time we spend getting to know God by reading His words to us in the Bible, and listening to that 'inner voice' in our hearts, the more easily we will recognise when God is speaking to us.

PRAY Loving Father, thank You for the help of Your Word and Your Spirit in leading me down the best paths. Help me to be able to recognise Your voice. Amen.

TALKING WITH GOD

KEEPING IT REAL

Read: Psalm 91:9–16

KEY VERSE: 'He will call on me, and I will answer him; I will be with him in trouble, I will deliver him and honour him.' (v15)

Some people think the Bible is unrealistic, but God is as real as it gets. He doesn't say we'll never have tough days; in fact John 16:33 says that we will have troubles!

Don't worry though, He has promised that through all of the ups and downs, He will be with us and give us what we need, and He will turn it all around for good for us.

So what's prayer got to do with this? Well, remember how prayer is talking to God? When we go through a tough time, God is often the last person we go to. Weird, isn't it? Especially when we know that He has all the answers and is able to help us overcome everything. Even people who have been Christians for decades have to be reminded of this. We don't need to face hard stuff on our own, we can do it with God.

So here's your reminder: stay on the line with heaven and don't hang up!

THINK Do you ever forget to go to God with your questions and concerns? Can you think of any practical ideas to help you to remember to talk to Him?

OPEN HEART SURGERY

Read: Psalm 66:16–20

KEY VERSE: 'If I had cherished sin in my heart, the Lord would not have listened' (v18)

Did you notice the key word in that verse? *Cherish*. What we cherish in our heart makes a big impact on our prayer life.

To cherish something is to let it grow, to put great importance on it, to give it lots of our attention. The psalmist knew sin, but he didn't *cherish* sin in his heart. Others had sinned against him, and he had sinned against others. But when others hurt him, he didn't take the pain, anger, and 'why me' questions to heart and give them room to grow: he took them to God and asked Him to deal with them. When he sinned, he didn't try to hide his guilt and shame from God: he laid it all out to God, asking for forgiveness.

There's nothing God can't deal with. By His sacrifice on the cross, Jesus has already paid the price for our sin, and His Holy Spirit comforts us in our pain caused by sin. We just need to take it all to God and ask Him to fix it.

PRAY Father God, forgive me for holding sin and anger in my heart. I give You all my sins and hurts now and ask You to deal with them. Amen.

STOP THE POISON

Read: Matthew 6:5–15

KEY VERSE: 'But if you do not forgive others their sins, your Father will not forgive your sins.' (v15)

If a venomous snake bit you, what would you do? Would you start shouting and attempt to get your own back on the snake? Or would you get away and get medical help ASAP?

Unforgiveness is a poison to your life – that's right, *your* life. Refusing to forgive someone is like choosing to die attacking the snake instead of getting help. That might seem like an exaggeration, but think about it: when you're angry at someone do you feel peaceful and like everything's going to be OK? No! You feel annoyed, unable to think about other things for long, trapped in this anger. Unforgiveness is bad for us.

It's also a huge blockage to your prayer life, because when you refuse to forgive completely – which is how God forgave us when Jesus died for us – you're saying that His sacrifice wasn't good enough. Forgiving someone doesn't mean what that person did to you was OK. It means that you're trusting God to sort out both your hurt and their sin, in His way and timing.

THINK Has a friend done something that really hurt you? Have you forgiven them for this? It's not easy to forgive, but God can help you.

STICK AROUND

Read: John 15:1–11

> **KEY VERSE:** 'If you remain in me and my words remain in you, ask whatever you wish, and it will be done for you.' (v7)

What fruit is Jesus talking about? It's the fruit of the Spirit – godly character traits that grow in us as we grow in our relationship with Him.

This fruit – love, joy, peace, patience, kindness, goodness, faithfulness, gentleness and self-control – is not something we have to work to produce ourselves. It's God who produces these things in our lives as we spend more time with Him. Wouldn't you love to be someone who has all of those things?

Well, you become like who you hang out with! The more we hang out with God, the better and better we'll become. Prayer is just being in constant communication with God as He walks with you through each and every day. It's allowing Him to get rid of your rough edges so that the new, healthy shoots can push through and produce good fruit. The thing is, if we want Him to keep sorting us out in order to produce these great things in us, we need to stick around!

PRAY Lord Jesus, it's so good to spend time with You! Help me to stick close to You so that You can produce Your goodness in me. Amen.

TALKING WITH GOD

PAY IT FORWARD

Read: Philippians 1:9–11

KEY VERSE: 'And this is my prayer: that your love may abound more and more in knowledge and depth of insight' (v9)

Prayer is a wonderful opportunity to talk about other people behind their backs. Not to gossip about them but to talk to God about their needs.

See, the more you hang out with God, the more like Him you become and the more interested you become in the things He cares about. And what does God care about more than anything? People. As your relationship with God grows, so does your love for other people. When Paul visited Philippi on his second missionary journey, several people became Christians. Lydia and a prison jailer were among those who became Christians and formed the first Christian church in Europe. Paul wrote to them to tell them that he was praying for them. Just look at his love and prayers for them.

We are blessed to be a blessing. We pray, not just for the sake of our relationship with God, but for the sake of those around us and their relationship with Him.

THINK Do you mainly pray for yourself or do you remember to pray for others as well? Challenge yourself to choose three people who you will pray for every day for a week.

FROM THE TOP

Read: Matthew 16:13-19

> **KEY VERSE:** 'I will give you the keys of the kingdom of heaven; whatever you bind on earth will be bound in heaven, and whatever you loose on earth will be loosed in heaven.' (v19)

Prayer is not a religious duty – it is part of an awesome relationship with God. It is powered by the same revelation that Peter had in today's reading: that Jesus is who He says He is – Son of the living God. Prayer is the key that opens the door to understanding the world from the view of its creator. With prayer, we end up walking in line with God, working with Him to bring the rule of heaven to earth.

Under the rule of heaven there is no more sickness, poverty, corruption, sadness, death, violence, conflict, confusion and pain. Under the rule of heaven, there is joy, love, peace, kindness, fun, life, health, goodness and every other good thing imaginable.

God has given us the keys to open any situation to His power. The question is whether we leave the keys in our pocket, or start turning the lock.

PRAY Lord Jesus, teach me how to pray so that Your power is unlocked in my life – not just for my benefit but for the benefit of others too. Amen.

THIRSTY?

Read: Psalm 42:1-11

KEY VERSE: 'My soul thirsts for God, for the living God.' (v2)

Today's psalm writer was probably writing this psalm as a refugee. A terrible war had destroyed Israel and the people had been dragged off as slaves to foreign countries. The Temple had been vandalised and smashed up. That was very, very serious. The Temple was more than just a building; it meant that God was with His people. So what did it mean if the Temple was a pile of rubble? Had God deserted His people?

The singer feels a long way from God's presence. He is sad and very low. But in the middle of all his sadness, all he knows is that he is desperate for God. He chooses to believe the impossible: that God loves him and that He will come to His people again.

Being thirsty means that you really want something that you haven't got just yet. Jesus said that He is looking for people who really want to be close to God but know that they haven't got there just yet (Matt. 5:6).

PRAY Lord, please come and be with me. If I'm thirsty, show me more of You. If I don't feel that thirst, give me a taste of just how amazing You are so that I will be! Amen.

PSALM

FIT FOR A KING

Read: Esther 1:1-9

KEY VERSE: 'For a full 180 days he displayed the vast wealth of his kingdom' (v4)

The dramatic story of Esther has so much to teach us girls about bravery, and shows us that real beauty isn't just skin-deep. She really is quite a girl – in fact, she saved the lives of thousands of her people, as you'll soon find out!

The story starts with a king called Xerxes – the man who would soon be Esther's husband. He was pretty much the most powerful man in the world at the time. He wasn't a particularly nice guy and liked throwing flashy parties to show off all his money. Xerxes would let his guests get as drunk as they liked, and things would get pretty rowdy and out of control.

All King Xerxes had going for him was his money, his nice palace and his expensive parties, but inside he was a bit of a rotten egg. The outside appearance didn't match up with the inside. The lesson here? Try not to form an opinion about someone based on their clothes, their house or their stuff. It's a person's character that counts!

PRAY Lord God, help me to remember that appearances can be deceiving. What looks like fun might actually be quite harmful for me. Help me to know the difference. Amen.

ESTHER

TROPHY WIFE

Read: Esther 1:10-12

KEY VERSE: 'Queen Vashti refused to come. Then the king became furious and burned with anger.' (v12)

After a seven-day party binge, the king was enjoying being the centre of attention. Still wanting to show off, he thought he'd bring out his beautiful wife, Vashti, so he could make all the other men jealous. He wanted to parade her around like a catwalk model – but Vashti wasn't having any of it!

The king treated his wife like an object, rather than the love of his life. So when she refused to come and join in with his wild party, Xerxes was absolutely furious! Because all his self-worth was wrapped up in his money and power, he simply couldn't handle it when he was publicly disobeyed. He threw an enormous tantrum – the party was over.

Because of Jesus, we don't need to be insecure like Xerxes was. Remember that you are precious and valuable not because of the way you look, but because you are a child of God! And the same goes for everyone else. It's so important that we treat other people with respect, and don't demand that they do whatever we want.

PRAY Dear God, thank You that I'm not an object to You, but You love me so much. Help me to find my worth in that. Amen.

BANISHED

Read: Esther 1:13-22

> **KEY VERSE:** 'let him issue a royal decree... that Vashti is never again to enter the presence of King Xerxes' (v19)

After Queen Vashti stood up to him (and quite right too!), King Xerxes threw a mega-tantrum. He was so angry that he had her thrown out of his kingdom forever. That's no way to treat your wife! And he didn't stop there. Worried that other women in the kingdom would start sticking up for themselves when they were treated badly, he passed a law that all wives in the country needed to stay put and stay quiet.

What do you think of the way the king handled things? Notice that he didn't even talk to Vashti and try to sort things out with her. Instead he used his power to punish her.

We all fall out with people we love sometimes, and it can be really hard to talk things through and mend things properly. But it's always worth trying to make amends, even if you're not the person in the wrong. Remember that your friendship with that person is more important than arguing over who was wrong in the first place.

THINK What's your temper like? Is it something you need God's help with? Talk to Him about it now.

ESTHER

QUEEN VACANCY

Read: Esther 2:1-4,12-14

KEY VERSE: 'Then let the young woman who pleases the king be queen instead of Vashti.' (v4)

After he kicked out Queen Vashti and banished her from the kingdom, Xerxes found himself wifeless and wanting a new one. He thought of a new bride as a thing to go shopping for, rather than someone to love and cherish – so he set up auditions so that he could choose the most beautiful woman in the kingdom. The new queen would be the winner of the Miss Persia beauty pageant, and, being a single young woman in the kingdom, Esther was forced to take part.

You might already be feeling pressure to look a certain way, or be told that you're only worth anything if you're pretty. But that simply isn't true! Of course it's enjoyable to be told that you look nice, but you'd never want that to be the only reason someone loves you. Yes, Esther was beautiful on the outside – but it was her bravery and courage that made her amazing. God simply used King Xerxes' shallowness and vanity to put Esther right where she needed to be.

THINK God values people for who they are, not the way they look, and we should do the same. There was so much more to Esther than just her looks, and the same goes for you too!

NOT JUST A PRETTY FACE

Read: Esther 2:5–11,15–18

> **KEY VERSE:** 'Esther won the favour of everyone who saw her.' (v15)

Now we've set the scene, we're ready to meet the leading lady herself: Esther!

Esther was actually an orphan who had been brought up by her relative, a really good guy called Mordecai (remember him, because he'll play an important part in this story). Esther was also an absolute stunner, and she turned a lot of heads. It wasn't just the judges of the beauty contests who admired her, but the other contestants, too. Despite being in a very competitive situation, Esther made lots of friends because of her good heart. She was soon crowned the winner – Esther would be queen!

But Esther was keeping a secret: although she lived in Persia, Esther was actually Jewish (and the Persians didn't particularly like Jews). How angry do you think Xerxes would have been if he'd known he was about to marry a Jew? For her own safety, Mordecai urged Esther to keep her true identity under wraps.

PRAY Father God, thank You that You always have a plan. Help me to be myself and honour You, just like Esther did. Amen.

ESTHER

WHAT A STAR!

Read: Esther 2:10–11

> **KEY VERSE:** 'Every day he walked to and fro near the courtyard of the harem to find out how Esther was' (v11)

Good old Mordecai — he kept a really close eye on Esther!

When her parents had died, Mordecai stepped up to the mark and raised Esther as his own daughter. Not only did he take on the role of a single parent, but he did a great job of it, too. Esther was born with the name 'Hadasseh', which is a Jewish name meaning 'myrtle' (a pretty flower), but he changed it to 'Esther', meaning 'star', so that she wouldn't be picked on by their Persian neighbours. Mordecai always looked out for Esther, and wanted to keep her safe.

The handy thing is that Mordecai worked as a guard at the palace gate, and although he was forbidden from going anywhere near the beauty contestants, he made sure he found out how Esther was doing every single day. How reassuring it must have been for Esther to know that there was someone nearby who cared for her so much.

In the same way, we have someone nearby who cares for us and watches over us — God.

THINK When you think about how God isn't far away but is right with you, how does that make you feel?

TREASON AND PLOT

Read: Esther 2:19–23

KEY VERSE: 'Mordecai found out about the plot and told Queen Esther, who in turn reported it to the king' (v22)

Because Mordecai had done such a great job of bringing Esther up, she trusted him completely and followed his advice.

Working the gate as he usually did, one day Mordecai heard of a plot to kill King Xerxes! A couple of angry guards had hatched a wicked plan to have him murdered.

Even though the king wasn't a particularly nice man, Mordecai knew that this would be a very wrong and terrible thing to happen. So he made sure he got the news to Esther, so that she could warn her husband straightaway and keep him safe from harm.

Well, what a scandal! When the truth came out, the two would-be murderers got their just desserts and Esther made sure Mordecai got all the credit.

Even though he didn't have to, Mordecai spoke up against evil and ended up saving the king's life. When you're faced with a tough choice, what moves you to do the right thing – what God thinks of you, or what other people think of you? What do you think made Mordecai do the right thing?

PRAY Lord, help me to always act out of love for You, and not with selfish motives. Amen.

ESTHER

MAN OF THE HOUR

Read: Esther 3:1–6

> **KEY VERSE:** 'When Haman saw that Mordecai would not kneel down or pay him honour, he was enraged.' (v5)

You might be thinking that King Xerxes is the bad guy in this story – after all, he's a bit of a bully, treats women really badly, drinks far too much and has massive tantrums whenever he doesn't get his own way. But today's reading introduces us to a far worse villain: a man called Haman.

There's no two ways about it: Haman was a nasty piece of work. As the king's right-hand man, he thought a lot of himself and expected everyone else at the palace to lick his boots.

Mordecai knew he would be expected to bow down every time Haman walked through the palace gates, but he had decided that he would only bow down and worship God. Being completely in love with himself, Haman was angry and insulted that Mordecai didn't go along with the kneeling-down routine. And when he found out that Mordecai was Jewish, he was even angrier. He hated the Jews and stormed off to think of a way to get rid of all the Jews in the empire who worshipped God.

THINK Do you feel under pressure at the moment to look or act a certain way? How could you stand up for God instead?

FACING EXTERMINATION

Read: Esther 3:7–15

> **KEY VERSE:** 'it is not in the king's best interest to tolerate them' (v8)

Yesterday we read about how Mordecai refused to bow down to Haman — he only worshipped God. Rather than simply having Mordecai sacked, Haman totally overreacted and hatched a plan to get rid of all the God-loving Jews in the empire! (See — we said he was evil.)

Haman knew he'd need a pretty huge and convincing reason to persuade the king to sign off on a death warrant for half of the people in the kingdom. In the end he managed to convince Xerxes that the Jewish people were dangerous to everyone else, and couldn't be trusted. So Xerxes allowed Haman to invent a law stating that all the Jews would be killed on the thirteenth day of the twelfth month. Because of the way the law was written, this was set in stone.

So now Esther and Mordecai were facing death, just because they were Jewish! But remember, God had placed them right where they were for a very specific reason, and the story isn't over yet.

THINK Has anyone given you a hard time recently because you're a Christian? How did you react? Ask God for the courage you need to stand up for Him and react in the right way.

ESTHER

PERFECT TIMING

Read: Esther 4:1-14

> **KEY VERSE:** 'who knows but that you have come to your royal position for such a time as this?' (v14)

Have you ever found yourself in just the right place at just the right time?

When they heard the terrible news that their people were facing death, Esther and Mordecai were devastated. How terrifying! But then they remembered how powerful and loving God is, and they took the mess to Him.

It occurred to Mordecai that maybe God had been prepared for this all along, and provided a solution before the problem even arose – Esther! Esther was married to the king, after all – surely she could do something about this terrible thing about to happen?

But it was still a very dangerous situation. Esther risked her life just by approaching the king without an invitation, even though they were married. It would take every ounce of her courage to arrange a meeting with him, and try to persuade him to let her people live. Of course, that would mean giving away her secret that she was a Jew herself. Would Esther keep quiet or speak out for God, even though it meant she might be killed?

PRAY Father God, help me to trust You no matter what. Help me to speak up for You when You want me to. Amen.

ALL YOU CAN DO IS PRAY

Read: Esther 4:15-17

KEY VERSE: 'Go, gather together all the Jews who are in Susa, and fast for me.' (v16)

Esther had to make the hardest decision of her life. Should she play it safe, do nothing and hope to live beyond the day when all the Jews would be killed? Or would she risk her own life to try to save God's people?

Esther knew she needed God's help and so she asked for it. More than that, she asked others to pray for her too. She also fasted by going without food for a little while. This is something Christians do sometimes when they are praying really hard for something. Esther really needed a breakthrough and she showed God she meant it.

When we have such an amazing and powerful God just a prayer away, we don't need to struggle on our own! Don't ever be embarrassed about asking other people to pray for you. God hears us when we talk to Him. He can turn any situation around for good.

THINK Is there a situation you are trying to muddle your way through at the moment? Why not talk to God about it? He loves to hear from you, and He always has the answer. Don't struggle on your own – let Him help you.

ESTHER

A FOOT IN THE DOOR

Read: Esther 5:1-8

> **KEY VERSE:** 'When he saw Queen Esther standing in the court, he was pleased with her' (v2)

After three days of praying her socks off, Esther knew it was time to talk to the king. Even though she was his wife, it was very dangerous for her to barge in without a proper invitation. If Xerxes did not hold out his golden sceptre to welcome her in, she would face the death penalty.

Fortunately, Xerxes was still head-over-heels for his new queen, and was so delighted to see her that he offered her half of his kingdom! But Esther didn't get distracted by the offer of wealth and power. All she wanted was freedom and safety for her people. So instead of putting herself first, she trusted God and invited Xerxes to have dinner with her so that she'd be able to make her real request.

God had proved Himself faithful in being with Esther as she approached the king, and making sure she'd have the chance to talk with him further.

Do you crave being popular and powerful? Don't forget that if you're with God, you're already the daughter of the king!

PRAY Heavenly Father, I want to put You and Your plans first, always. Help me not to focus on stuff and status, but on what You want to teach me. Amen.

PRIDE BEFORE A FALL

Read: Esther 5:9-14

KEY VERSE: 'But all this gives me no satisfaction as long as I see that Jew Mordecai' (v13)

Who do you want to serve – yourself or God?

Haman was so full of himself, it's a miracle he could even stand up! Enjoying his status as a royal big cheese and looking forward to the day that the Jews would be killed, nothing was going to rain on Haman's parade. Except, that is, for Mordecai.

Even though his people were facing death, Mordecai carried on as normal. He still trusted God, still went to work every day, and still refused to bow down to Haman. And it drove Haman nuts!

Too impatient to wait for the thirteenth day of the twelfth month, Haman plotted to have Mordecai executed sooner rather than later.

Haman was only interested in fulfilling his own ambitions, no matter who he had to walk all over to get to the top. But Mordecai was only interested in serving God, trusting Him and doing the right thing. He knew that God was in control and would work things out for good. He was prepared to worship God even if it cost him his life.

PRAY Father God, thank You that I can be confident that no matter what happens, You are always around. Help me to worship You no matter what the cost. Amen.

ESTHER

BEING PUT IN YOUR PLACE

Read: Esther 6:1-11

KEY VERSE: 'Get the robe and the horse and do just as you have suggested for Mordecai the Jew' (v10)

Here's something great about God: He works in favour of the humble people, not the arrogant lot.

The king's bedtime reading was about to change everything. Unable to sleep one night, Xerxes was reading over some old royal documents and noticed a short mention of Mordecai's name.

Do you remember that Mordecai had exposed a murder plot against the king and saved his life? Xerxes was keen to reward the guard who had done him such a huge favour.

He decided to ask Haman how he should go about publicly thanking a loyal servant. But Haman, being so full of himself, assumed that the king was looking to honour him! So he suggested an extravagant parade, complete with cheerleaders and fireworks (well, something like that). Imagine his horror when it turned out that instead of executing Mordecai, he would be parading him through the city as the man of the hour. How humiliating for Haman, and how marvellous for Mordecai! Serves Haman right for being so arrogant.

THINK Who do you admire who's really humble and servant-hearted? Why not find a way to encourage that person and tell them how highly you think of them?

DON'T RAIN ON MY PARADE

Read: Esther 6:12-14

> **KEY VERSE:** 'Mordecai returned to the king's gate. But Haman rushed home, with his head covered in grief' (v12)

Haman rushed home after the parade — he had never felt so humiliated and angry in his life! And it all had been his own going. His perfect plan for power and status was going horribly wrong. What was going on?!

Meanwhile, Mordecai returned to his ordinary day job as a guard at the king's gate. Even though there was still a law in place ruling that he and his people would soon be destroyed, he continued to serve God faithfully and get on with life, trusting that things would work out in God's perfect timing. Why do you think he was able to keep calm?

It can be tempting to faze God out of our lives a bit when things are going well for us, as if we don't really need Him. But God wants more of a relationship with us than for Him to be like a paramedic — only called in when there's an emergency! He wants to be part of your life, every day.

THINK How would you describe your relationship with God? Do you spend more time with Him when things are going well, or when things are going wrong? Why do you think that might be?

ESTHER

AN UNEXPECTED TURN

Read: Esther 7:1–8:2

KEY VERSE: 'So Haman was hanged on the very gallows that he had built for Mordecai. And the king's hot anger cooled.' (7:10, *The Message*)

Haman couldn't sit and strop forever – he had Esther's royal dinner party to get to! Getting all dressed up as a guest of honour might have lifted his spirits for a little while, but if he'd known what was in store for him, he might have called in sick...

The evening began well – until Esther was ready to talk. The timing could not have been more perfect. First, she revealed her true identity as a Jewish woman who loved and worshipped God– much to Haman's horror! Then she revealed that she was a relative of Mordecai.

In a dramatic turn of events, everything changed. The king imploded with rage at the discovery of Haman's plot against his beautiful wife, Esther. He instantly ordered for Haman to be put to death, and promoted Mordecai to the highest position in the kingdom (Haman's old job!).

The Bible is full of stories of God turning hopeless situations around for His glory. Is there anything you need His help with today?

PRAY Father God, You are awesome! Help me to remember that You are so much bigger and more powerful than any danger or threat I will ever face. Amen.

SELF-DEFENCE

Read: Esther 8:1-11

KEY VERSE: 'Now write another decree in the king's name on behalf of the Jews as seems best to you' (v8)

Haman may have been out of the picture, but the royal order to kill all the Jewish people on the thirteenth day of the twelfth month still stood. The laws of the Medes and Persians could never be changed, so Mordecai and Esther were still facing a pretty big problem – their lives were in danger.

So they persuaded the king to pass another law so that Jews would have the right to defend themselves against anyone who dared to attack them. They even had the new law printed in several languages so that everyone in the kingdom would get the message.

As Christians, we too have an enemy that wants to hurt us. But we also have a powerful God who helps us fight through our struggles. Just like Esther's people we're stronger together, armed with the Bible and prayer. Are you feeling under attack at the moment or know someone else who's struggling with their faith? Get together with some Christian friends and remind yourself that God's already got this.

PRAY Heavenly Father, thank You that You never leave us to fight on our own. Help me to stand with fellow Christians and face down any challenges without fear. Amen.

ESTHER

D-DAY

Read: Esther 8:15-9:4; 10:3

KEY VERSE: 'he worked for the good of his people and spoke up for the welfare of all the Jews' (10:3)

So, would the Jews be brutally wiped out on the thirteenth day of the twelfth month? Or would the right to defend themselves be enough to save their skin?

God used the nine months leading up to that day so that Mordecai, in his new fancy job, would have the chance to speak up on behalf of the Jewish people. In the end, most Persians sided with the Jews because of the respect they had for Mordecai. Anyone who dared to fight against the Jews lost the battle. Death Day became Deliverance Day!

Just as Esther had been in a position of privilege and honour but risked it all to help others, Mordecai used his power and influence for the greater good and the sake of God's plans, rather than simply enjoying a life of luxury as Haman had. Do others benefit from the gifts God has given you? Think of some people in need and plan practical ways you can care for them.

THINK What gifts do you have that you most want God to help you use for His glory? Talk to Him now — He gave you those talents and resources for a reason!

BEHIND THE SCENES

Read: Esther 9:20–28

> **KEY VERSE:** 'And these days of Purim should never fail to be celebrated by the Jews' (v28)

To make sure the Jewish people didn't forget how God had saved them from being wiped out, Mordecai made it a custom to have a two-day celebration every year. Freedom is worth celebrating! To this day, Jews still celebrate the Feast of Purim by dressing up and giving gifts.

As human beings, we can have quite short memories and soon forget the good things God has done for us, especially when we're finding things a bit tough. But just like Esther's people, we too faced a death sentence (cut off from God forever because of our sin) until Jesus our Saviour rescued us. Because of His bravery and sacrifice, we can be restored to God forever. Now *that's* worth celebrating!

The book of Esther is an epic story of God's power, and yet God's name is never mentioned! Did you notice that as you've been reading? But His name is written all over it in the way that He was there all along, working behind the scenes for the good of those who love Him.

THINK Is God asking you to do something brave at the moment? What can you learn from Esther's story that will give you courage?

ESTHER

SORRY

Read: Psalm 51:1-19

KEY VERSE: 'Create in me a pure heart, O God' (v10)

When things go wrong, when we mess up, we can't just press a button to make everything right again – we have to sort things out and that usually involves saying sorry.

Of course, this can be one of the toughest things to do. We naturally want to pretend we've done nothing wrong by saying, 'It wasn't my fault.' Or, 'That person deserved it.'

The psalm today is believed by many to be written by King David. He messed up big time. He was a cheater and a murderer. He tried to carry on as normal, pretending he'd done nothing wrong, but eventually it all hit him. He'd behaved badly, not only against other people, but against God. He felt terrible! He couldn't turn back time, but at least he could get right with God.

If we don't admit we've done anything wrong then we're trapped – we can't grow as Christians. That's a shame and it can even tear us away from God. But when we admit our mistakes to God, the burden of guilt is lifted and we can feel so much better.

PRAY God, You love me so much and forgive me freely. Thank You. Please clean out my heart and make me new today. Amen.

RELAX

Read: Psalm 131:1-3

KEY VERSE: 'I have calmed and quietened myself, I am like a weaned child with its mother' (v2)

So, you've just been born and what happens? Suddenly you are thrown out of a lovely, safe, warm and comfortable home and into the cold, fresh air. Where's your lovely warm home gone? And what about your endless supply of food? Now you have to ask for it (cry a lot!).

The thing about babies is that when they finally get fed, they relax. Cuddled up with their mums, nice and smug, they are very, very happy!

Weaning is the stage of a baby's life where they are no longer on milk but start to eat other food. This psalm shows us a picture of a happy child who has learnt to trust his mother to provide this food for him. It shows us that when we come close to God and relax in His company, then we are a bit like a happy child. God loves us, protects us and feeds us. Just like a mother enjoy the bond that grows between herself and her child, so God enjoys it when we chill out and enjoy His company.

THINK What do you think it means to spend time relaxing with God? Take some time now to enjoy just hanging out with Him – it's so good for you!

PSALM

INNER CIRCLE

Read: Mark 14:12–21

KEY VERSE: 'But woe to that man who betrays the Son of Man!' (v21)

Let's jump right in at the deep end of the days before Jesus' crucifixion. It's a dinnertime scene, and Jesus is having dinner with His closest friends for the last time before His arrest.

As Judas was one of the disciples, he was one of Jesus' *best friends*. Think about that for a moment. He had followed Jesus for three years, seen Him perform miracles, and heard Him preach about the incredible love of God. Jesus loved Judas, and at some point Judas must have loved Jesus.

We read today that Jesus knew that Judas would betray Him (v20), but had still loved him as one of His best friends. He warns Judas of how bad things would be if he did betray Him. But Judas still goes through with his plan to handover Jesus.

Jesus allowed Judas into His inner circle, and loved Him, despite knowing that he would hurt Him. That's pretty incredible. In the same way, God brings us close to Him even though we sometimes mess up!

PRAY Lord Jesus, thank You for allowing me to be Your friend even though I get things wrong. Your forgiveness and love for me are amazing. Amen.

CROSSROADS

THE NIGHT SHIFT

Read: Luke 22:47–53

KEY VERSE: 'But Jesus answered, 'No more of this!' And he touched the man's ear and healed him.' (v51)

So, picture this...

It's the middle of the night – something like 2am. You're a temple guard out on night patrol in Jerusalem. You're tired and crabby, but you've received a tip-off from Judas that Jesus – the 'trouble-maker' the authorities have been after for ages – is close by. This should be the easiest arrest of your career (and may earn you a promotion!).

When you get to the Garden of Gethsemane, Judas signals to you which man is Jesus. Your moment has come: time to jump in and arrest Him.

He doesn't resist. But the next thing you know, pain is blasting the right-hand side of your head. A very angry man – one of Jesus' friends – has chopped off your ear!

This was pretty much the experience of the temple guard in today's reading. But in the midst of chaos and horrible pain, Jesus – the man he has just arrested – places His hand on the spot where the guard's ear had been, and heals him. No questions asked.

That's how the Son of God responded to being arrested.

THINK How do you react when someone starts an argument with you? Do you lash out, wanting to hurt them back? Or do you show them kindness?

TRIAL AND ERROR

Read: Matthew 26:57-67

KEY VERSE: 'But I say to all of you: from now on you will see the Son of Man sitting at the right hand of the Mighty One and coming on the clouds of heaven.' (v64)

Let's fast-forward a couple of hours from the ear-chopping incident...

Jesus has been taken to a make-shift court. Everybody there wants Him killed. There's just one problem – Jesus is perfect. They don't have any dirt on Him to have Him crucified. They resort to calling false witnesses. The trial was clearly illegal and was part of the plot to get rid of Jesus.

Caiaphas, the high priest, was completely disgusted by Jesus' claims that He was the Son of God – so much so that he tore his own clothes in anger (as you do!). He then decided to go with the charge of blasphemy, which meant acting or speaking in a way that disrespects God. Caiaphas couldn't have been more wrong.

Jesus faced all of this for us. He willingly went through this unfair trial so that we could go free. Jesus, now our high priest, sets out to free us and not condemn us.

PRAY Lord Jesus, thank You so much for going through such an awful situation so I could be free. I praise You for what You have done. Amen.

PASS THE SOAP

Read: Matthew 27:11-26

> **KEY VERSE:** 'So when the crowd had gathered, Pilate asked them, "Which one do you want me to release to you: Jesus Barabbas, or Jesus who is called the Messiah?"' (v17)

The next man to step in was Pilate. He had the authority to pull the plug on the plot against Jesus, but he didn't have the backbone.

By this point it was early morning. The crowd wanted to see Jesus crucified by lunchtime, and they wouldn't stop yelling until they got their way. In stepped Governor Pilate. He tried to get Jesus to defend Himself, but Jesus made 'no reply, not even to a single charge' (v14).

It was a holiday weekend in Jerusalem, and tradition allowed the release of a prisoner, decided by public vote. So Pilate offered the mob the choice: a perfectly innocent man from Nazareth, or a convicted scumbag called Barabbas. But the crowd screamed all the louder and chose to release Barabbas. Pilate then washed his hands of the situation and gave the order for Jesus to be crucified.

THINK The mob wanted Jesus' blood out of hatred for Him, but Jesus was willing to go to the cross out of love for them. Is love what drives you to make the decisions that you make?

CROSSROADS

FRENEMIES

Read: Luke 23:4-12

KEY VERSE: 'That day Herod and Pilate became friends — before this they had been enemies.' (v12)

Today's reading shows just how Pilate liked others to take the blame for him. He didn't like the decision he was being forced to make. So he packed Jesus off to Herod, and ended up making a friend out of an old enemy.

To cut a long story short, Pilate and Herod had not exactly been best buddies. They had probably hated each other. But when Pilate signed the death warrant of Jesus — top of Herod's hit list — he was back in his old enemy's good books. However, their jolly reunion was based upon a shared dislike for the Son of God. Not exactly a friendship built to last.

This can be a hard passage to read when you really think about what is happening here. Jesus is 'ridiculed and mocked' (v11). He was dressed up and humiliated, and no doubt shouted at and spat upon. They wanted Him to fight back. But look at Jesus' reaction — He 'gave Him no answer'. His love for us kept Him standing firm, taking all our punishment on His shoulders.

PRAY Lord Jesus, thank You for going through so much to have a friendship with me. Help me to always remember this. Amen.

THE LONG ROAD

Read: Mark 15:21-32

> **KEY VERSE:** 'A certain man from Cyrene, Simon, the father of Alexander and Rufus, was passing by on his way in from the country, and they forced him to carry the cross.' (v21)

The trek to Golgotha wouldn't have been an easy one, and Jesus had been beaten up so badly that He barely had the energy to carry His cross.

We don't know all that much about Simon, except that he was from North Africa. We can guess that he was on his way to the city for the feasts happening that weekend. He would have passed Jesus' execution parade on his travels.

The Bible tells us that Simon was 'forced' to carry the cross (v21). We don't know why, but whatever the reason, he walked alongside Jesus to the place where He was killed. He felt how heavy that cross was, and it may have given him splinters and blisters. He was there, right there, when the Son of God was nailed to the cross he had carried, suffering a punishment on behalf of the human race.

THINK It's a horrible scene to think about, but it's important for us to remember everything our Saviour did for us. If you were walking with Jesus up to the cross, what would you say to Him?

CROSSROADS

THE GAME OF THE KING

Read: Matthew 27:27–31

KEY VERSE: 'After they had mocked him, they took off the robe and put his own clothes on him. Then they led him away to crucify him.' (v31)

Let's be clear about one thing: the Roman soldiers we are talking about here were not nice people. They were dangerous, cruel and enjoyed killing people. In today's passage, the whole company of soldiers gather together in a large building and are tormenting Jesus before He is crucified.

A few of the men dress Jesus in a robe. A crown of thorns is put on His head. The rest of the soldiers shout insults at Him and a staff is placed in Jesus' hand as a mock iron sceptre. The soldiers mock Jesus more by shouting, 'Hail, king of the Jews.' Then, they begin to spit on Him and hit Him.

Again, this passage is pretty hard-going. But the thing to remember is that Jesus died for every single soldier tormenting Him. He suffered at their hands so that He could save them. People still mock Jesus today – maybe you know some people who do this. But Jesus' mission was to save everyone, no matter how bad.

PRAY Lord, it's amazing to know that no one is too bad for You to save them. Thank You for wanting to save everyone. Amen.

THEY DO NOT KNOW

Read: Luke 23:23-43

KEY VERSE: 'Jesus said, "Father, forgive them, for they do not know what they are doing."' (v34)

It can be pretty shocking to think about what human beings are capable of. Watching the news on TV can make us very aware of this. In today's passage, we read more about the soldiers who seemed to enjoy executing people so much that they even started gambling while doing so.

We've already mentioned about their cruel behaviour. But look at the plea that Jesus shouts out to His father on their behalf: 'they do not know what they are doing'. That's love right there. The soldiers have no idea that they still have the chance to be saved and forgiven – all because of the man they are killing.

Then we see 'the criminal' – that's all we know about this guy. He's unknown, but he's clearly not one of the good guys. Despite that, he sees who Jesus is, and that's enough for Jesus – He tells the criminal that he will be welcomed into paradise.

PRAY Lord Jesus, I believe You are who You say You are. Thank You for dying such a horrible death for me. I believe You are alive today, and I want to live the rest of my life following You. Amen.

CROSSROADS

GOD'S UNDERTAKER

Read: Luke 23:50-56

KEY VERSE: 'There was a man by the name of Joseph, a member of the Jewish High Council, a man of good heart and good character.' (v50, *The Message*)

So — where have all the good men gone? Today we meet one of them: Joseph of Arimathea.

The other Gospel accounts tell us that Joseph was 'a rich man' (Matt. 27:57), and a member of the council (Mark 15:43). We also know that he was a 'disciple of Jesus' (John 19:38).

Joseph was there when Jesus was on trial, but did not agree with the decision that was made. We don't know if He spoke up for Jesus or not, but going to Pilate and asking for Jesus' body would have taken some guts.

Joseph was pretty rich, too. Rich enough, in fact, to own a family tomb in Jerusalem. He believed that Jesus' body deserved a proper burial, not to be dumped in an unmarked grave. So that's what He did. He took Jesus' body down from the cross, wrapped it in cloth, and buried it.

Joseph might have felt like He'd let Jesus down, but he knew that there was still something he could do to worship Jesus — bury His body properly.

THINK Do you ever feel like you've let Jesus down? Don't let your past mistakes make you feel like you can't serve Jesus right now.

THE SPICE OF LIFE

Read: John 19:38-42

KEY VERSE: 'He was accompanied by Nicodemus, the
man who earlier had visited Jesus at night.' (v39)

Joseph didn't have to bury Jesus by himself. We are told
that he had the help of another guy, Nicodemus, who
was an important Jewish leader. Nicodemus had tried to
get Jesus a fair trial when he heard about the plot against
Him. And here, we see him again, giving Jesus a funeral fit
for a king.

Do you know what John 3:16 says? Lots of Christians
love this verse! It says: 'For God so loved the world that
he gave his one and only Son, that whoever believes in
him shall not perish but have eternal life.' And do you
know who Jesus was speaking to when He said that?
Nicodemus! Now that's a conversation he wouldn't easily
forget. Perhaps those amazing words were going through
Nicodemus' head as he poured expensive myrrh and
spices onto Jesus' body, prompting him to take care as
He buried God's Son.

The words that are now on church walls all over the
world were first spoken to good old Nic — what a brilliant
claim to fame!

PRAY Lord God, thank You that I also get
the chance to hear the message You shared
with Nicodemus. Help me to always remember
the truth of this and live by it. Amen.

CROSSROADS

WAY AHEAD OF YOU

Read: Matthew 28:1-15

KEY VERSE: 'He is not here; he has risen, just as he said. Come and see the place where he lay.' (v6)

It's been quite a weekend in Jerusalem... but the worst is over. Today we look back at the very first Easter Sunday, when it would have been a great day to be called Mary!

Picture the scene: two Marys go to visit the tomb of Jesus. They both would have really loved Jesus, and their emotions would have no doubt been all over the place. It had been one heck of an upsetting and scary few days. But just when they thought they'd seen it all, they find an angel sat on the tomb stone, having rolled it away!

Imagine that! The tomb is wide open and empty and an angel is there just chilling out, waiting to speak to you! Team Mary were told, 'He has risen from the dead and is going ahead of you into Galilee. There you will see him' (v7).

Sorry – what?! Is this the right tomb? Is the angel talking about the same Jesus? Is this a joke? No! Jesus took death on, and He smashed it.

THINK Mary and Mary were the first to see Jesus alive again, and they fell at His feet. What would your reaction have been if you were in their shoes?

A GIRL CALLED JO

Read: Luke 24:1-12

> **KEY VERSE:** 'It was Mary Magdalene, Joanna, Mary the mother of James, and the others with them who told this to the apostles.' (v10)

Today we meet another woman who played a big part in the news about Jesus' resurrection going viral: Joanna.

Joanna was one of the women who gave money to support Jesus in what He was doing. The disciples had quit their jobs to follow Jesus, so the money needed to come from somewhere. Joanna had definitely helped here. She'd seen Jesus' miracles and have given Him her time, money and gifts.

What makes Joanna super interesting is that her husband, Chuza, was the manager of Herod's household! That's right, the money Joanna was giving to Jesus came from none other than the man who had pushed for Him to be killed.

Joanna got to be one of the first people to hear that Jesus was alive – most definitely not the sort of thing her husband's boss would like to hear! But did she care? Probably not, because she ended up being one of the first members of the Church – ever.

PRAY Dear God, I want to be part of the team that makes Your good news go viral. Please use me to spread the word to other people. Amen.

CROSSROADS

DAY
136

A MYSTERY GUEST

Read: Luke 24:13-35

KEY VERSE: 'It is true! The Lord has risen and has appeared to Simon.' (v34)

Cleopas was making his way to Emmaus, a few miles out of Jerusalem. We don't have many clues as to who his friend was (one theory suggests Mrs Cleopas) – but the two of them walked and talked together, getting on with their journey.

Reading this story, we know that it is Jesus who joins them on the road, but as far as Cleopas and his friend are concerned, they've picked up a mystery guest. Look at how Jesus just 'came up and walked along with them' (v15). He doesn't demand to be bowed down to; He just joins His friends where they are, and asks them questions. And Jesus definitely has a sense of humour here – He gets them to tell Him everything that's happened over the past few days!

Did you also notice that Jesus doesn't barge into Cleopas' home and expect to be fed? Instead, He waits for an invitation, just like He waits to be invited into our lives. It isn't until dinner is served that He is recognised for who He is. And what a shock it was!

THINK Jesus is walking alongside us, waiting for us to chat to Him even though it means telling Him things He already knows. Will you have a conversation with Him?

SOMETHING IN THE WATER

Read: John 21:1–14

KEY VERSE: 'None of the disciples dared ask him, "Who are you?" They knew it was the Lord.' (v12)

The resurrected Jesus still isn't done revealing Himself to His followers.

Before the disciples met Jesus, they had been professional fishermen. Then Jesus told them to throw their nets over the other side of the boat, and they caught so many fish their nets broke. After the best catch of their lives, they quit their day jobs to follow Him.

In today's reading, it looks as though the disciples have tried to re-enter the fishing business. Their master wasn't with them anymore, they thought it was all over, and they needed to keep a low profile and put some food on the table. They'd spent the whole night fishing, still to be left fish-less, when Jesus showed up. Performing the same miracle in front of the disciples was the perfect in-joke. They realised who He was, and couldn't refuse His offer to 'Come and have breakfast' (v12).

Jesus is full of surprises and is always doing new, exciting things in people's lives. Why not ask Him to show you what He's doing in yours?

PRAY Father, I know You have so many good things in store for me. Help me to notice when You are doing something new in my life. Amen.

CROSSROADS

THE NEW GUY

Read: Acts 1:15–26

KEY VERSE: 'the lot fell to Matthias; so he was added
to the eleven apostles' (v26)

Warning! This one isn't pretty. Judas didn't get a happy
ending at all. But his departure left a spot open in the 12
disciples — and prophecies from years and years ago said
that this spot would need to be filled. So, who got the job?

Picture this: you've been around in Jerusalem for a
while, and are well aware of the awesome stuff that
Jesus has been doing. You know about the healings and
miracles, His death and resurrection, and you want that
spot on the dream team. There's only one other guy
who's in with a chance. Of course, you'd prefer it if they
didn't decide by throwing dice, but you trust that it's God
who gets the final say.

That's what it was like for Matthias! But God knew how
loyal Matthias had been behind the scenes and pulled
him into the group at the right moment. The disciples
had started their decision-making off with an important
prayer: 'Lord, you know everyone's heart. Show us' (v24).
Wow — what a prayer!

THINK The next time you face a
decision, why not try praying a similar prayer?
'Lord, You know my heart. Show me what You
think.' Give Him the ultimate control.

RELEVANT

Read: Acts 5:27-42

> **KEY VERSE:** 'For if their purpose or activity is of human origin, it will fail. But if it is from God, you will not be able to stop these men' (vv38–39)

Here we meet a chap called Gamaliel. He was a Pharisee but in today's reading the man speaks sense.

Reading on through the book of Acts, the good news about Jesus is spreading fast. Jesus has returned to heaven, the Holy Spirit has come on the day of Pentecost, people are getting healed from sickness, many are accepting Jesus as their Saviour, and the anti-Jesus club is getting nervous. Once again, the Temple guards are blood-thirsty.

Gamaliel was 'a teacher of the law who was honoured by all people' (v34). And whether he meant to or not, he saved the disciples. What he said went something like this: 'Leave them be, chaps. If this is all a big lie, it will blow over. Don't go mad about it. That way, just in case it's actually true, you won't have picked a fight with God.'

We know that it wasn't a lie. Jesus is alive! Over 2,000 years later we're still talking about Him. He's relevant, He's amazing and He's full of love for you.

THINK Write down some of the ways that Jesus has had an impact on the world we live in today.

CROSSROADS

NO MISTAKE

Read: Psalm 8:1-9

KEY VERSE: 'what is mankind that you are mindful of them, human beings that you care for them?' (v4)

The writer of this psalm is taking a look up at the sky and thinking about how big the world is, and it's made him realise some big stuff about God's big love for His people.

We are a very special part of God's creation. In the middle of all the fantastic things in creation, like the moon and the stars, God chose to 'crown' humans with 'glory and honour' (v5). Amazing! We are so tiny compared to the moon and the stars, but who is it that God has a big place in His heart for? Us. And who is it He does the most for? Us! That's how much He values us.

Lots of people live their lives wondering what they are worth and if they are loved. Well here's the truth: the creator of the universe, the same one who put the sun in the sky, loves you more than words can say. He cares so much about us that He watched His own Son, Jesus, suffer on a cross so that we could be set free.

THINK God cares for us, so let's care for each other. Is there anyone you know who could do with being made to feel cared about today? Think of something you could do for that person.

PSALM

OBEDIENT TO GOD

Read: Genesis 11:27–32; Hebrews 11:8

KEY VERSE: 'By faith Abraham, when called to go to a place he would later receive as his inheritance, obeyed and went, even though he did not know where he was going.' (Heb. 11:8)

When you just can't wait for something to happen, having to hang around for it can be really tough. We live in a world of next-day delivery – we hate the wait! The story of Abraham and Sarah tells us of some amazing promises that God made. But the promise they wanted God to keep the most was the one thing they had to wait for.

Let's start at the beginning: before God changed his name to Abraham, our main guy was called Abram. He and his family lived in a rich town called Ur, but what made them leave?

Even though it hadn't been long since God sent the huge flood, the people had once again turned away from Noah's God. Even Abram's dad worshipped idols. Yet Abram realised the God of Noah was real and for him. So Abram, Sarai (his wife – soon to be known as Sarah), Terah (his dad) and Lot (his nephew) left Ur and headed towards Canaan.

THINK Change can be really hard, but God is there to talk about it. Are you finding it hard to adjust to changes in your life?

PROMISES

GOD OF PROMISES

Read: Genesis 12:1-9

KEY VERSE: 'I will make you into a great nation, and I will bless you; I will make your name great, and you will be a blessing.' (v2)

While Abram was at Harran, God made some promises to him. These were not your everyday 'I promise I'll tidy my room' type of promises, they were *big* promises. Four thousand years later, let's see if God kept them.

Did Abram's descendants become a great nation?
Abram became the father to several nations, but the great nation God was on about is Israel. Attempts to destroy the Jews have failed. They are still in the land promised to Abram.

Was Abram blessed? Yep! Abram had wealth and power. However, his biggest blessing was being able to talk with God about anything.

Has Abram's name become great? It's not only Jews and Christians who respect him, but Muslims too. He's honoured by millions of people around the world.

Has everyone been blessed through Abram's descendants — the Jews? Jesus was born as a Jew. Through Jesus, anyone in the world can be forgiven and become friends with God. So yes, we've all been blessed.

THINK God keeps His promises. Can you think of any promises He's made to you?

GOD OF TRUTH

Read: Genesis 12:10-20

KEY VERSE: '"What have you done to me?" [Pharaoh] said. "Why didn't you tell me she was your wife?"' (v18)

Abram was settled in the Promised Land when the land dried up and there was no food. With these problems, did he wonder if he and Sarai had been right to leave Ur?

Abram and Sarai headed south into Egypt in search of food. News that there was a beautiful woman in town reached Pharaoh, who wanted to add her to his collection. At this point, Abram bottled out of trusting God. He was afraid to say that Sarai was his wife in case Pharaoh had him killed in order to marry her. So he pretended Sarai was his sister. God, however, was having none of it. He had plans for Sarai to be the mother of a great nation. So Pharaoh was taken out of action with a serious illness until the truth came out.

Abram got himself into a big mess by telling lies. But although he let God down, God made sure Abram and Sarai were allowed to return to the Promised Land with all the food they needed.

PRAY Lord, thank You that You love to help me and are always there. Please help me to live my life relying on You, not lies. Amen.

PROMISES

GOD KNOWS

Read: Genesis 13:1–13

KEY VERSE: 'Abram called on the name of the LORD.' (v4)

After a lot of bother in Egypt, Abram hit the road, returned to Bethel and sorted things out with God. But the problems didn't stop there.

The issue was that Abram and his nephew, Lot, had so many sheep and cattle that they couldn't all fit on the fields in that area. Abram had the right to first choice on the land. After all, God had promised it to him, not Lot. But he offered Lot first choice instead, and Lot got greedy. He decided to take the fertile Jordan valley, leaving the dried up mountains to Abram. Abram knew he was getting a rubbish deal but didn't complain. He wanted to part ways on good terms.

But was it such a bad deal? Lot had not talked with God about the decision. Had he done so, God would have pointed out the dangers of going to live near Sodom and Gomorrah. The people there were bad news. Lot's decision gave him fat cattle but brought him and his family a lot of sadness.

THINK God knows things that we don't know. Do you talk to Him about decisions you have to make? It makes sense to because He always knows what's best.

GOD FIRST

Read: Genesis 13:14–18

KEY VERSE: 'Go, walk through the length and breadth of the land, for I am giving it to you.' (v17)

Ever felt like you've become worse off for doing the right thing? Lot had made his choice; did that mean Abram was left with second best? Lot rushed off to claim his land, a 25-mile stretch of the Jordan valley. Abram remained on the hilltop with land that was wild and rocky. How would his sheep survive?

God always works for the good of those who put Him first. There was no way Abram would come out of this second best – not with God in charge. God told Abram to look up, then look around. He could see for miles and miles in every direction, right out to the coast, along the Jordan valley, and over the hills. God promised that all this land would be his – including Lot's patch!

So how did Abram celebrate? He built an altar and worshipped God.

Going God's way might not always make us popular at the time, but you can guarantee this: if you put God first, you'll come out on top. Who or what comes first in your life?

PRAY Dear God, I know that You want the best for me and I am deciding to put You first in my life. I trust You. Amen.

PROMISES

ABRAM TO THE RESCUE

Read: Genesis 14:8–16

> **KEY VERSE:** 'He recovered all the goods and brought back his relative Lot and his possessions, together with the women and the other people.' (v16)

Lot found that things were far from easy in the land he'd chosen. His get-rich-quick plans took a setback when Kedorlaomer, a tough-nut outlaw, forced the local businessmen to cough up protection money. They paid him off for 13 years before deciding to gang together and refuse to pay anymore. Lot's gang came off badly in the mob fighting that followed, and he and his family were captured.

How did Abram react to the news? Did he laugh and say, 'Serves him right'? Lot had been really selfish in grabbing the best land for himself, so he had it coming, didn't he?

Nope, Abram got a gang of 318 men ready to go on a search and rescue mission. In a daring night raid Abram, with God's help, chased the mob out and rescued Lot, his family and all their belongings! Abram risked his life to save his selfish nephew. That sounds a lot like what someone else we know did – Jesus!

THINK Jesus gave up His life to set us free from sin and death. If He doesn't hold grudges, even when we've messed up, are there any grudges you need to let go of?

PRIEST-KING

Read: Genesis 14:17-24

KEY VERSE: 'praise be to God Most High, who delivered your enemies into your hand' (v20)

Abram returned as a hero, and Melchizedek, the king of Jerusalem, congratulated him. Melchizedek wasn't only the king, but a priest of the most high God. He gave credit where it was due – to God.

At a time when most people worshipped the sun or man-made idols, Melchizedek knew better. He didn't congratulate Abram for winning the battle. He congratulated him for having God on his side. He didn't praise Abram for being successful – he praised God. Melchizedek, the first recorded priest-king of Jerusalem, believed that God who created everything could do anything. He praised God for simply being the best.

Abram showed his thanks to God by giving 10% of the goods he had captured to Melchizedek. He returned the rest to its rightful owners in Sodom, refusing to keep any for himself. He had already promised God he wouldn't accept any gifts from the dodgy characters in Sodom. He didn't need their help (which probably wouldn't be very helpful) or money – he had God on his side!

PRAY Lord Jesus, I also think You are the best. I praise You for all the things You do in the world and in my life, both big and small. Amen.

PROMISES

COUNT ON IT

Read: Genesis 15:1–6

KEY VERSE: 'Do not be afraid, Abram. I am your shield, your very great reward.' (v1)

As soon as Abram turned down the king of Sodom's offer, God arrived on the scene as Abram's 'very great reward'.

Abram opened his heart to Him. He shared with God the things that were really bothering Him. He and Sarai had tried to have children but hadn't been successful. And let's face it, all God's promises about Abram becoming the father of a great nation were depending on him having children. If God didn't make him a dad soon, all would be lost. If he had no heir, one of his servants would inherit everything from him.

But God knew what He was going to do. He asked Abram to look up and open his eyes. As Abram star-gazed, he took in God's promise. He would have a son! Impossible as it might seem, he would finally be a real father with so many descendants that there would be too many of them to count! God said so, and Abram trusted that He would make it happen – somehow.

THINK Do you ever wonder if God really cares about the things that bother you? Here's something to remember: if it's bothering you, He's bothered.

SAFE

Read: Genesis 15:7–21

> **KEY VERSE:** 'I am the LORD, who brought you out of Ur of the Chaldeans to give you this land to take possession of it.' (v7)

God promised childless Abram that his family would grow into a great nation — and with that promise was a guarantee that they would have their own land. God's promise was huge. How about Abram's faith?

Abram knew that the land God promised was full of tough-talking tribes who wouldn't want him marching in and settling down. He just couldn't work out how his family would ever be strong enough to take them all on. After making sacrifices to God, he fell into a deep sleep. But what God told him as he slept scared him. He learnt that although he would enjoy a long and peaceful life, his descendants would spend 400 years as slaves in a foreign land.

But then God threw a light on the situation, and suddenly the future looked far, far brighter. God promised to rescue the Israelites and help them claim their land from those troublesome tribes. Abram's family *would* live where God had promised.

PRAY Heavenly Father, when the future scares me, please remind me of how far You've already brought me and of how safe I am in Your hands. Amen.

PROMISES

THE WRONG PLAN

Read: Genesis 16:1-6

> **KEY VERSE:** '[Sarai] said to Abram, "The LORD has kept me from having children. Go, sleep with my slave; perhaps I can build a family through her."' (v2)

Ten years after arriving in Canaan, Abram, (now 86) and Sarai still had no children. They had waited for God to give them a son but nothing had happened. What now?

God's plan – Plan A – was that Abram and Sarai would have a son. And Abram believed God would work to that plan. But after years of waiting, the couple came up with Plan B. The result would be the same – a son – but via their servant Hagar, not Sarai.

Abram and Sarai didn't speak to God. They just put Plan B into action and Hagar became pregnant. But they hadn't read the small print for Plan B: family problems were guaranteed. There was trouble from day one. Jealous Sarai treated Hagar badly and eventually the young, pregnant servant ran away from home.

God hadn't forgotten about Plan A, He just had it on hold. Abram made the big mistake of rushing ahead of God. Instead of trusting Him, Abram put his own plan into action.

THINK Do you sometimes want to do things your way without speaking to God? Next time you're tempted to rush into something, try talking and praying with a Christian friend first.

SPOT ON

Read: Genesis 16:7–16

KEY VERSE: 'She gave this name to the LORD who spoke to her: "You are the God who sees me"' (v13)

Abram and Sarai's Plan B was a disaster that left Hagar on the run and alone. What did God make of it all? He sent an angel to find Hagar. God still cared about her and her baby. He wasn't going to leave her to fend for herself in the desert. The angel asked Hagar to talk about what happened and what she planned to do. God knows it's important that we have someone to talk to.

The young girl needed a lot of support and love, and the best place for her to be was at home. But there would have to be changes. Hagar should begin by working things out with Sarai and helping her. But she was understandably worried about the future and what would happen to her baby, so God let her in on a secret. She was expecting a boy – a son who would grow up to have many descendants.

When we are going through a hard time, God sees us. He wants us to talk to Him about how we feel. We can trust Him.

PRAY Thank You, God, that You will always see and care for me. Please remind me to always talk to You in hard times. Amen.

PROMISES

FULL STOP

Read: Genesis 17:1-8,15-22

KEY VERSE: 'Yes, but your wife Sarah will bear you a son, and you will call him Isaac.' (v19)

Remember this? Abram is 99 years old. Sarai is 90. God now explains that the time is right for them to have a son. Abram just laughs. Well, what would you have done? Looked it up in a science textbook?

There was no way it was humanly possible for this retired couple to have children. Abram struggled to get his head around it. He didn't tell God about his doubts but God knew about all of them.

God had to put in a 'Yes, but...'; yes, but you WILL have a son and you WILL call him Isaac. There were no doubts as far as God was concerned. He went into detail about Isaac's future and even gave the couple an arrival date.

God had a new name for Abram – Abraham, meaning 'special dad to loads of children'. He also had a new name for Sarai – Sarah, meaning 'princess'. With all their faults and failings, God still loved this couple.

THINK Sometimes we have a hard time believing that God cares for us when things don't work out in the way we had hoped. How can you help yourself to trust in God's care in future?

NO LIMIT

Read: Genesis 18:1–15

KEY VERSE: 'Is anything too hard for the LORD?' (v14)

There are some people who let whatever you say to them go in one ear and out the other. It's like talking to a brick wall! No matter how many times God promised Abraham and Sarah, the doubts were still lingering.

When three strangers turned up, Abraham invited them in for a bite to eat. Little did he know he was entertaining the Lord.

As Sarah eavesdropped on the mealtime conversation, she heard one of their guests say she would give birth to a son in a year's time – and she had a quiet chuckle. 'No chance,' she thought. Sarah believed she was way past her sell-by date as a mother. But the Lord didn't lay into her for her lack of faith. Instead he asked them a question: 'Why did Sarah laugh? Is *anything* too hard for the Lord?'

Rather than answering the question, Sarah lied about her sniggering: 'I didn't.'

'Yes, you did,' the Lord replied. He knows everything.

God had answered His own question by saying 'I WILL return next year... and Sarah WILL have a son.' He has no limits. He can do anything He wants!

PRAY Lord, when life gets tricky, thank You that there's no limit to what You can do. No problem is too hard for You. Amen.

PROMISES

REAL

Read: Genesis 18:16–21

KEY VERSE: 'I have chosen him, so that he will direct his children and his household after him to keep the way of the LORD.' (v19)

As Abraham walked his guests out, he got some good news and some bad news.

The good news was that Abraham really would become father to a powerful nation. God also told him the secret of being the best dad – teaching your children to love and follow God. God wanted Abraham's family to set an example to all other families by doing things His way.

The bad news was that Lot and his family, living in Sodom, were about to be burnt to a crisp. Sodom and Gomorrah had become cities full of evil. God wasn't going to tolerate the people's behaviour any longer. Lot and his family hadn't joined in with the wild partying, but they hadn't walked away from it. They lived a double life – one to please the bad guys and another to please God. It didn't work. God wants us to be real and for Him all the time.

PRAY Father, I'm sorry for times when I care more about what other people think of me than about what You think of me. Please help me to be loyal to You. Amen.

GOD OF FORGIVENESS

Read: Genesis 18:22–33

KEY VERSE: 'For the sake of ten, I will not destroy it.' (v32)

God is about to detonate the dynamite – His judgment on the 'sin cities'. Abraham knew God was serious about dealing with the wickedness in Sodom and Gomorrah.

God's still against sin today. So the Bible warns us to get right with Him while we have the chance. God hates the wrong things we do and wants to save us from them because He loves us. We can work this out for ourselves as we read what Abraham asked the Lord: would those who obeyed God get the same deal as those who didn't? Even if there were only 50 of them – or fewer? Not at all.

God is tough on sin but He's also kind. He gives people time to think through the way they live, and escape. That's why two angels were on their way to Sodom – to help Lot and his family get out.

God sent Jesus into our world to give us a way out of danger too. When we trust Jesus, we're safe.

THINK Is there anything that you need to ask God to forgive you for? It can be difficult to own up to sin, but it's easier when we realise that God loves us and wants us to go to Him.

PROMISES

DON'T LOOK BACK

Read: Genesis 19:12–29

KEY VERSE: 'But Lot's wife looked back' (v26)

It was make-your-mind-up time for Lot and his family.
How seriously would they take God's warning to leave
their homes as He was about to destroy the city? At first,
Lot seemed in no doubt that God would do as He said. He
rushed round to his future sons-in-law and told them to
pack their things. Sadly, they treated Lot's words as a big
joke. They didn't care about obeying God.

Perhaps this affected Lot's own opinion. Suddenly he
didn't seem so keen to get out either. God's angels had
to practically drag him, his wife and two daughters away.
Even then Lot argued over where they were told to go to
be safe!

As for Lot's wife, she went along with God to start with,
but didn't really want to leave her life in Sodom. Her heart
was still in the city and so she became a pillar of salt.

Despite Lot's hesitation, he and his daughters reached
safety because they'd finally done as God had asked them to.

PRAY Heavenly Father, I want to give
You control of my life today — not just part of
it, all of it. Thank You for sending Jesus to let
me escape from sin. I am so grateful! Amen.

FAITHFUL FRIEND

Read: Genesis 20:1–17

KEY VERSE: 'he is a prophet' (v7)

Some people have a hard time learning their lesson. Remember how Abraham lied to Pharaoh to save his own skin? Remember the trouble that caused? Well, surely he wouldn't pull the same trick again to Abimelek?

Believe it or not, Abraham did. He said he was Sarah's brother to keep himself safe (again!), and let her be taken off to the palace. All God's promises were forgotten as Abraham pushed God out and looked after number one.

But once again, God came to the rescue. God couldn't let Abimelek ruin His plans to start a great nation, so He warned the king. Abimelek was horrified and returned Sarah home immediately.

Was God's friendship with Abraham spoilt by Abraham's lies and lack of faith? Not at all. God told Abimelek that Abraham was a prophet (v7). You see, He still had big plans for His friend and nothing would change that. God even came up with a way to deal with the aftermath. He told Abimelek to ask Abraham to pray for him, and Abraham's prayers brought good results not just for Abimelek, but for Abraham too.

THINK God knows we let Him down but He doesn't write us off. We are still His children even when we get it wrong, and He loves us just the same.

PROMISES

GOD OF LAUGHTER

Read: Genesis 21:1-7

KEY VERSE: 'the LORD did for Sarah what he had promised' (v1)

At last Abraham really is going to be a dad. He's 100 years old and Sarah is expecting their child – just *as* God promised and just *when* God promised.

Only a year before, when God had told Abraham he'd be a father, Abraham had laughed. God had fed him this line for over 20 years, and the joke was starting to wear thin. When Sarah heard that God planned to make her a mother, she'd laughed too. At her age she thought there was no chance.

And now both Abraham and Sarah were laughing again because God had kept His promise. But this was a different type of laughter. It didn't come from their doubts, it came from God Himself. Sarah said as much: 'God has brought me laughter!' Finally, they had a son. God had exchanged their zimmer frames for a pram!

So – is anything too hard for God? Not a chance! God had already named the baby, and Abraham didn't object to the choice. His son was called Isaac – which in Hebrew means 'He laughs'.

PRAY Holy Spirit, please change me so that I learn to trust You in all situations. Let Your goodness be seen by others through my life. Amen.

NO FAVOURITES

Read: Genesis 21:8-21

KEY VERSE: 'God heard the boy crying, and the angel of God called to Hagar from heaven and said to her, "... Do not be afraid"' (v17)

Sarah v Hagar was a rivalry like no other.

God had promised that Abraham's heir would be the father of a great nation – a nation into which He would send the Saviour of the world. Would this special nation come from Hagar's son, Ishmael, or Sarah's son, Isaac? Ishmael was the eldest, but God had always said His promises to Abraham would be fulfilled through Sarah.

Abraham was upset over the family squabbling. He loved both his sons – so did God. And God had the answer. Isaac's children would become the special nation God had chosen to show His ways to the world – the Jews. Ishmael's children would become a great nation too – the Arabs.

God didn't love Isaac more than Ishmael. He proved it by looking after Hagar and Ishmael in the desert all those years ago. God has different plans for all of our lives, but that doesn't mean He loves us any more or less than others.

THINK Do you ever think that God seems to have favourites? He has no favourites, He just chooses to use people in different ways.

PROMISES

PEACEMAKER

Read: Genesis 21:22-34

KEY VERSE: 'Abraham planted a tamarisk tree in Beersheba, and there he called on the name of the LORD, the Eternal God.' (v33)

Remember King Abimelek, the second person Abraham fooled into thinking that Sarah was his sister? (A weird habit of Abraham's!) Some of his men had hijacked a well that Abraham had dug.

Both Abraham and Abimelek had taken an oath agreeing not to work against each other, and this was the first test of their agreement. Would Abraham keep his promise or would he use force to take back the well?

Abraham wisely decided to talk the matter through with Abimelek. He discovered that the king knew nothing of the hijacking, nor did he approve of it. Abraham's attitude as he went into the talks was important too. He didn't storm in all guns blazing. Instead he brought gifts. Abimelek, completely shocked, accepted the gifts and confirmed that the well was Abraham's. The situation was resolved.

When a friend appears to be doing something against you, it's best to calmly talk to them — most of the time this is enough to sort the situation out.

PRAY Lord, when I get caught up in an argument, help me to remain calm and be a peacemaker so that the situation can be worked out. Amen.

THE TEST

Read: Genesis 22:1-8

> **KEY VERSE:** 'God himself will provide the lamb for the burnt offering, my son.' (v8)

We're back at this story again. Having waited so long for a son, Abraham had his faith tested to the limit. God asked him to sacrifice Isaac... *What?* This didn't make sense. First, although some people in Canaan did make human sacrifices, God *hated* this. Second, all God's promises to Abraham depended on Isaac being alive and having children of his own.

Clearly, God had no intention of any harm coming to Isaac. However, he wanted to test Abraham's faith in a dramatic way. He had an incredible lesson to teach him that would explain how God can rescue us from death. Even the place God chose was significant — Mount Moriah. Years later the Jews would sacrifice animals here to avoid the death penalty for their sin.

So what did Abraham make of God's request? Incredibly, he decided to trust God and took Isaac up the mountain. There was no way God would break His promises. It had taken Abraham 100 years to believe God that much, but now he did.

THINK Are you having a tough time at the moment? God always keeps His promise to be with you. Keep talking to Him and to other Christians.

PROMISES

GOD'S GREATEST BLESSING

Read: Genesis 22:9-19

KEY VERSE: 'through your offspring all nations on earth will be blessed, because you have obeyed me' (v18)

Abraham's faith was being stretched to the limit. God had asked him to sacrifice his only beloved son, Isaac.

All Abraham could do was trust in God's unchanging character and His unchanging promises through Isaac. Abraham even believed God could raise him from the dead (Heb. 11:18). And his faith was rewarded! The moment the knife was drawn, God moved in to spare Isaac's life. 'Do not lay a hand on the boy,' said the angel of the Lord.

God then showed Abraham an alternative sacrifice: a ram trapped in a bush by its horns. God hadn't changed, nor had His plans; Isaac would live to have millions of descendants. The Lord hadn't let Abraham down.

God told Abraham that everyone on earth would be blessed because Abraham had obeyed Him (v18). That includes us today. How? Because Abraham's greatest descendant, God's own Son, Jesus, was born a Jew. Just like the ram died instead of Isaac, Jesus died so that we can live. He is the Lamb of God who takes away our sin.

PRAY Lord Jesus, I thank You with all my heart for giving up Your life so that I can spend mine with God forever. Amen.

BEST WIFE

Read: Genesis 24:1–9

> **KEY VERSE:** 'The LORD, the God of heaven... will send his angel before you so that you can get a wife for my son' (v7)

Abraham had a problem. Isaac needed a wife... but who? Abraham didn't want Isaac to marry any of the local girls. He knew they had no time for God. They worshipped false gods and lived only to please themselves. He feared that if Isaac married a Canaanite, his son would drift away from God and begin worshipping idols. God had told Abraham to teach his children right from wrong, and that included in their love lives.

Abraham wanted his son to marry a girl who loved God. That narrowed down the field a bit. Abraham knew the right girl for Isaac would be God's choice. He wanted God to play matchmaker because he trusted that God always has our best interests at heart. God's choice would be the best person in the world for Isaac. So Abraham sent his servant out with the task of bringing back God's choice of wife for his son.

THINK Is there someone you've got your eye on? Take a minute to think about the effect that getting involved with that person would have on your relationship with God.

PROMISES

PRAYER FIRST

Read: Genesis 24:10-27

KEY VERSE: 'Lord, God of my master Abraham, make me successful today, and show kindness to my master Abraham.' (v12)

We all face choices. What should I have for breakfast? What outfit should I wear today? What subjects should I pick at school? Abraham's servant travelled up north on his quest for God's choice of wife for Isaac. He headed straight to the local spot that was popular with the girls – the well. When he was almost there, to make sure he wouldn't get confused, the servant said to God, 'When I ask a young woman for a drink, if she gives me a drink and waters the camels too – let that mean she's the girl You've chosen for Isaac.' (See verse 14.)

Now when Rebekah appeared, that's exactly what happened. And Rebekah was not only beautiful, but kind and caring too. As God made His choice, the servant couldn't help but worship Him.

The reason the servant's quest was successful was because he prayed before doing anything else. He asked God to be in charge. Then he waited patiently for God to lead him to the right person.

PRAY Dear Lord, You know what decisions I have to make right now. Please show me the right way to go, and give me the patience and understanding I need. Amen.

FROM GOD

Read: Genesis 24:28-52

> **KEY VERSE:** 'Laban and Bethuel answered, "This is from the LORD; we can say nothing to you one way or the other."' (v50)

Abraham's servant was certain he'd met the perfect bride for Isaac. He'd even given her a ring — a nose ring, but still a ring! Now what would her family make of this? When Rebekah came home showing off her new piercing, big brother Laban rushed out to see the man Abraham had sent.

No, he wasn't in overprotective big brother mode — he welcomed him with open arms. Laban knew straight away that Abraham's servant was a man who loved God. And in the discussions about the marriage proposal, the servant name-dropped the Lord multiple times. He couldn't stop talking about all that God had done.

When Rebekah's family had listened to the whole story, it was learn there was nothing at all to argue about. God had clearly planned all of this out. All they could do was agree with Abraham's servant and say, 'This is from the Lord.'

THINK When you look back, can you see times when God was clearly working in your life? If you're waiting for Him to make something clear at the moment, be patient and keep talking with Him.

PROMISES

HAPPY ENDING

Read: Genesis 24:53-67

> **KEY VERSE:** 'Isaac... married Rebekah. So she became his wife, and he loved her' (v67)

So, between the servant and the family, the marriage was agreed. But Rebekah and Isaac had never met each other. This could have been very, very awkward! Would they be as happy about the match as Abraham's servant was?

Rebekah was keen to marry someone who loved God, which she knew Isaac did. Even so, how did she feel about marrying an unknown man and moving far away from her home? That was a lot of change. But, given the choice of another ten days at home or catching the next camel to meet Isaac right away – she was on the next camel!

As for Isaac, when the camel arrived at the platform, he was spending time with God in a field (one way to make a good impression!). He saw Rebekah and rushed to meet her. When he learnt how God had brought them together, he was over the moon. The couple married and the Bible simply tells us that Isaac loved his wife (v67). A happy ending all round.

PRAY God, when I can just see a small piece, You see the whole puzzle. Help me to trust You more with the big decisions in my life. Amen.

PROMISES KEPT

Read: Genesis 25:1-11

KEY VERSE: 'His sons Isaac and Ishmael buried him in the cave of Machpelah near Mamre' (v9)

Sarah had passed away, and Abraham had remarried and had six more sons. And with these, six smaller nations were born. However, Isaac was still Abraham's heir and the father of the special nation God had promised.

God said Abraham would have a long and peaceful life, and He was right – as always. Abraham lived to be 175 years old – and that is *old*! After he died, both Ishmael and Isaac were at their father's funeral. Family fights had caused the two boys to live apart but they were reunited by Abraham's death. And there is no record of any argument between them over Abraham leaving everything to Isaac. The sons worked together to make the funeral arrangements.

Isaac's descendants are still living in the land God promised them all those thousands of years ago.

But God's promise to bring freedom to all families in the world (Gen. 12:3) is what it's all about. God has kept His promise in Jesus, Abraham's greatest descendant. If there's one thing that can never be argued about, it's this – God keeps His promises.

PRAY Lord, thank You that because of Jesus, You accept me as Your child. I love belonging to You! Amen.

PROMISES

MUCH MORE

Read: Psalm 132:1–18

KEY VERSE: 'The LORD swore an oath to David, a sure oath he will not revoke: "One of your own descendants I will place on your throne."' (v11)

Symbols are things that point to something much more than what they actually are themselves. A good example is a national flag. It's only a bit of cloth, but it symbolises so much more. In Old Testament times, the name 'David' wasn't like any other name, it symbolised something much more.

David, as we know, was God's chosen king of Israel. As the king, he would be used in a special way to bring about God's promise to rescue the world. God spoke through the prophets to say that he would use a 'Son of David' to carry out His rescue mission. So when this psalm talks about David, everyone who first heard it knew what it meant. 'David' was a symbol for everything God had done, and all that he was going to do to rescue His people.

As Christians, we know that the 'Son of David' is in fact the Son of God: Jesus. He is now ruling the universe as the eternal king!

PRAY Lord Jesus, I can never thank You enough for what You did for me by dying on the cross, and for how You still help me each and every day. Amen.

WE ARE FAMILY

Read: Psalm 133:1-3

KEY VERSE: 'How good and pleasant it is when God's people live together in unity!' (v1)

Imagine two sisters. They argue constantly about the tiniest things. One day, a girl comes along and starts shouting at one of them. The other sister sees the threat and immediately jumps to her sister's defence! Even though they were more than happy to argue with each other, when someone else came against one of them, their true loyalty shone through. They suddenly realised who they were – sisters who loved each other.

Today's reading is all about how important it is for us, God's children (who are a family), to love each other. Because together we are a light showing God to the world. When we fight we look just like any other family. But if we love each other, we will shine – and others will see God through us.

Obviously it's not always easy to love people, even other Christians! Sometimes, like the sisters in the story, we need to remember who we really are – God's children – before we can do it.

Do you find it easy to get on with other Christians? Are there some you don't like so much? Talk to God about it.

PRAY Father God, please help me to be patient with other Christians especially. Please remind me that we're all family. Amen.

PSALM

ASSURANCE

Read: 2 Timothy 3:14-17

KEY VERSE: 'continue in what you have learned and have become convinced of' (v14)

Long Bible words can make your brain feel like a tin of mushy peas, unless you know what they mean. We're going to take a look at some of these words and make sense of the jargon. First up is the word 'assurance'.

Christians might sometimes have doubts that they really belong in God's family. Does He kick us out when we mess things up? How can we really *know* that we are saved?

The Bible says that if we love Jesus and follow Him, He forgives us and gives us eternal life. And when you become a Christian, the Holy Spirit makes His home inside you! The Holy Spirit helps us to know that God is with us.

Timothy wasn't convinced he was a Christian just because Paul said so. He knew he was saved by Jesus because the Holy Spirit was at work in him, making him more like Jesus. He knew God's Word and believed it too.

Satan hates it when we start to understand just how loved we are by God – and he'll do anything to persuade us otherwise! But you can be 100% confident that God loves you.

THINK Have you ever doubted that God has actually forgiven you? His forgiveness is real when we turn to Jesus. Believe it! Know it! Live it!

JARGON BUSTER

ABUNDANT LIFE

Read: John 10:1-10

> **KEY VERSE:** 'I have come that they may have life, and have it to the full.' (v10)

Jesus came to earth to deliver abundant life – a way of living that is longer and deeper than anyone thought possible.

Although most us will live happily into our old age, the sad truth is that life can end at any moment. But abundant life doesn't go out of date. When our human bodies switch off, God gives us a new body and a new home with Him forever.

Lots of people feel like something is missing from their life. When Jesus talks about abundant life, He means living a life that is full of the Holy Spirit. Now that's living!

The Bible is full of God's promises to give us a future and a hope (Jer. 29:11); to never leave us (Heb. 13:5); and to make things work for good (Rom. 8:28). Until we let God into our lives, they are incomplete. But when we invite God's Spirit to live in us (wow!) our emptiness becomes full to the brim with good stuff – God's stuff. Abundant life.

PRAY Holy Spirit, come and fill me with life – abundant life. Please show me the best way to live, full of You. Amen.

ADVOCATE

Read: John 14:15–27

KEY VERSE: 'I will ask the Father, and he will give you another advocate to help you and be with you for ever – the Spirit of truth' (vv16–17)

The word 'advocate' might not crop up as often as some other biblical words. Other Bible translations might say 'Counsellor' or 'Helper' in this verse instead. But what does it mean?

Put simply: the Holy Spirit stands alongside us. God fights our corner. When we're up against it in life, we can ask the Holy Spirit for help. He makes us winners, because Jesus has won. We get to share in His victory and raise the trophy with Him! If we trust Jesus it means that when God looks at us, He sees Him!

The Holy Spirit advocates for us in prayer to. In Romans 8:26, it says the Spirit even helps us when we know we want to pray, but we can't think of the right words. He steps in and prays on our behalf – how amazing is that?! When we just don't have the words, our advocate fills in the blanks. He is on our side.

THINK How often do you speak up for other people? Is there someone who needs you to stand alongside them at the moment?

CONSCIENCE

Read: 1 Timothy 1:18-20

KEY VERSE: 'holding on to faith and a good conscience, which some have rejected and so have suffered shipwreck with regard to the faith' (v19)

Our conscience is a partnership with God that helps us know right from wrong. Have you ever done something you shouldn't have and felt regret afterwards? That's your conscience speaking.

In today's reading, Paul talks about two men who had ignored God's warning and made a right mess of their lives because of this. Instead of admitting they had messed up and asking God to forgive them, they'd shut Him out. If we don't want to make a mess out of our faith, we need to keep listening to God.

Paul told Timothy to hold on to a good conscience. When you know God wants to draw your attention to something, don't avoid the issue – sort it out with Him. He's given us a Bible packed with info on right and wrong – so get to know it! If we get closer to God, we'll become more like Him. Hold on to God and you'll hold on to a good conscience.

PRAY Dear God, help me to get Your ways into my head, so that my conscience lines up with what's right. I want to listen. Amen.

JARGON BUSTER

CONFESSION

Read: 1 John 1:1-10

KEY VERSE: 'If we confess our sins, he is faithful and just and will forgive us our sins and purify us from all unrighteousness.' (v9)

When we think of confession, we might think it just means confessing our sins, but really, there's more to it. We do need to confess where we've gone wrong to God. But it's also about lining ourselves up with God's truth and living (and speaking) according to the truth.

We're not perfect. We never will be. We can't do this on our own. Put bluntly: without Jesus, we're not good enough for God. But remember what we said about our advocate? God doesn't look at us and want nothing to do with us. He sent His Son to save us so we can be forgiven.

Confession is also accepting the truth about God. He's awesome. Perfect. Holy. Spotless. Loving. Above everything. In charge. Forever. He is God.

The first Christians made sure they were openly 'confessing' that Jesus is Lord. It wasn't a secret they kept. So many people have the wrong idea about God. They don't understand who He is. Let's spread the word about how great God really is. If we really believe that this is the truth, then let's confess it!

THINK Is there anything you know you need to confess *to* God? Is there anything you know you need to confess *about* God?

DISCIPLE

Read: John 8:31–36

KEY VERSE: 'Jesus said, "If you hold to my teaching, you are really my disciples."' (v31)

Did you know that the word 'disciple' is used nearly three hundred times in the Bible? Depending on your Bible translation, the word 'Christian' is only used about three times. So, what is a disciple? It's a follower or learner.

The first 12 disciples of Jesus dropped everything to follow Him. They literally *followed* Him everywhere He went. They watched how He lived. They asked Him questions. They learned all they could about life; how to love people; how to change the world.

Jesus is a great teacher. He knows learners make mistakes. His first 12 were always messing up. James and John had anger problems, Peter was always saying the wrong thing, none of them were perfect. And after three years together, they all ran away! They should have been crossed off the list of suitable disciples, but Jesus loved them, helped them with their issues, and turned them into world-changers. And it's the same for us too. We are all disciples of Jesus when we decide to follow Him.

PRAY Lord Jesus, thank You for being the best teacher ever. You know the areas that I need to grow in, so help me to learn from You. Amen.

JARGON BUSTER

FAITH

Read: ROMANS 10:9-17

> **KEY VERSE:** 'faith comes from hearing the message, and the message is heard through the word about Christ' (v17)

God doesn't leave fingerprints. You can't take photos of Him, record His voice, or touch Him. People will tell you there's no 'proof' for God. How do you deal with that?

God's creation is living, moving, growing, talking evidence of His power (Rom. 1:20). But people today aren't impressed, and instead they see our existence as a gigantic cosmic accident. Why doesn't God show His face every now and again? The truth is that God did make an appearance through Jesus coming to earth. Witnesses wrote down what happened, and that's how we've got a lot of the New Testament. And God wants us to trust what the Bible says about Him.

We become Christians by believing that Jesus can save us from our sin (v9) – we trust that He means what He says. That's what we call *faith*. There's so much about life that we don't understand – and may not ever understand until we make it to heaven. But no one who trusts God will ever be let down (v11).

THINK Have you had anyone tell you that there's no proof for Christianity? What would be a good way to respond to this? Tip: start by looking at the life of Jesus.

GRACE

Read: 1 Corinthians 15:1–11

KEY VERSE: 'But by the grace of God I am what I am, and his grace to me was not without effect.' (v10)

Grace isn't that prayer you quickly mumble so you can tuck into your dinner. In the Bible, 'grace' is what is meant by God's love for us. A love we don't deserve.

Paul is a star example of God's grace in action. He'd hated followers of Jesus, even ordering for them to be killed. Paul was basically a terrorist, targeting Christians. If there was ever a guy who deserved to be shown no mercy from God, it was Paul.

So what did God do — let him rot away in jail? Send a lightning bolt strike him down? No! God introduced him to Jesus and forgave him! Amazing or what?

Paul knew that he didn't deserve God's kindness. So he didn't want to waste it or take it for granted. The more Paul understood God's grace, the more he became like Jesus and told others about Him. Let's do the same with God's grace to us — become more like Jesus, and tell more people about Him.

Remember this: if God could love Paul, He can love anyone.

PRAY Lord Jesus, I just can't thank You enough for grace! Thank You for saving me even though I don't deserve it. Amen.

JARGON BUSTER

GOSPEL

Read: ROMANS 1:8–17

> **KEY VERSE:** 'I refuse to be ashamed of sharing the wonderful message of God's liberating power unleashed in us through Christ! For I am thrilled to preach that everyone who believes is saved' (v16, TPT)

The news is often so full of bad news that we can wonder where the good news has gone. Well, here's some incredible news!

The word 'gospel' means 'the good news about Jesus'. What a great news story to tell! God sending Jesus to die for us so we could live. Jesus told His disciples to release this story everywhere. The bad news is that we were cut off from God. The good news is that Jesus has made a way for us to get together with Him!

In Greek, the word for 'gospel', *euggalion*, became the Latin word *evangel* – where we get the word 'evangelist' from. An evangelist is someone who tells the good news. That someone includes you and me. We've got a job to get on with. The most important job in the world – telling everyone about Jesus. Paul says he wasn't ashamed of the gospel. Why would we ever be ashamed of our incredible, powerful God who saves us?

THINK Who could be the first/next person you tell this good news to? Pray for them to listen and then share with them what Jesus has done for them!

JUSTIFIED

Read: Romans 5:1–9

KEY VERSE: 'Since we have now been justified by his blood, how much more shall we be saved from God's wrath through him!' (v9)

Every morning millions of people get up and head for the mirror. Why? Because we care what we look like, don't we?

Before we became Christians we looked pretty bad in God's sight. Sin had made us a right mess – and there was nothing we could do about it. But God stepped in and sent Jesus, who died and rose again – providing a way for our mess to be cleaned up. Because of Jesus, when God looks at us now it's like we've never messed up. He died so we could be forgiven! His sacrifice has made everything all right again. Jesus wipes the slate clean.

In verse 6, Paul explains it really simply: 'just at the right time, when we were still powerless, Christ died for the ungodly.' We can't make ourselves right again, only Jesus can do that. And He did – even though we didn't deserve it. Are you thankful for that?

PRAY Thank You, Jesus, for justifying me by dying on the cross and rising again. I praise You for making a way for me to be forgiven! Amen.

JARGON BUSTER

LOVE

Read: John 21:15-19

KEY VERSE: 'The third time he said to him, "Simon son of John, do you love me?"' (v17)

The Bible uses two Greek terms when talking about of love: *phileo* and *agape*. *Phileo* love means to like someone or be friends with them. *Agape* love is loving others without expecting anything in return. *Agape* love is used to describe God's sacrificial love for us.

Love. What comes to mind when *you* think of it? Red fluffy love-hearts, chocolates and general soppiness? Well, the kind of love that the Bible shows is actually a strong, powerful love that sent Jesus to the cross for us. So let's see what He thinks about love.

Before this meeting in John 21, Peter had disowned Jesus on three occasions to save his own skin. The New Testament was originally written in Greek, in which several different words (each with a different meaning) are used for the English word 'love'. Jesus asks Peter, 'Do you love me?' He's talking about the *agape* form of love. Peter responds the first two times saying, 'I love you' using the *phileo* word. Jesus doesn't want us to just *like* Him, but *love* Him – with an all-out love that overtakes everything else in our lives.

THINK How would you describe your love for Jesus – is it *agape* or *phileo*?

MEDIATOR

Read: 1 Timothy 2:1–7

KEY VERSE: 'For there is one God and one mediator between God and mankind, the man Christ Jesus' (v5)

Have you ever been in the middle of two people who are having issues?

The word 'mediator' is made up from two words, 'middle' and 'go'. And that's why Jesus is described as our mediator – He's the middle man going between us and the Father.

In order to come close to our holy God, we need to get our problem of sin sorted. Jesus Himself took the punishment for our rejection of God. What an amazing friend He is! He built a bridge in the gap between us and God, and takes us over it. We could never do that without Him. Because of Him, there's no issue between us and God.

Today's passage also tells us that Jesus gave Himself 'as a ransom for all people'. He came for *all people*. So once again, we're reminded this isn't a gift to be greedy with, but to share with other people. The greatest favour we can show anyone is to introduce them to Jesus. Jesus said 'I am the way' (John 14:6). He meant it. He is the only middle man, and everyone needs to know this.

THINK How could you be a mediator today? What would it look like to be the mediator between your friends and Jesus?

JARGON BUSTER

PRAISE

Read: Ephesians 5:18-33

KEY VERSE: 'always giving thanks to God the Father for everything, in the name of our Lord Jesus Christ' (v20)

Praise is saying thanks and giving God credit. The Bible is always reminding us to 'praise the Lord'. That's because we need reminding!

God doesn't need us to pat Him on the back or raise His self-esteem. What we say doesn't make God feel any better about Himself. But praise helps us to focus on God instead of ourselves, and that's good for us! Praise says out loud that God knows best. He's the King! He cares about us. He deserves to be at the top!

By praising God in tough times, we avoid the trap of feeling sorry for ourselves. By giving thanks in every situation, we announce that God is in control. He won't let anything happen to us that He can't turn around and work out for our good.

Praising God can be hard at times when your friends are being weird, you're grounded, or you've missed out on something you really wanted. But the Holy Spirit can help us to praise God throughout everything.

So let's give God thanks and be grateful to Him – with a great, full heart!

PRAY Lord Jesus, You are worthy of my praise! It's impossible to say everything You have done for me, but I am so grateful. Amen.

REDEEMED

Read: 1 Peter 1:13-21

> **KEY VERSE:** 'it was not with perishable things such as silver or gold that you were redeemed from the empty way of life' (v18)

When the New Testament was written there were over six million slaves in the Roman Empire. Some slaves had the option of buying their freedom for a sum of money. But sometimes the owner would arrange that slaves would only have enough money to buy their freedom when they were too old to work.

The price of a slave's freedom was agreed, and when it was paid they were redeemed. As slaves were poor, this often meant someone else paying for them. We still use the word 'redeemed' to mean 'settling the cost'.

The Bible says that Jesus is our redeemer – He paid the ransom to set us free. And the cost of our freedom was not paid with a cash, coupons or clubcard points – it was paid with the blood of Jesus on the cross. What does He want in return? Us to love Him.

THINK Do you ever feel like you're not very valuable? Lots of us can feel like that, but here's the truth: you are so valuable that Jesus died just so you would be His friend!

JARGON BUSTER

REPENTANCE

Read: Acts 3:17–20

KEY VERSE: 'Repent, then, and turn to God, so that your sins may be wiped out' (v19)

Some people confuse the word 'repent' with 'remorse'. Remorse is simply feeling sorry for what we've done. Repenting is more than that — it's a big U-turn in God's direction. Have you ever seen someone walk down a street, realise they're going the wrong way, and awkwardly turn right back round? In the Bible, to repent is to change your heart and mind — to choose to walk away from your sin and accept that God's way of doing things is right and perfect.

In today's passage from Acts, Peter is explaining the gospel to people — that they need to turn away from their old ways of living.

But that's not all — Peter says that when they do repent, God doesn't keep a big folder in a filing cabinet in heaven with a record of what they've done wrong. God wipes their sins away. That's right — He gets a big shredder out and destroys those records! So when we repent, we tell God we're sorry and run away from our sin, and He forgets all about it. That's how amazing God's forgiveness is!

PRAY Father God, help me to see the things in my life that are wrong. I want to leave them behind and live the way You want me to. Amen.

REVIVAL

Read: Psalm 85:1-6

KEY VERSE: 'Will you not revive us again, that your people may rejoice in you?' (v6)

Most first aid courses teach you how to give the 'kiss of life'. Those who have only just stopped breathing can sometimes be revived if you can get air back into their lungs.

Not only can bodies be revived, but relationships can be too. When the Bible uses the word 'revival' it's usually to do with our friendship with God. When we drift off into disobeying God, we need Him to wake us, shake us and breathe His new life into us.

We all need to be revived – woken up by God. Throughout history there have been huge revivals where thousands of people have asked Jesus into their lives! Psalm 85 is a prayer for revival. God's people had gone off to do their own thing. Their relationship with God had fizzled out and the joy had gone missing from their lives. So they humbly asked God to forgive and revive them. They needed reviving, not just help surviving!

THINK Do you feel a bit 'sleepy' in your faith? Maybe it's become the same old, same old? Think and ask God about ways that you can wake up a bit more in your faith.

JARGON BUSTER

RIGHTEOUSNESS

Read: John 16:5–15

KEY VERSE: 'When he comes, he will prove the world to be in the wrong about sin and righteousness and judgment' (v8)

Mutter the words 'right' and 'just' very quickly and you get the word 'righteous'. To be righteous means to be completely right because we are right with God.

God knows what is good – He *decides* what is right, and He thinks right and acts right.

So, are we righteous? We all like to think we're right. We even say we are. But that's our opinion. Righteousness is being right by God's standards. Jesus told His disciples that the Holy Spirit would show them right from wrong. Without His help we can't appreciate how good God is and how much we fall short in comparison. It's the Holy Spirit who shows us that we are not as smart as we think, and guides us to Jesus to sort it out.

Jesus is our righteousness – our way of being made right with God. We can't become righteous by just doing what we think is best. Only Jesus has the power to deal with the 'not right' and make us all right. So where are you? Just not right? Or right with God – and just thankful to Jesus?

PRAY Jesus, thank You so much for making me 'right'. Help me to live the right way – for You! Amen.

SANCTIFICATION

Read: John 17:1–19

KEY VERSE: 'Sanctify them by the truth; your word is truth' (v17)

Have you ever used a pen that leaks? The ink gets on your fingers or stains the lining of your pockets. It's a real pain. We're like a leaking biro when our lives are not fully put in God's hands. Instead of being focused on doing what God wants, we leak off to do our own thing, often leaving a mess behind us.

To be sanctified is to be made holy, completely washed clean by God – and that means to be set apart, different from everyone else, for God. In a pocket full of leaking biros, the sanctified pens are the good-as-new ones.

The moment we become Christians, we are 'justified' – forgiven and made right. God has made us holy, but we still need to chase after holiness. In today's reading, before His death, Jesus is praying to His Father (God!) to sanctify us 'by the truth' (v17). That's His prayer for us – that we be pure and set apart. We'll mess up, but we can keep on trying.

THINK Do you ever feel pressure to follow the crowd and do things that you know aren't good? Make a plan for how you will try to be different, because of God, next time this happens.

JARGON BUSTER

SALVATION

Read: Acts 4:8-12

KEY VERSE: 'Salvation is found in no one else' (v12)

It's at the centre of our faith, but what does salvation actually mean?

We can't get into heaven on our own – there's no way we'll ever be good enough. The Bible says that the 'wages [penalty] of sin is death' (Rom. 6:23) – we need a Saviour! We need salvation: to be saved from an eternity spent separated from the love of God, and to have our relationship with God mended now.

Peter and John risked their lives to tell the Jews that Jesus – the man they'd crucified – was alive, with the power to give them eternal life instead of death! The Jews hoped their good work would save them, but there is only one way to be saved, and that is through Jesus. After speaking about the penalty of sin, Romans 6:23 goes on to say, 'but the gift of God is eternal life in Christ Jesus our Lord'. Wow!

But salvation is optional. We have to grab hold of this gift. Jesus died in our place and came out on top – He can save us and sort our relationship with God out, if we ask.

PRAY Lord Jesus, thank You for saving me! I want You in my life today and every day. I receive Your forgiveness and choose to follow You. Amen.

WISDOM

Read: 2 Chronicles 1:7–12

> **KEY VERSE:** '"Give me wisdom and knowledge, that I may lead this people, for who is able to govern this great people of yours?"' (v10)

If you could ask for anything in the world, what would it be? King Solomon didn't come up with a wish list to make him rich, popular or a style icon. He asked God for something very rare – wisdom.

Wisdom is using knowledge the right way – God's way. It's seeing life from God's point of view. Usually when we are faced with a decision, we look at the options from our own point of view. What's best for me? Wisdom looks at things differently. It knows that God knows best and turns to Him for answers. Wise people put God first.

Wisdom views others as God sees them. It sees what people really need. And being wise isn't about being popular, but about doing right. Whose view on life are you going with? Yours or God's? Solomon put God in the top spot and found that all the other things he needed came his way too.

THINK
What's more important to you – being popular, or doing right? Which one do you think would be the best way of living life, and why?

JARGON BUSTER

ON TOP OF THE WORLD

Read: Psalm 134:1-3

KEY VERSE: 'May the LORD bless you from Zion' (v3)

The singers of this psalm had climbed up the hill to Jerusalem, and now they're worshipping God in the Temple. Not only are they on top of the mountain, they're on top of the world!

Some people think that Christianity is all about suffering and hard work. Well, admittedly there is some of that, but this is knocked out the park by joy! The joy of being in God's presence is like nothing else. He is so amazing and yet He's so keen to be close to us.

Worship isn't just an extra bit added onto our Christian life, it's the whole point of being a Christian. That doesn't mean it's all about just singing songs; it means knowing God is close to you, loving being with Him and listening to Him (reading the Bible and listening to good Christian teaching can help you worship God too).

You could perhaps say that our main reason for being alive is to praise and give glory to God by enjoying knowing Him forever. When we enjoy knowing God, we are worshipping Him!

THINK Do you enjoy knowing God?
We can know and worship God more when we include Him in every day of our lives, talking with Him and living in His joy-filled way.

DUST YOURSELF OFF

Read: Psalm 130:1–8

KEY VERSE: 'If you, LORD, kept a record of sins, Lord, who could stand? But with you there is forgiveness' (vv3–4)

Have you ever tried really hard at something only to find it's not worked? Well, most people know what it feels like to fail every now and then! It's actually a good thing! Realising we've failed is a very good place to get to know Him better. That is what this psalm is all about.

The people of Israel knew what failure was. God had rescued them and given them His law. Because of this they knew the world was in a total mess, broken, sick and damaged beyond repair. They knew they could never fix things and that, deep down, human beings had failed! Their only hope was that God would do something to help. In verse 8, you can see how strong that hope was.

God has chosen to forgive those who admit their failure to Him. This is not because we have a right to forgiveness, but because He is extremely loving and kind. We can have a completely fresh start, thanks to God.

PRAY Lord, thank You that You love us so much, however many times we make a mess of things. Thank You that I don't have to be scared of failing. Amen.

PSALM

SETTING THE RECORD STRAIGHT

Read: 1 John 1:1-4

KEY VERSE: 'we proclaim to you the eternal life, which was with the Father and has appeared to us' (v2)

Jesus is the Son of God. Fact. He came to earth, born as a tiny baby to a human mother, fulfilled hundreds of Old Testament prophecies, preached love, set people free, was crucified, buried, rose again and returned to heaven. Awesome! But what happened after that? How did those first Christians protect their message of truth from the other strange ideas around at the time? Well, it's partly down to the writings of a man called John.

John had been one of Jesus' disciples, and by the time he was an old man, people were starting to get a little hazy on the facts around Jesus. But John, who had worked closely with Jesus and witnessed His death and resurrection, decided to expose the lies and reveal the truth instead. It all starts off with today's Bible reading. The rest of his letters set the record straight about who Jesus was – and is. Do you have doubts about your faith? Let's jump in and discover the truth!

PRAY Lord Jesus, thank You that I can talk to You honestly about my doubts. Help me to deepen my faith in You as I read Your truth in the Bible. Amen.

TRUTH TELLING

TOO BAD

Read: 1 John 1:5–10

KEY VERSE: 'If we confess our sins, he is faithful and just and will forgive us our sins and purify us from all unrighteousness.' (v9)

We don't often hear the word 'sin' outside of church. The rest of the world gets by with its own slightly blurry sense of right and wrong. But John cuts to the chase in today's verses: we've all messed up, but God's forgiveness is there for us when we ask for it.

There are two lies that John busts open:
1. You're a perfect person and can ignore all the God stuff.
2. You're too bad to be forgiven.

John puts the truth out there like this:
1. Sin is real and affects us all. We all mess up. There's no point in trying to gloss over the things we do wrong. There's no way we could ever match up to God's standards for holiness. But the good news is...
2. We can be forgiven! John says, 'the blood of Jesus... purifies us from all sin' (v7). Yep – really – ALL sin! When God says He'll forgive us, He means it. All we need to do is be truly sorry.

THINK Is there something you need to confess to God? Why not talk to God about it and let Him deal with it right now.

WALKIE-TALKIE

Read: 1 John 2:1-6

KEY VERSE: 'whoever claims to live in him must live as Jesus did' (v6)

There are lots of people who make out they are speaking the truth about God, but how do you spot a fake? John says you can tell by the way they walk – not literally one foot in front of the other, but whether or not they walk through life obeying God and following His ways.

The false teachers in John's day claimed to know God, but they didn't really follow Him. They put on the 'God has told me' act very heavily so that people didn't dare to question them – even when they ignored all of God's commands. They talked the talk but didn't walk the walk. Their words didn't match up to their actions.

Those who speak the truth want to live the truth. They don't say 'I'm right', but 'God's right'. They don't give their opinions but God's directions. They don't rewrite the rules but live by God's laws.

That's a challenge for us too! People watch the way we live. Does your behaviour line up with your beliefs? Can people tell that you're a Christian from the way you live your life?

PRAY Lord Jesus, help me to live well and behave in a way that honours You. Amen.

A LESSON IN LOVE

Read: 1 John 2:7–11

KEY VERSE: 'Anyone who loves their brother and sister lives in the light, and there is nothing in them to make them stumble.' (v10)

Holding grudges is a very dangerous habit. Sadly, some people say they love Jesus, but behind the scenes, they knock other Christians with nasty comments or gossip. People like that will never be the kind of Christian that Jesus wants them to be until they learn to love those in God's family (and everyone else!). If we only want to knock others down to build ourselves up, we're seriously missing Jesus' point about love.

Those who live for Jesus learn to love like Jesus. And loving like Jesus means not making ourselves out to be better than we are. It means going out of our way to befriend other people. It means focusing on people's good points rather than their not-so-good points. It's getting on with people and praying for them, even if they really wind us up. It's being ready to forgive people, even if we think they don't deserve it.

Is there someone at your church who you find it difficult to love? Why not ask God for His help.

PRAY Lord Jesus, help me to love and forgive other people, just like You love and forgive me. Amen.

TRUTH TELLING

SOMETHING FOR EVERYONE

Read: 1 John 2:12-14

> **KEY VERSE:** 'I write to you... because... the word of God lives in you, and you have overcome the evil one.' (v14)

John was writing down all this truth for everyone – new Christians, young Christians, older Christians... he had something to say to all of us.

Have you recently become a Christian? John reminds you that you have been totally forgiven because of Jesus. You are a member of God's family and He is your heavenly Father. Never forget that – it's the core of your faith! Mix with other Christians and learn what you can from them.

Even though you're only young, you can still be a strong Christian. The young'uns John was writing to knew God's Word well. If you want God's truth written on your heart, get stuck into as much of the Bible as you can!

The most wonderful thing about becoming a Christian when you're young is that you have a lifetime ahead to get to know Jesus. If that's you – if you've been Christian for quite a long time now – keep that friendship with Jesus at the centre of your life.

THINK Jesus has something to say to all of us! What do you think He wants to say to you today?

WHAT DO YOU LOVE?

Read: 1 John 2:15–17

KEY VERSE: 'Do not love the world or anything in the world.' (v15)

It's really important that we don't get the wrong end of the stick with today's verses! John's not telling us that we shouldn't care for planet Earth and everything in it. When he tells us not to love 'the world', he's talking about worldly values that aren't heavenly values. It's a warning not to get side-tracked by anything that isn't good for us.

'Love of the world' is doing whatever makes you happy, even if it might hurt someone else. It's getting your hands on as much stuff as you can, and using whoever you want. Because of sin, a lot of the good things in life have become distorted, and can be bad for us if we don't respect God's rules. Happiness, prosperity and relationships are all good things – but the world's way of getting them often doesn't fit in with God's ideas.

'Love of God', however, is putting Him first. Having lots of stuff might be nice, but it isn't everything. Loving God is being all about what you can give, not what you can get. It's treating others the way we want to be treated, even if we don't think they deserve it.

THINK What are your priorities? How can you ask God to help you set them straight?

TRUTH TELLING

FOR OR AGAINST?

Read: 1 John 2:18–23

KEY VERSE: 'Who is the liar? It is whoever denies that Jesus is the Christ.' (v22)

Another important way of sussing out who's really a Christian and who isn't is what they make of Jesus. If someone says that Jesus isn't who He said He was, then they've missed the whole point of what Christianity is about.

To be anti-Jesus doesn't always mean publicly saying bad things about Him. Lots of people say He was simply a nice guy, a great man, a good prophet... but not that Jesus is God's Son, who died to save us from sin and then rose to life again. John doesn't mince his words – if you don't believe Jesus is God's Son, you are against Jesus.

Those who know Jesus speak the truth about Him. They don't size Him down to being just a good, kind man, but the Saviour and Lord of all!

So this is one big truth that John wants to make sure everyone gets into their heads: Jesus is God. No two ways about it.

PRAY Jesus, thank You for being You!
I believe that You are who You say You are.
I love You. Amen.

THE END...?

Read: 1 John 2:24-29

> **KEY VERSE:** 'And this is what he promised us – eternal life.' (v25)

So, what happens when you die?

It's a big question, and one that people seem to have lots of different ideas about. But here John brings us back to what God has promised us through Jesus: eternal life.

What's your view about heaven? Some say that if you're a 'good person', you're in. Some might think of a full-on, cloudy, chubby-babies-playing-harps experience. Other people might believe heaven is just a feeling of peace after you die.

But the Bible tells us that heaven is so much more than that. It's not going to be a disappointment. And it's where we will be with Jesus forever.

You are a unique person with one lifetime to make up your mind about God. John's advice is to trust in Jesus. Hold on to what the Bible says about the future. Death is not the end! Because of Jesus' sacrifice, if we trust in Him, we have eternal life. It's the most valuable gift in the world, and it comes free from God to all those who love Jesus. And no one else can ever take it away!

THINK What do your friends think about heaven? Is it something you ever talk about?

TRUTH TELLING

LAVISH LOVE

Read: 1 John 3:1–3

> **KEY VERSE:** 'See what great love the Father has lavished on us, that we should be called children of God! And that is what we are!' (v1)

Everybody wants to be part of something and feel important. Faith in Jesus does that in the best way possible – we are part of God's family. Now that's important!

Have you ever felt that God doesn't care about you? Or doubted whether you are really part of His family? You're not alone in feeling that way. But here's the truth... God has a great love for you!

John gets so excited when he talks about God's love – he really gets it. Do you?! God loves you! And it's not a one-off show of care when we become a Christian. God *lavishes* His love on us. That means He keeps dishing it out in huge helpings. Our love for Him may sometimes run cold but His love for us never changes.

John is gobsmacked to think he is a child of God – a part of God's family. He knows he doesn't deserve to be, but God's love is so amazing that those who trust Jesus are not only forgiven but made children of God (however old they might be!).

THINK How do you know that God loves you? How does God know that you love Him?

BELIEF AND BEHAVIOUR

Read: 1 John 3:4-10

> **KEY VERSE:** 'The reason the Son of God appeared was to destroy the devil's work.' (v8)

A bunch of dodgy teachers were telling Christians that as long as they believed the right things, how they behaved wasn't important – as if breaking God's rules with their bodies wasn't important because He would save their souls. So John sets the record straight, again...

Doing what God says is a way of showing Him that we trust and love Him. When you become a Christian, you turn away from the things that displease God and you choose to live His way instead. That's not as easy as it might sound, but there's forgiveness for when we mess up.

In order to be forgiven, though, we need to admit when we've done wrong and be truly sorry. A person who thinks they can go through life doing whatever they want might not realise they're wrong. But a true child of God knows they need to get right with God and then live right with Him, and won't be happy until they do!

PRAY Lord Jesus, thank You for loving me, even though I mess up sometimes. Thank You for Your forgiveness and for never giving up on me. Help me to line up my behaviour with Your values. Amen.

TRUTH TELLING

LOVE. ONE. ANOTHER.

Read: 1 John 3:11–15

KEY VERSE: 'this is the message you heard from the beginning: we should love one another' (v11)

What do you think the world would look like if people treated each other nicely? How do we even take a step in that direction? The answer: love.

As you read through the book of 1 John, you might notice a certain catchphrase popping up now and then. It's a solid one, and easy to get the hang of. All together now: Love one another!

Hatred is at large in the world, and it's toxic. John uses the example of a man called Cain, who you can read about in Genesis 4:1–8 (his parents were Adam and Eve). Cain was full of hatred, and as a result he couldn't control his anger. He let jealousy take over, and murdered his own brother. This might be an extreme example, but John shows us Cain to remind us the truth about hatred. It began with jealousy, and then spiralled out of control.

God's way is to show love, not hatred — especially to other Christians. Gossip can quickly get out of hand, and the hurt can last a lifetime. So John repeats his catchphrase again: 'we should love one another.'

PRAY Lord, help me to let go of anger and hatred. I want to love people like You do. Amen.

WHAT LOVE LOOKS LIKE

Read: 1 John 3:16–18

KEY VERSE: 'This is how we know what love is: Jesus Christ laid down his life for us.' (v16)

Do you think John's catchphrase 'love one another' sounds a bit cheesy? Well, John certainly wasn't a lovey-dovey kinda guy. He was a rough, tough fisherman with a quick temper. You didn't mess with him.

But John knew exactly what love is. He showed God's love to others by rolling up his sleeves and helping those in need. When Jesus was dying on the cross, it was John who comforted Mary. He looked after her by letting her stay at his house and made sure she was properly fed.

John had seen God's love in action through the life of Jesus. Jesus fed the hungry, befriended the lonely and helped the poor. So John's advice to us is this: if you want to know what 'love one another' means, just copy Jesus. We can get so caught up in trying to be 'good Christians' that we end up just caring about ourselves. But Jesus' kind of love is caring about others, wanting the best for them.

THINK How could you show someone love over the next few days? Perhaps through a kind word, by helping them out, or a small, thoughtful gift? Have a think!

TRUTH TELLING

FACTS, NOT FEELINGS

Read: 1 John 3:19-24

KEY VERSE: 'And this is his command: to believe in the name of his Son, Jesus Christ, and to love one another' (v23)

Have you ever struggled with your faith? Many of us feel like that from time to time. But John has a tip for beating the blues, and it's a simple one to remember: rely on the facts, not your feelings.

God's promises don't change. He is greater than our feelings and the things that get to us. The Bible is full of amazing truths from God that we need to get into our heads and hearts so that our emotions don't get the final say. God is good — even when we don't feel good.

Here's the truth: if you trust in the name of Jesus, the fact is that you are forgiven and are a member of God's family, whether you feel like it or not! It might be that you need to check if you are living in line with God's commands. Sometimes the reason we can feel low in our faith is that we've gone off track a bit. Try spending some time with God to put things right in your life.

PRAY Father God, thank You that however I feel, the facts still tell me that You love me. Let those facts stick in my head and my heart. Amen.

WHO'S FAKING IT?

Read: 1 John 4:1-6

KEY VERSE: 'every spirit that acknowledges that Jesus Christ has come in the flesh is from God' (v2)

We know that God speaks to us today — all the time, in fact! He does this through His Word, pictures, dreams... However, when someone claims to have heard from God, how can we be sure that's really the case? How do we know they're not misled, confused, or just lying?

John's advice: measure it up to the truth about Jesus. If the message denies who Jesus is, or tries to lead you away from Him, it's a load of rubbish!

Our enemy, Satan, hates that Jesus paid the price for us on the cross. It drives him mad to see Christians worshipping Jesus, knowing that they'll have eternal life with Him forever. So he's trying to ruin things for as many people as possible, and part of his plan is to persuade people to reject or ignore Jesus. So John's test is a good one — what we think about Jesus is the most important thing about us.

PRAY Lord Jesus, I believe that You are God's Son. Help me to hear Your voice when You are speaking, and to be wise when other people are lying. Amen.

TRUTH TELLING

ALWAYS WORTH IT

Read: 1 John 4:7–12

KEY VERSE: 'This is love: not that we loved God, but that he loved us and sent his Son... for our sins.' (v10)

People search in all sorts of places for love. But what really is life-changing is knowing that you're loved just as you are.

God loves you so much that He sent Jesus to die for you.

Think about that for a minute; let that thought go from your head into your heart. It's incredible!

John's got more to teach us. He knows how quickly we forget, so he keeps repeating his catchphrase: 'Love one another'. And he has another truth test to help us to work out who is following God and who isn't: anyone who knows God shows love (because God *is* love!).

The love that Jesus showed us on the cross can never be topped by anyone, but that doesn't stop us from doing all that we can to show others that same love. God gives us the Holy Spirit, and when we let Him into our lives, we become more caring. He gives us a greater ability to love others, even when we don't feel like it. Even if it's hard, loving other people is always worth it, and it's really quite simple.

THINK What's the most loving thing anyone outside your family has ever done for you?

A MATTER OF TRUTH

Read: 1 John 4:13–15

> **KEY VERSE:** 'we know that we live in him and he in us; he has given us of his Spirit' (v13)

Does God ever seem distant to you? Does it ever feel like He's not interested in your life? Well, get this...

John jumps straight in with his next truth-bolt: 'If anyone acknowledges that Jesus is the Son of God, God lives in them and they in God' (v15). That includes YOU! If you believe that Jesus is who He says He is, that means His Spirit lives in YOU!

John had heard Jesus promise to send the Holy Spirit (see John 16:5–16). On the day of Pentecost, John and the others praying together were filled with the Holy Spirit. Immediately they were up and doing the things God wanted them to do.

Jesus had also told John that the Holy Spirit would show them the truth. So they then went and preached that Jesus is God's Son (true!), that God had raised Jesus to life (also true!), and that we need to turn to Jesus for forgiveness (definitely true!). We need the Holy Spirit if we're ever going to begin to get our heads around all this amazing truth.

THINK Have you ever had an experience of the Holy Spirit when you have noticed His presence? What was it like?

TRUTH TELLING

NO FEAR

Read: 1 John 4:16-21

KEY VERSE: 'There is no fear in love. But perfect love drives out fear, because fear has to do with punishment.' (v18)

As we continue reading, John is *still* going on about love. And why? Because love is powerful. Love forgives. Love wins. Love drives out fear.

We all experience fear at times. A lot of this is to do with thinking that we might not be accepted by someone. We might worry about how people will treat us and if people actually like us. And sometimes we do that about God. But those who know Jesus have no reason to fear anything. If you truly believe in Jesus, there's no need to doubt that you are forgiven and accepted by God, now and forever!

Today's verses from 1 John say that God's love 'drives out fear'. When we focus on our problems instead of on God, we worry, forgetting that God is looking after us and working things out for our good. But when we focus on Him, all that fear loses its power over us.

What's your biggest doubt? What's your biggest fear? If you're fretting about anything, talk to Jesus. Remember just how much He cares for you. He is love.

PRAY Lord Jesus, thank You for Your perfect love. Thank You that I don't need to be afraid of anything. Amen.

IT'S ALL GOOD

Read: 1 John 5:1-5

> **KEY VERSE:** 'True love for God means obeying his commands, and his commands don't weigh us down as heavy burdens.' (v3, TPT)

John's still not ready to change the subject – he's still talking about love! And he has another way for us to test our love for God: those who love their fellow Christians love God, those who love God follow God.

John didn't dream this up – it was what Jesus had taught him. John knew that Jesus loved God not because He said so, but because He did what God said, even when it was difficult. When we talk about obeying God and keeping His commands, it might sound like a bit of a drag. But when we look at the rules God has given us, every single one of them is for our own benefit. God gives us rules because He loves us, and wants us to love Him back.

Just like a person might show their love for someone else with a present on their birthday, we can show our love for God by keeping His rules and loving His people. That's how we can really worship Him.

THINK Which of God's commands do you find hardest to keep? Why not ask God to help you?

TRUTH TELLING

ONE WAY

Read: 1 John 5:6–12

KEY VERSE: 'Whoever has the Son has life; whoever does not have the Son of God does not have life.' (v12)

Lots of people think it's OK to believe in something, but that doesn't have to be Jesus. They say that as long as you're a 'good person', you'll go to heaven. But that's not what the Bible tells us. John tries to clear things up in today's verses: Jesus is the way to heaven. That's pretty much it.

We can't make ourselves good enough for God simply by being kind, generous and loving (although of course that's important!). All sin comes with a punishment – being separated from God – that Jesus has paid for us.

Let's have a think about what we mean by 'heaven'. John is talking about eternal life, with Jesus, in paradise. That's three key things: Jesus, perfection and eternity. So how would you get there except through Jesus Himself? Other 'gods' won't cut it, nor will wishy-washy beliefs. Only Jesus. And all we have to do is believe by His Spirit that He is our Saviour, and thank Him!

PRAY Lord God, thank You for sending Jesus to show me the way to You. Help me to speak to the truth about You to others. Amen.

ABSOLUTE CONFIDENCE

Read: 1 John 5:13-15

KEY VERSE: 'This is the confidence we have in approaching God' (v14)

So... what? Why did John bother to write all this truth down? The answer is this: because the truth can so easily get twisted or watered down. But having spent so much time with Jesus, John knew this stuff was the real deal.

John wrote his Gospel (the book of John, without any numbers in front of it!) so that people could study the evidence about Jesus and discover the truth. He put pen to paper so 'that you may believe that Jesus is the Messiah, the Son of God, and that by believing you may have life in his name' (John 20:31). He wrote his letters (the John books with the numbers 1, 2 and 3 in front!) to encourage those who 'believed in the name of the Son of God'. He wanted to remind them that eternal life was theirs, they could talk to God about anything, anytime, and that He would always answer their prayers.

What's the main truth that John has reminded you of? How can you remind yourself of it in the future?

PRAY Father God, thank You for Your amazing promises. Thank You for always hearing my prayers. Amen.

TRUTH TELLING

IN CONCLUSION...

Read: 1 John 5:16–21

KEY VERSE: 'If you see any brother or sister commit a sin... you should pray and God will give them life.' (v16)

John concludes his truth round-up with a challenge to get alongside Christians who are out-of-sorts with God. So how should we react when a Christian breaks God's rules – and may not seem to care about it? Here are John's guidelines.

First of all, let's remember that we all mess up, and sometimes we need someone to gently point out to us where we're going wrong. But being judgmental of others is never OK. Second, however badly a person might be behaving, we have to keep on loving them the way Jesus does and try to show them understanding. Finally, keep on praying for them. God has promised to answer.

It's easy to judge people when they get it wrong, but it can be harder to notice when we ourselves are going off track. God's way isn't to talk about someone behind their back, but to their face. As Christians, we're a team, and we need to help each other up when we fall down. In our love for each other, let's not keep a list of failings, but show forgiveness.

THINK Has anyone ever tried to talk to you about something you'd done wrong? How did they go about it? What was your response?

HONESTLY

Read: Psalm 123:1–4

KEY VERSE: 'I lift up my eyes to you' (v1)

Today's psalm starts off cheery, talking about friendship with God, but then it goes downhill a bit as the psalmist talks about how tough things have been... is this alright? When we worship God, should we really talk about our struggles too?

Do you ever find that you can't be yourself with people? Maybe it's like that in your class at school, with some of your friends or even at home with your family. We can all be guilty of telling people what we think they want to hear. Why do we do it? Well, it's usually because we're worried of what they'll think of us if we're honest.

The sad thing is that we can get so used to doing this with other people that sometimes we hide our feelings from God. We can worry that He won't accept us if we're really open with Him.

But that's the amazing thing about psalms. They're honest to God. Yes, about how great He is, but also about how incredibly tough life can be at times.

So to answer that question, yes we can talk to God about our struggles. We can talk to Him about anything!

THINK There's no better time than now to start being honest with God. Try writing down whatever you want to say to Him.

PSALM

THREE FOR THE PRICE OF ONE

Read: Genesis 1:1-5

KEY VERSE: 'and the Spirit of God was hovering over the waters' (v2)

There is one God but He is three persons — each one unique. God the Father, God the Son (Jesus) and God the Holy Spirit. We learn a lot about God as our heavenly Father, and we appreciate Jesus as God in human form. But what about God the Holy Spirit? What do we know about Him?

Well, the Holy Spirit didn't just arrive on the scene at Pentecost. He is God, and has always existed. At the beginning of time, God the Holy Spirit was involved in planning out our universe. The Spirit was hovering over the waters, ready for action! Before He started work, there was nothing except darkness. After He started work, there was light, power and purpose.

At just the right time, God got the wheels moving on a plan for creation and humanity that is still going on. We may not totally understand the 'how' of creation but we know 'who' made it possible — 'God created' (v1). The Holy Spirit is never dull or boring. He is amazingly creative, and out-of-this-world powerful!

PRAY Father in heaven, I want to let Your Holy Spirit work powerfully to carry on Your incredible, creative work in my life. Amen.

POWER UP!

DIVINE INSPIRATION

Read: Exodus 31:1-11

KEY VERSE: 'I have filled him with the Spirit of God, giving him great wisdom, ability, and expertise in all kinds of crafts.' (v3, NLT)

When we look at the incredible diversity in creation we realise that God was not a dull, unimaginative creator. For example, it is estimated that there are over a million different species of worm alone. God could have made one worm and thought, 'That'll do' but oh no, God wanted to make a million different types!

The Holy Spirit doesn't only inspire and help preachers and teachers, He inspires the imagination of creative people such a Bezalel and Oholiab who were more the artistic sort. The work on the tabernacle was to be of the highest standard – God never accepts second best. So, He sent His Holy Spirit to be with the craftsmen to give them the creative ideas and skills needed to achieve excellence. Just look at the range of artistic skills that the Holy Spirit got involved in: design, metalwork, wood carving, jewellery making, sewing... the list goes on! It was the craft show to end all craft shows.

THINK God has unlimited ideas and He wants you to be creative too. Whether you are good at art, sport, music, writing or something else, think how you could use your skills to serve God.

GODLY INFLUENCER

Read: Numbers 11:16–25

KEY VERSE: 'I will take some of the power of the Spirit that is on you and put it on them' (v17)

God had sent His Holy Spirit to help Moses be a great leader. The Holy Spirit made Moses bold, wise and fair. People respected his leadership and took all their problems to him.

Realising that he was a few steps away from turning into an over-worked agony aunt, Moses asked God for help. God responded by choosing 70 men to share the work. And to make sure that they would do a good enough job, God gave hem His Holy Spirit. The Holy Spirit rested on Moses and the 70 leaders, giving them the management skills and power that they needed.

When God tells a Christian to do something, He never leaves them to do it on their own. The Holy Spirit lives in Christians to help them succeed in carrying out God's plans. God has a plan for each one of us. But He doesn't dump the plan on us and run. He gives us what we need, and is there every step of the way.

PRAY Lord, I thank You for giving me Your Holy Spirit. Help me to rely on You to show me the best way to deal with the people and situations in my life. In Jesus' name. Amen.

WHO LET THE DONKEYS OUT?

Read: 1 Samuel 10:1–8

KEY VERSE: 'The Spirit of the LORD will come powerfully upon you' (v6)

Israel wanted a king. Meanwhile, Saul, a country chap from one of the least important families in the land, was asking Samuel for his help locating some runaway donkeys. Saul had no idea that God had told Samuel to anoint him as king. So he was amazed when Samuel got the oil out to put on his head and told him that God wanted him to rule over His people. Saul was only looking for his donkeys, not looking to become king!

Samuel told him not to worry about the donkeys – they were fine. God even gave Saul some reassurance that He was with him, ending with Saul being filled with the Holy Spirit. All of this happened so that Saul could be absolutely sure that this was God's work.

If He was to become king, Saul needed to know God powerfully in His life. And God provided. The Holy Spirit was God living inside of Saul, and that was a game-changer.

THINK Do you need God to reassure you that He is with you today? Speak to Him and tell Him how you're feeling.

POWER UP!

HEART TRANSPLANT

Read: 1 Samuel 10:9-11

KEY VERSE: 'God changed Saul's heart' (v9)

Saul's life was turned upside down and inside out by God's Holy Spirit. One minute he was a loser, running around after lost donkeys; the next, he was a winner, the first king of Israel, speaking God's words like a prophet.

Saul was tall, dark and handsome (1 Sam. 9:2). He would look great in all the royal pictures. But this was not the main thing the nation wanted – they wanted a leader to unite them and defeat their enemies. God needed to change Saul from the inside out to make him into the person He wanted him to be. Where did God start? He gave Saul a new heart, then He sent the Holy Spirit to power up his life. The change was sensational. Saul felt and acted like a new person.

God still changes lives in the same way today. First He has to deal with our hearts. That's why we need to ask God to forgive us and make us holy. Jesus died on the cross so that God could do just that for us. Not only does God clean out our lives, but He sends His Spirit to give us the power to live for Him.

PRAY Father God, maker of everything, please help me to welcome the Holy Spirit to come and power up my life. Amen.

WARNING SIGNS

Read: Nehemiah 9:6,21–31

KEY VERSE: 'By your Spirit you warned them through your prophets.' (v30)

How often do you get told off for doing something wrong? Those who do the telling off are often actually helping us by making us realise our mistake, and that's what the Holy Spirit is like.

Today's reading is part of Ezra's prayer in which he gives a ten-minute history of the Jews. It's a sad cycle of events. First, God rescues the Jews from Egypt and cares for them. But the Jews turn away from God. So, God warns them He will punish them if they do not turn back to Him. He gives them time to do this. However, when the Jews continue to disobey, He takes away their freedom. The Jews then cry out to God to forgive and save them. God, being a loving God, rescues the Jews and cares for them... and so on.

The Holy Spirit sometimes shows His love for us by warning us when we are heading into dangerous territory. He might do that through something we read in the Bible, our conscience, or through other people. God patiently gives us time to change our ways because He only ever wants what's best for us.

THINK Has God been trying to get your attention about something you've been doing recently? Take time to sort it out with Him.

POWER UP!

GOD'S SPIRIT BRINGS LIFE

Read: Psalm 104:1-4,27-30

KEY VERSE: 'When you send your Spirit, they are created' (v30)

Have you seen any of the episodes from the *Blue Planet* or *Planet Earth* series? These really popular documentaries captured amazing footage of nature and animals, often never seen before, from around the world. Using the best cameras, they show the spectacular variety of living creatures on our planet. The sea, air and land are filled with life – and it's amazing to see this.

Of course these programmes show how important it is that we all take care of our planet, but who's making sure that creation is all being held together still? David, the writer of this psalm, knew the answer. It is God the Holy Spirit who continues the cycle of life, generation after generation. God's Spirit brings colour, variety, laughter, enjoyment and purpose to creation.

David knew that every creature looks to God to give them the food that they need (v27). Similarly, we can look to our Father to provide for us.

THINK Are you a creative person? Take a look at the world around you – what do you think is the best part of God's creation?

HERE, THERE AND EVERYWHERE

Read: Psalm 139:1-12

KEY VERSE: 'Where can I go from your Spirit?' (v7)

The Holy Spirit knows all about us. He even knows what we are going to say before we say it. Can we do a runner and get away from Him if we want? This Hebrew worship song explains that we can't get away from God's Spirit. There's nowhere we can go to avoid Him. But the writer didn't see that as a problem, instead he'd found a reason to party!

Why should we want to avoid someone who only wants the best for us – someone who cares, guides, protects and helps us? This song is raving about the fact that God the Holy Spirit is here, there and everywhere. Whatever the situation, God is around to support us through it. Isn't that awesome?

The writer was bowled over at the thought of God's Spirit going ahead of him to guide and also following behind to protect. Christians have the excitement of knowing the Holy Spirit lives within them, giving all the support and strength they need. Who wouldn't want that extra help in their lives? Let's not shy away from the Holy Spirit but welcome His guiding presence.

PRAY Father, You know everything about me and You still accept me! Help me to be completely open with You. Amen.

POWER UP!

SPIRIT-LED PATHWAYS

Read: Psalm 143:1-10

KEY VERSE: 'may your good Spirit lead me on level ground' (v10)

David was trapped. His enemies were hunting him down. He was surrounded. He felt weak and scared as he hid in a dark cave. A meeting of the escape team was called.

David knew he could only move under the cover of darkness and along dangerous mountain trails full of bumps, ditches and drops. So he invited the Holy Spirit onto the escape team. He wanted the Holy Spirit to show him the next move he should make; to guide him along safe routes. And with the Holy Spirit's help, David was able to plan ahead knowing that God would be with him every step of the way. The great escape was a success. His enemies never caught up with him.

Sometimes we too don't know what to do next. Thankfully, we have God's Holy Spirit to lead us. We can talk with God about all our plans and ask for His advice, and then wait for the go-ahead from Him. Then, we can be sure that the Holy Spirit is moving in front of us, removing any obstacles from the path ahead.

THINK What are your future plans? It's always best to keep God in our planning, so why not talk to Him about these plans?

CARING HOLY SPIRIT

Read: Isaiah 61:1–3

KEY VERSE: 'The Spirit of the Sovereign LORD is on me' (v1)

One of the jobs of the Holy Spirit is to teach us what God wants us to know, and show us what God wants us to do. The Holy Spirit gave Isaiah some exciting challenges. The prophet knew exactly what God wanted from him. Isaiah had been given a pretty long job description, but he was eager and felt honoured to have been selected by God for the task. God knew that there was a lot of sadness and he wanted Isaiah, His man on the ground, to 'comfort all who mourn' (v2).

Years later, in His hometown of Nazareth, Jesus stood up in the synagogue and read the same words the Holy Spirit had given Isaiah (Luke 4:18–19). Jesus knew that God had sent Him to do all these things too. Look through the list in the reading again. Can you think of examples when Jesus preached good news to the poor, comforted those with broken hearts etc?

The Holy Spirit can show you what God wants *you* to do – that's really exciting!

PRAY Holy Spirit, I want to be like Isaiah and Jesus who knew that they should care for others. Help me to know exactly how You want me to do this. Amen.

POWER UP!

HAS THE HOLY SPIRIT GOT YOUR ATTENTION?

Read: Ezekiel 1:1,26–2:2

KEY VERSE: 'the Spirit came into me and raised me to my feet, and I heard him speaking to me' (2:2)

We have discovered that the Holy Spirit is incredibly creative. He has many ways to grab our attention and communicate with us. Just look what happened to Ezekiel...

Each person's experience of being filled with God's Spirit is different. Ezekiel was shown a vision of God that sent him flat on his face, and then was whooshed to his feet to hear the Holy Spirit. It was an absolutely bonkers (in a good way!) story. God also works in far less dramatic ways; it could be a gentle nudge or feeling like we should say something to someone. While we may not have visions like Ezekiel, his experience helps us understand the Holy Spirit more.

The Holy Spirit reveals God to us. He helps us understand what the Father is like. And He transforms us. Like a tornado swirling around us to lift us up, He can change the way we think, feel and act to make us more like Jesus.

THINK The Holy Spirit speaks to us, showing us how to live. Are you open to hearing from Him? What might He be giving you a nudge about?

OUT WITH THE OLD, IN WITH THE NEW

Read: Ezekiel 36:24-28

KEY VERSE: 'I will give you a new heart and put a new spirit in you' (v26)

Some people spend a long time thinking about what they look like, what shoes they've got, how their hair is styled – the list goes on. There's nothing wrong with making an effort to look good, but it is good to be aware that what really matters is what our heart looks like.

God is more concerned with our hearts than appearance. And it's actually sometimes our hearts that need a revamp. This is where the Holy Spirit comes in!

He can replace our cold hearts with hearts that have love and joy in them. Doesn't that sound good? And we don't get any old second-hand heart either. Did you notice the number of new things the Holy Spirit wants to bring to His people? New hearts, new desires, new Spirit, new love... So often our hearts are cold and ignore God. But ignoring Him is like ignoring a notification to update your phone – if you ignore it, you're missing out! Allow the Holy Spirit to update your life and bring new things into the mix.

PRAY Father, please help me to be willing to change. Fill me with Your Holy Spirit and give me a heart update. Amen.

POWER UP!

DRY BONES

Read: Ezekiel 37:1-10

KEY VERSE: 'I will make breath enter you, and you will come to life.' (v5)

It's a spooky reading, this one. Skeletons rattling around in a valley. You've been warned!

No, it's not a movie — it's a dramatic picture of God working in people's lives. Here we have a fantastic picture of how God would gather the currently land-less people of Israel together in their own land, and give them the power to live for Him! At that time, the Israelites must have felt like dry bones — lifeless and useless. But God wanted them to know that He could bring them back to life.

This is also a dramatic picture of what God does for us today. Without God we're skeletons — lifeless. When we come to God for forgiveness, He not only puts our lives back together but He also send His Holy Spirit to give us life and power. God loves to bring life to His people. When they fall apart, He wants to bring them back to life through His Spirit, and turn them into world-changers.

THINK Do you feel like you need more of God's power and life? If so, ask God for that extra zing — ask for more of the Holy Spirit.

OFFER OPEN TO ALL

Read: Joel 2:15,28–32

KEY VERSE: 'I will pour out my Spirit on all people.' (v28)

We have breezed over some Old Testament examples of God's Holy Spirit empowering people to do fantastic things. But it was only a few people who experienced the Holy Spirit so powerfully. They were Holy Spirit 'limited editions'. Then God gave Joel a Holy Spirit forecast: the heavens would open and the Holy Spirit would pour down all over the world. He would flood the lives of young and old, rich and poor, male and female. Yep, everyone would be getting a holy drenching! No longer would God's Spirit be limited to one nation. Anyone, anywhere, anytime, would be able to experience God working in them.

Then, when Jesus came to earth, He forecast that the Holy Spirit would be like a stream of living water flowing through those who believed in Him. After Jesus had returned to heaven, the Holy Spirit came as promised. He flooded into the lives of the early Christians. And today the Holy Spirit is still ready to flow through anyone who trusts in Jesus as their Saviour – anywhere, anytime.

PRAY Holy Spirit, It's amazing that You are alive in all Christians. I want to know more of You, so please flood my life today. Amen.

POWER UP!

ACCESS ALL AREAS

Read: John 14:15–24

> **KEY VERSE:** 'the Father... will give you another advocate... the Spirit of truth' (vv16–17)

Jesus knew He was about to be captured and killed, and that afterwards He would rise from the dead and return to heaven. But what would happen to His disciples? How would they cope without Him to help them? Jesus had some comforting news.

   God wasn't going to abandon the disciples. He loved them too much to do that. They would not be left alone with no one to care for them. Once Jesus had returned to heaven, God was going to send the Holy Spirit. The disciples had already experienced the Holy Spirit living *with* them – now they were going to experience the Holy Spirit living *in* them!

   Jesus described the Holy Spirit as a comforter or counsellor. Not someone to say, 'There, there, never mind,' but a close friend to help, advise, lead and just be there, just as Jesus had done. The best news? When we become Christians, the Holy Spirit sets up a home in us too. He's with us all the time and is eager to be our guide through life!

THINK If the Holy Spirit is living inside you, are there any areas of your life that you don't want Him to have access to? Why?

PERSONAL TUTOR

Read: John 14:25-27

KEY VERSE: 'the Holy Spirit... will teach you all things and will remind you of everything I have said to you' (v26)

Have you ever wondered what it was like when Matthew, Mark, Luke and John started writing the books about Jesus? Were they panicking, knowing how many people would eventually read these books, desperately trying to remember all the details? No, God sent the Holy Spirit to teach and help those who wrote the Bible. He reminded them of the things that Jesus had said and done.

The Holy Spirit is not the kind of teacher who comes in ready to tell someone off. Instead he is a one-to-one personal tutor. He works at our pace and is very patient. If we don't understand something, He won't bite our heads off but will take time to explain. He knows what is in the Bible and what it means. And if something is too hard for us to understand at the moment, He'll come back to it with us another time.

The Holy Spirit treats life as one big lesson in getting to know God. The more we ask Him to teach us, the more we learn.

PRAY Holy Spirit, please explain to me the things that I don't understand about the Bible. Thank You for being so patient. Amen.

POWER UP!

HOLY SPIRIT BACK-UP

Read: John 15:18-27

KEY VERSE: 'the Spirit of truth who goes out from the Father—he will testify about me' (v26)

Jesus had warned His disciples that they were in for a hard time. Some people would absolutely hate them. Christians would be picked on for no reason. And they could expect to be beaten up, put in prison, teased, robbed, and possibly murdered — just because they loved Jesus. But why? Jesus explained that He is the reason people would hate them. God's enemies really, *really* hate Jesus and will do everything they can to make life hard for people on His team.

What does this look like for us today? Well, it's different. But let's be realistic, we still might be picked on and have horrible things said to us just because we are Christians.

So should we quit now before it gets too personal? No way! Jesus promised He would send the Holy Spirit to comfort those who are having a hard time for loving God. The Holy Spirit would encourage Christians, remind them of Jesus and give them strength to carry on living for Him.

THINK Do you get scared that if people know you're a Christian they'll give you a hard time? Lots of people feel like this, but the Holy Spirit can help you and be with you — speak to Him!

KEEPING US ON TRACK

Read: John 16:5-11

KEY VERSE: 'When he comes, he will prove the world to be in the wrong about sin and righteousness and judgment' (v8)

The Holy Spirit acts as God's police force on earth. He knows when we break God's laws. There is no need for an investigation, He calls us out straight away – He makes us feel uneasy about what we've done.

Scared? You shouldn't be! The Holy Spirit wants to set us free from our bad habits so that we can live well. Sadly, we can ignore the Holy Spirit's attempts to help us out, and keeping on doing the wrong thing. But if we go down that path, the evidence against us piles up. The good news is that as followers of Jesus, we can ask for forgiveness. Then when God the judge looks at us, He says, 'not guilty'!

The passage today talks about sin and righteousness. We are given an awesome, exciting relationship with God, and the Holy Spirit wants to keep us on the right path so that we can experience all the good stuff He's got in store for us!

PRAY Holy Spirit, thank You for looking out for me and pointing me in the right direction. When I mess up, help me to sort things out with You. Amen.

POWER UP!

JESUS' NO. 1 FAN

Read: John 16:12–15

KEY VERSE: 'He will glorify me' (v14)

Many people seem to have a low opinion of Jesus. Some use His name to swear. Others laugh at what He's done for us. Most people seem to want nothing to do with Him.

But not the Holy Spirit! He has a message for the world: Jesus is God! Treat Jesus' name with respect! Jesus is the greatest! Give Jesus credit for all He has done. Look at Jesus! Come to Jesus! Praise Jesus! Give glory to Jesus!

The Holy Spirit runs Jesus' fan club. He helps us to show our love for Jesus.

He supplies us with information about Jesus and updates us on what He is doing. He likes us to go to events where Jesus is praised and talked about, and where everyone there loves Him. He arranges VIP access to Jesus for us, and starts off some great conversations.

The Holy Spirit works non-stop behind the scenes to bring our attention to Jesus. He absolutely loves it when we respect and praise Jesus – so do that now!

PRAY Jesus, You are so amazing. I never want to forget how You died on a cross for me so that my sins could be forgiven and I could follow You. Thank You. Amen.

A HOLIDAY TO REMEMBER

Read: Acts 2:1-4

> **KEY VERSE:** 'They saw what seemed to be tongues of fire' (v3)

Before Jesus returned to heaven, He made a promise: 'In a few days you will be baptised with the Holy Spirit.'

Jerusalem was full of Jews from all over the world who had come to celebrate a festival. Jesus' followers were all together waiting for Jesus' promise to happen. First, there was a sound like a tornado. Jesus had described the Holy Spirit as being like wind (John 3:8) – invisible, but the effects of it can be seen. Like this, the Holy Spirit is invisible, but we can see what He does in people's lives.

Next came fire! It appeared over their heads. John the Baptist had predicted that Jesus would baptise His followers with Holy Spirit fire. Fire symbolised spotlessness and power.

The Holy Spirit powered up the first Christians to tell the holiday crowds about Jesus. They started speaking to them, but the words coming out of their mouths were not Greek, they were the languages of the people they spoke to – it was a miracle! There's nothing that can stop Jesus being talked about when the Holy Spirit is at work.

THINK The Holy Spirit can help you talk to the people you know about Jesus too. In what way do you need His help for this?

POWER UP!

COMMON LANGUAGE

Read: Acts 2:4-13

KEY VERSE: 'Amazed and perplexed, they asked one another, "What does this mean?"' (v12)

Have you ever tried to learn a new language? At Pentecost, the Holy Spirit helped the first Christians express their love for God in languages they hadn't even had lessons in.

After Jesus went back to heaven, the disciples got together and kept a low profile. They didn't want to be recognised now it seemed to be all over. The Holy Spirit changed all that. The disciples were able to speak, with no fear, in languages they'd never learnt a word of! Their cover was blown. Holiday-makers rushed to find out what on earth was going on.

'Hello! Bonjour! Güten tag! Welcome to our talk about the miracles of God, available in all languages!' It was like God had invaded the school language department. Holiday-makers were listening in their own languages, and Google translate didn't get a single hit!

The Holy Spirit wants to bring Jesus out into the open in our lives too. He wants to take away our fear and give us bravery to tell people about Him.

PRAY Holy Spirit, You are the giver of the best gifts. Please give me exactly what I need right now so that I can show the world Jesus. Amen.

REASONS TO BE THANKFUL... 1,2,3

Read: Acts 2:14-21,37-39

KEY VERSE: 'The promise is for you and your children and for all who are far off' (v39)

Remember Joel? He was the prophet who preached that the Holy Spirit was coming to live in anyone who had been forgiven by God. At Pentecost, Peter remembered Joel's words, stood on a chair and started preaching...

The Holy Spirit fired up Peter to preach a long (but hardly boring) sermon. It was deep stuff! Not even one joke was cracked. Peter launched straight into his first point. He said that in God's eyes, everyone was out of order. And it was time to turn back to God.

The time came for the radical second point – only Jesus can deal with our sin and can forgive us. And to complete the original three-point sermon – those who turned from doing whatever they wanted, to believe in Jesus would receive the Holy Spirit. As 3,000 people responded and said 'Yes' to this, they all received the Holy Spirit. Joel's prophecy was beginning to be fulfilled.

There is only one way to get right with God – by turning to Jesus and receiving the Holy Spirit.

THINK What tends to turn your attention away from God the most? Ask the Holy Spirit to help you overcome this.

POWER UP!

RIGHT SKILLS
FOR THE JOB

Read: Acts 6:1–15

KEY VERSE: 'choose seven men from among you who are known to be full of the Spirit and wisdom' (v3)

As the Early Church grew, problems occasionally cropped up. Christians from Greek backgrounds felt they were not being treated as well as those from Jewish backgrounds. New leaders would need to be chosen to sort out these problems so the apostles could concentrate on teaching and praying. These leaders would need to make sure things were managed fairly, properly and effectively.

A leader had to be a certain sort of person, living their life in a good way. But most of all, they needed to be full of the Spirit and known for being like this.

Being a church leader is a very important job. It's also a very hard job – think about everything they have to do! Sundays are just the tip of the iceberg. So it's essential that leaders are filled with the Holy Spirit so that they can be successful not just in the main service, but in everything else they are called to do.

THINK Do you know any of the leaders in your church? Whether it's the main leader or the youth leader, why not pray for them now? They need a lot of support and encouragement.

CHANGE OF HEART

Read: Acts 8:1-8

KEY VERSE: 'Philip went down to a city in Samaria and proclaimed the Messiah there.' (v5)

Do you have any rivalries or ongoing arguments?

One of those chosen to be a leader was Philip. He was a man powered up by the Holy Spirit. Jewish people like Philip avoided going to Samaria. Years of rivalry and arguments had meant that Samaritans and Jews hated each other. But the Holy Spirit changed how Philip saw the Samaritans. They were people that Jesus had come to save, just like Philip. Samaritans needed to hear about Jesus and receive the Holy Spirit. So Philip boldly went where no Jew dared to go – Samaria. The Samaritans could not get enough of Philip. A Jew who loved them... this was amazing! A Jew who performed miracles in Jesus' name... this was jaw dropping! A Jew who wanted them to be filled with the Holy Spirit... this was just incredible!

Philip was a man with an attitude. An attitude of love to those he had once hated. It led to a great revival (remember that word? Look at day 185 if you've forgotten). Samaria – a place with a bad reputation – became the place to be!

PRAY Father, I know that You love absolutely everyone. Through Your Holy Spirit, please help me to shine Your light to anyone and everyone. Amen.

POWER UP!

DESERT, ANYONE?

Read: Acts 8:26-40

KEY VERSE: 'So he invited Philip to come up and sit with him.' (v31)

Philip is leading the most successful Jesus mission outside Jerusalem. Hundreds have turned to Christ. Where next? A bigger mission in a larger city? No, a dusty road in the desert. Why had God called Philip away from the crowds to wander among the cactus plants? Philip knew God had a purpose in sending him to a giant sandpit, and he soon found out what it was.

God had made an appointment for Philip to meet an African man who as searching for Him. Philip chatted to him and used the Bible to explain that Jesus had died as a sacrifice for sin. The man was so keen to learn more that Philip sat with him and shared the good news of Jesus.

This man was convinced Jesus was God's Son. He even found a water hole to be baptised in then and there. Afterwards, he set off to share the good news with the rest of Africa. Philip's one-to-one chat hand launched the gospel to a new continent – a day well-spent!

THINK When there's an opportunity to talk about Jesus, do you take it? The Holy Spirit will give us 100% support when we want to bring glory to God's Son.

LET'S GO

Read: Psalm 122:1-9

KEY VERSE: 'I rejoiced with those who said to me, "Let us go to the house of the LORD."' (v1)

This psalm was sung by Old Testament believers as they climbed a hill to Jerusalem, where they worshipped God. In the Old Testament, Jerusalem wasn't just a capital city, it reminded the people of these promises of God:
1. That God would bring healing to the whole world through Abraham's children.
2. That God is with His people.
3. That God was going to do something miraculous to sort out Israel's problems and, at the same time, the problems of the whole world.

Today we are reminded of those promises when we talk about Jesus. He is bringing healing to the world, He has given us the Holy Spirit to be close to us, and He is the great king who mends our lives.

We don't have to climb a hill to meet with God, He is with us all the time. But what we can do is 'go to' His promises. When we *feel* God is distant, even though we *know* He's not, let's go to His promises and trust Him. He's never broken a single one – and he never will.

THINK Do you ever experience times when God doesn't feel near? What ideas do you now have of what to do when this next happens?

PSALM

NICE JACKET

Read: Genesis 37:1-4

KEY VERSE: 'Now Israel loved Joseph more than any of his other sons' (v3)

We're going to spend a couple of weeks looking at the story of Joseph (the Old Testament one, not the man who brought up Jesus!). You might have heard of this Joseph as being a dreamer with a snazzy coat. That's true — but there's a bit more to him than that.

It was no secret that Joseph was his dad's favourite, and that caused all kinds of problems within the family. His other brothers hated his guts because of the special treatment he got (such as his amazing coat). You see, Joseph's dad, Jacob (aka Israel) had more than one wife (quite normal for the time), and Joseph's mum was the favourite wife. It's easy to see why the other brothers were jealous, but their jealousy was about to grow into the strongest hatred imaginable.

Do you have feelings of jealousy towards someone at the moment? Maybe even someone in your family? If so, ask God to take away those feelings of bitterness and replace them with kindness. You'll feel a whole lot better for it!

PRAY Lord Jesus, please fill my heart with your love so that there is no room for jealousy. Amen.

BIG DREAMER

DREAM-TELLER

Read: Genesis 37:5-11

KEY VERSE: 'And they hated him all the more because of his dream' (v8)

He may have been his father's favourite but Joseph was hated by his brothers. And the situation was about to get much worse when he started having special dreams from God.

All the bowing down going on in Joseph's dreams was a picture of what was to happen in the future. But Joseph, a little bit cocky and not fully able to understand what his dreams meant, wasn't shy about telling his brothers that they would one day all bow down to him. True as that might have been, he didn't go about it in the right way. Even Jacob felt the need to give his favourite son a telling off for showing off.

Sometimes we need to be a bit more mindful of the way we speak to people, especially when we want to share our faith with our friends. Sometimes we can say the right things in the wrong way. It's important that we can talk about God, but we need to be respectful when we do so. How might you change the way you speak to people about Jesus?

PRAY Lord, help me to think before I speak. Give me the words You want me to speak today and help me to say them in the right way. Amen.

A DAUNTING TASK

Read: Genesis 37:12-17

KEY VERSE: 'I am going to send you' (v13)

What do you think went through Joseph's mind when his dad asked him to find his brothers and check that they were OK? Do you think he tried to come up with an excuse? Was he nervous about meeting with his brothers without backup from Dad?

It can't have been easy for Joseph to trust all would be fine — he must have picked up on the negative vibes he was getting from his brothers since all the dream business. He knew they hated his guts. But he didn't squirm his way out of what his father was asking him to do. He simply answered, 'Very well.' He might have been a little bit cocky with his brothers, but he was obedient to his dad.

God is our Father and sometimes He might ask us to do things that seem pretty tough — that's when we have to be brave and trust Him. He wouldn't ask us to do something if He didn't think we were capable of doing it. He is always with us!

THINK How do you react when others ask you to help them? Do you start making excuses or do you get stuck in? If God asked you to do something challenging in order to help others, what would you say?

SELL-OUTS

Read: Genesis 37:18–30

KEY VERSE: 'When Reuben heard this, he tried to rescue him from their hands.' (v21)

Joseph's brothers hated him so much that before Joseph had even reached them, they had decided to get rid of him – forever. That's right – they were prepared to kill their own brother! So they threw him in a pit while they ironed out the finer details of their plan.

The only brother with any heart was Reuben. But even though he believed killing Joseph was a step too far, he still wanted him out of the picture. Reuben came up with Plan B: selling Joseph to slave traders. That way, they could make money *and* get rid of Joseph. Despicable!

How do you think Joseph felt when he realised his brothers, who were supposed to love and protect him, betrayed him like this? Remember, he was only 17 at the time – not that much older than you. Have there been times in your life when things (perhaps things that you had no control over) have left you feeling confused or worried? Talk to God, and know that He loves you and understands.

PRAY Thank You, God, that no matter what happens to me, You are still God and You love me. Help me to never forget that. Amen.

BIG DREAMER

WEB OF LIES

Read: Genesis 37:31-35

KEY VERSE: 'We found this. Examine it to see whether it is your son's robe.' (v32)

The problem with telling a lie is that you usually have to tell another lie to support the first lie. Then the lies spin out of control and before you know it, you're in so deep it would have been easier to just tell the truth all along.

This is the situation Joseph's brothers now found themselves in. They had to fib their socks off to their father, Jacob, who was completely devastated by Joseph's 'death'. The brothers smeared Joseph's beautiful coat in animal blood to make it look like he'd been killed by a wild beast. It was a web of lies that they would all have to stick to for years to come. While Joseph had been sold as an actual slave, his brothers became slaves to their own lies and had to live with the mess they had made.

All of us have told lies at some point, but it's never too late to come clean. God loves the truth – in fact, the Bible says He *is* truth, and there's nothing He can't forgive. Talk to Him truthfully now.

PRAY Lord, help me to be honest and truthful in all I say, and to talk to You when things are hard. Amen.

EMPLOYEE OF THE MONTH

Read: Genesis 39:1-6

KEY VERSE: 'the LORD gave him success in everything he did' (v3)

Having spent his entire childhood as the golden boy and favourite son, you might assume that Joseph would be doing some serious complaining now that he was a slave. But he didn't – in fact, he worked very hard, even when no one was watching. And it didn't go unnoticed.

Joseph was sold to a man called Potiphar, and he was impressed by Joseph's attitude. It wasn't long before he offered Joseph a promotion, so that he was in charge of the rest of the household!

Even though things were grim and he was far from home, Joseph remained faithful to God and did his best in difficult circumstances. He knew that God was with him, and it showed in the way he lived his life.

It can be so hard to keep going with a good attitude when we're in a situation we don't like. Maybe it's in a school lesson we find boring or difficult, or having to spend time with people we'd rather not hang out with. But people notice when we try hard and do our best for God and other people.

THINK Success is often the result of doing normal things abnormally well. Have you got any boring jobs to do? Why not try to do them really well?

BIG DREAMER

TEMPTATION

Read: Genesis 39:7-10

KEY VERSE: 'after a while his master's wife took notice of Joseph' (v7)

Potiphar wasn't the only one to be impressed with Joseph – so was his wife. After all, Joseph was good-looking guy...

To start off with, Mrs Potiphar (we don't know her proper name!) just liked to look at Joseph, but the small-talk soon turned to full-blown flirting – awkward. One day, she decided to kick things up a notch and tried to get Joseph to go to bed with her (yep – even though she was married, and Joseph was a slave).

Joseph was miles from home, and probably could have given into temptation without getting caught. But he respected his boss too much, and knew that sleeping with Mrs P would be very, very wrong, so he stuck to what he knew was right.

We live in a world where we're constantly told that if you can get away with doing something, you'd be mad not to do it. But God knows our hearts and wants us to honour Him, and others, in the way we live and the choices we make. It would have been difficult for Joseph to do the right thing, but he did it anyway.

PRAY Lord, thank You for being interested in all areas of my life. Help me to be strong and to put You first, no matter what. Amen.

ACCUSED

Read: Genesis 39:11–20

KEY VERSE: 'Joseph's master took him and put him in prison' (v20)

Despite the non-stop flirting from Mrs Potiphar, Joseph refused to give in and betray his boss. He did the right thing. Unfortunately, however, the lady in question wasn't accustomed to being told 'No'. Potiphar's wife hit the roof, and made it look as though Joseph had been the one making the moves on her. She used Joseph's cloak to frame him, and went crying to her husband. What a nerve!

Although he may have had his doubts, there's no way Potiphar could have believed a slave over his own wife, so he had Joseph thrown in prison. It was a horrible situation for Potiphar, too – either his wife was a liar, or his best servant was a good-for-nothing cheat.

Even though it landed him in prison, Joseph still did the right thing. It can be so hard not to go along with what everyone else is doing, but it's better to run in the opposite direction than to play with fire. Potiphar might not have known the truth, but God did, and He never left Joseph's side.

THINK What situations have you been in where you've found it hard to resist pressure to do something you knew was wrong or didn't want to do? Next time that happens, ask God to help you.

BIG DREAMER

A MODEL PRISONER

Read: Genesis 39:20-23

KEY VERSE: 'But... the LORD was with him' (vv20-21)

Sometimes, things get worse before they get better. Joseph was totally innocent, but had found himself thrown in jail. He had obeyed God, but was still unfairly punished. So, did Joseph turn his back on God?

No! Quite the opposite in fact. As we continue reading the story of Joseph in the Bible, keep an eye out for how many times it says, 'the LORD was with him'. Yes, the situation was unfair, and he was worried about his future. But deep down Joseph knew God was in control and that's the truth he clung to.

Joseph may have been a prisoner but he kept himself free of any bitterness or malice. His attitude and hard work impressed the chief jailer, who eventually handed over the entire prison management to Joseph. Just like Potiphar had done, the jailer trusted him. There was something different about Joseph – the Lord was with him!

Do you feel like life's a bit unfair sometimes? Remember – God is with you. Ask Him to help you with what you're facing.

PRAY Lord, thank You for always supporting me. Please give me a positive attitude in dealing with tough situations. I want to serve You where I am. Amen.

JAILBIRD JOE

Read: Genesis 40:1-8

'Why me?' 'What have I done to deserve this?' 'It's so unfair!'

When we've been treated unfairly, we can end up totally focused on ourselves. But even though Joseph had every reason to be self-absorbed, he took an interest in those around him. He was responsible for the other prisoners, which included a baker and a cupbearer, and Joseph took his job seriously. He was no longer the cocky dreamer who rubbed people up the wrong way – he was a sensitive young man, and noticed that his fellow inmates were a bit low. He cared enough to want to help them.

This change in Joseph's life didn't come about overnight. But his experiences as a slave and a prisoner were used by God to reshape his outlook on life. That's what happens when we trust God with our lives. He changes us from thinking about ourselves all the time to caring for others.

Who might God be asking you to be caring towards today? Helping someone else might both do that person a favour and change you at the same time!

THINK Are you aware of the needs of other people? Be open to opportunities to help people who are going through difficult times.

BIG DREAMER

TUNE IN TO GOD'S VOICE

Read: Genesis 40:9-13

KEY VERSE: '"This is what it means," Joseph said to him' (v12)

Egypt was a land full of mystics and sorcerers claiming to be able to tell the meaning of dreams. Even though they were a bunch of phoneys, they charged a fortune for their services.

When Joseph was told the dreams of Pharaoh's baker and cupbearer, he knew where to go for the answer: God. God had given him dreams before, and the gift of interpreting them.

God knows the past, present and future – and we can ask Him to advise us in everything we do! But hearing Him is something that can take a bit of practice. Do you ask God to guide you but find that you're struggling to hear from Him? Try turning down the volume a bit – all the noise that is going on around you (for example, distraction from TV, social media, and general busyness). It's not that God doesn't speak, it's that we can't hear or don't take the time to try.

Joseph hadn't forgotten how to listen to God. He knew that God can speak to us through dreams, the Bible and even through other people.

PRAY Lord, I want to hear Your voice. Help me to know when You are speaking to me, and to listen with my whole heart. Amen.

FORGOTTEN

Read: Genesis 40:14-23

KEY VERSE: 'The chief cupbearer... forgot him' (v23)

'Don't forget...!' How many times have you heard these words from a parent or teacher?

Well, they're the last words Joseph said to the cupbearer as he was released from prison. And what do you know? The cupbearer forgot him!

Joseph went through one of life's most cruel experiences – hopes raised and then dashed into a million pieces. This was a real opportunity for him to get out of that stinking prison, but nothing came of it. If ever he was tempted to despair, it must have been then.

The weeks turned to months, months turned into years and there seemed little hope of release. His patience in God was being tested to the limit. But God did not forget Joseph in prison and He will not forget you. God has a perfect memory. He may not answer our prayers as we would like, but He never forgets anything we ask Him. We can trust Him.

THINK Have you ever felt let down by someone? Maybe they made a promise they didn't keep? Try to forgive anyone who has let you down – and ask God for His help if you find it hard.

BIG DREAMER

GET-OUT-OF-JAIL CARD

Read: Genesis 41:1-16

KEY VERSE: 'I cannot do it... but God will give Pharaoh the answer' (v16)

It was Joseph's dreams that had got him into trouble. But God had an amazing escape plan for Joseph! He gave Pharaoh two vivid and puzzling dreams, but no clue as to what they meant. Pharaoh assembled all the wise men and told them his dreams, but no one could tell him what they meant.

At long last, the cupbearer remembered Joseph. He knew that, with help of the one true God, Joseph would be able to work out the meaning. And that's exactly what happened!

During the two previous years that Joseph sat in prison, imagine how many times he must have thought God had forgotten him. Do you sometimes pray to God but nothing appears to happen... nothing changes? God has answers to all the things that puzzle us, and at the right time He will show them to us. Even when life is a bit confusing, we can talk to Him and ask Him to help us understand — and even if we don't understand, we can still trust Him. He is a good and perfect God.

PRAY Lord, help me to understand Your timing and to trust in Your response. Amen.

EXCITING TIMES AHEAD

Read: Genesis 41:17–36

KEY VERSE: 'God has revealed to Pharaoh what he is about to do.' (v25)

When you let God guide you through life, you never know what might happen next! Exciting as well as challenging things might happen. For Joseph one minute he was in prison, the next he was talking to royalty with messages from God.

Pharaoh's dreams contained both good news and bad news. The good news was that Egypt was going to have seven years of bumper crops and brilliant harvests. Everyone would have more than enough to eat and the barns would be bursting at the timber beams. The bad news? Well, those seven good years would be followed by seven not-so-good years. There wouldn't be a crumb to eat.

But God had been warning Pharaoh through these dreams, and had a plan. During the years of plenty, advised Joseph, the people should save one fifth of all the good grain and lock it away safely. That way, by the time the famine struck, there would be enough stored up for everyone to eat for the seven bad years.

THINK Joseph didn't take any of the credit for what he said to Pharaoh. He gave all the glory to God. When you do something well, do you thank God for the gifts and skills that He has given you?

BIG DREAMER

STRAIGHT TO THE TOP

Read: Genesis 41:37-40

KEY VERSE: 'there is no one so discerning and wise as you' (v39)

Joseph had suggested a very sensible plan for the next 14 years: prepare for the future famine by storing up food now. The plan seemed like a very good idea to Pharaoh, but who would be in charge of making sure everything was put in place?

The job was up for grabs. But notice that Joseph didn't put himself forward – even though he might have done when he was a teenager and his father's favourite son. Instead, he stood back and waited for those in authority to recognise his gifts. And they did. Pharaoh could see how wise he was, and knew that God was with him.

So Joseph was immediately put in charge of the palace and all the people were to obey his orders. The only person with more power than him was Pharaoh. Wow! That morning, he'd been in prison, and now he was the second most important person in the country!

No matter how hopeless a situation might seem, God can turn anything around. Do you need God to change some things for you? Talk to Him, and remember that His timing is always perfect.

PRAY Lord, thank You for always having a plan. Please help me to remember that You can turn even the worst situation around. Amen.

DON'T LOOK BACK IN ANGER

Read: Genesis 41:41-52

KEY VERSE: 'Joseph named his firstborn Manasseh [meaning "made to forget"]' (v51)

Do you ever feel bitter, even after the situation has been sorted out? Joseph had gone from the very bottom of the pile to the absolute top! But would he ever be able to get over the terrible way he had been treated?

Joseph had suffered rejection by his brothers, the humiliation of being a slave and being wrongfully imprisoned. He had been forgotten by people he had helped, and left in prison for years on end. But God had turned his life around and made him into a respected and successful leader with a family of his own. So what about the pain of the past?

Well, look at the names he gave to his children: 'Manasseh' means 'made to forget'. God had blessed him so much he was able to forget all the pain he had been through. 'Ephraim' means 'fruitful'. Joseph had entered Egypt as a slave and God had helped him rise to the top. Joseph was trying to put the past behind him – he was thanking God for today, and trusting Him for the future.

PRAY Lord, please take away the hurt and bitterness I sometimes feel. Thank You for bringing new opportunities each day. Amen.

BIG DREAMER

SAVING FOR A RAINY DAY?

Read: Genesis 41:53-57

KEY VERSE: 'Go to Joseph and do what he tells you.' (v55)

It's great to sometimes have money to spend but we need to learn to use it wisely. When we've got more of it than we need, it can be tempting to blow it all on something fancy or fun. There's nothing wrong with enjoying ourselves or having nice things, as long as we're sharing and being sensible. But the Bible tells us to think about the future, and it's a very good idea to save some money for when we might unexpectedly need it.

The people of Egypt could have eaten like kings for the seven good years, and totally ignored God's warning through Joseph. But then they'd have been wiped out by the famine! But because they'd stored up grain while they had plenty, they had more than enough to live on (and even sell to people from other lands) when the hard times came.

God cares about every aspect of our lives, including how we spend our money and share what we have. Why not talk to Him about how you could use money wisely?

THINK There are many ways you could use your money — what needs are there around you? Could you support a food bank or give to a charity working with people who are going through tough times?

A DREAM COME TRUE

Read: Genesis 42:1–7

KEY VERSE: 'Joseph… recognised them, but he pretended to be a stranger' (v7)

Remember those dreams Joseph had as a teenager? Well, they really did come true! Yes, Joseph was now Prime Minister (ish), but the bit about the brothers bowing down hadn't yet happened. That is, until the famine spread to Canaan (Joseph's homeland) and his brothers were forced to travel all the way to Egypt to buy grain.

How do you react when you see someone who has treated you badly?

Despite all that he had been through, the Bible doesn't say anything about Joseph being bitter or wanting revenge. He had moved on, had a wife and family, and was happy. But the sight of his brothers – the ones who betrayed him – must have been like a sucker-punch to the chest.

Why do you think he pretended not to know them? Perhaps he wanted to watch how they behaved.

Rather than letting his feelings take over and reacting hastily, Joseph decided on a plan that would allow the truth to come out on its own. This was a delicate matter with a lot of emotions involved, and he wanted to handle it carefully.

PRAY Lord, when someone has upset me, help me to see that revenge won't take the pain away, but getting closer to You will help. Amen.

BIG DREAMER

HONESTY -
THE BEST POLICY

Read: Genesis 42:8-20

KEY VERSE: 'Your servants are honest men' (v11)

A hypocrite is someone who pretends to be something they are not. As Joseph's brothers grovelled to buy grain, they tried to make out that they were honest men. Unfortunately for them, they were talking to someone who knew the truth about them.

Joseph probably didn't know whether to laugh or cry. Honest men?! He didn't think so! None of them had the courage to admit they had tricked their father into thinking he was dead, right after they had sold him as a slave. Maybe they were just kidding themselves, after years of living with their secret swept under the carpet. How difficult it must have been for Joseph not to feel betrayed all over again!

Whatever we might have done wrong in the past, we can always ask God to forgive us. Then we have no need to lie about who we are, or pretend to be someone else. God loves you so much, and wants you to know that you are not defined by what you have done wrong.

PRAY Father, I'm sorry for the times I've messed up. Thank You for sending Jesus and forgiving me. I want to move on from these things, with Your help. Amen.

PAST MISTAKES

Read: Genesis 42:21-28

KEY VERSE: 'What is this that God has done to us?' (v28)

The past suddenly caught up with Joseph's brothers. They immediately thought that they were being punished by God for what they had done to Joseph, all those years before, when they sold him to slave traders and told their father he'd been killed by a wild animal. They remembered how distressed Joseph had been – how he'd begged them not to do it.

As the brothers discussed what they'd done many years ago, they were speaking in their own language. Because they didn't recognise Joseph, and assumed that he was a native Egyptian, they had no idea he was listening to their conversation and could understand every word. He was so emotional that he left the room so that no one would see him crying.

But Joseph still wanted to test them further. His brothers seemed more concerned about what would happen to them, rather than being truly sorry for what they had done to him. So he waited a little longer before telling them who he really was.

THINK Is there something you could do to repair a past mistake? It's never too late to try and make amends. Why not talk to God about it first?

BIG DREAMER

LESSON LEARNT

Read: Genesis 44:1-6,15-34

KEY VERSE: 'We are now my lord's slaves' (v16)

There's been a lot going on in this story, so here's a quick recap: Joseph's brothers have returned to their father in Canaan with food. Simeon has been kept in jail in Egypt until they bring Benjamin, the youngest son, to see Joseph. Jacob doesn't want to let Benjamin out of his sight, but when they run out of food again, he has to agree.

Back in Egypt, Joseph releases Simeon once he has seen Benjamin with his own eyes. The brothers set off for home again with more food, but Joseph has one more test for them. He's framed them to look like thieves, and says he wants to arrest Benjamin (just to see what his older brothers will do). And at long last, they show a change of heart. The brothers won't let anything bad happen to Benjamin – and Judah offers to become a slave if they will release him.

Joseph can finally see how devastated his brothers are. They don't want to put their father through any more grief. They have learnt their lesson.

THINK God loves families and wants everyone to be treated well in them. If we love those close to us we will find it easier to love others also. Pray for each person in your family today.

THE GRAND FINALE

Read: Genesis 45:1-15; 46:28-30

KEY VERSE: 'So then, it was not you who sent me here, but God.' (v8)

What an incredible drama. Joseph cannot hide who he is from his brothers any longer. He orders all his attendants out of the room so that he can be alone with his brothers. He then completely loses it, weeping so loudly that everyone in the palace can hear!

Joseph makes his brothers come closer so that they can see him better and announces, 'I am your brother Joseph'. His stunned brothers stand in silence and shame.

But instead of piling on the guilt for their past cruelty, Joseph says that God had a purpose and a plan in it all. He had made him Prime Minister of Egypt so that his family would not starve to death during the great famine. Joseph realised that God had a plan for his life right from the beginning. Joseph's brothers had divided the family, but God's love had brought them together again.

Looking back over Joseph's story, what has made the biggest impact on you?

PRAY Lord, thank You for the story of Joseph and what I can learn from it. Help me to remember that whatever happens in my life and wherever I find myself, You are always with me. Amen.

BIG DREAMER

LOSE CONTROL

Read: Psalm 127:1-5

KEY VERSE: 'Unless the LORD builds a house, the work of the builders is wasted.' (v1, NLT)

Do you like rollercoasters? Some people love them, some absolutely hate them! Part of the reason for their hatred of them is the feeling of having no control.

The singers of today's psalm were on their way to worship God. They were getting themselves ready by remembering that they are totally in God's hands. He controls everything, we don't. This can be a scary thought!

No one likes to admit that they can't control things. But the simple fact is we don't have complete control over anything – what's going to happen today, tomorrow or even what happens inside our own bodies. But the great thing is we don't need to. Because someone far more qualified is in control.

God is in charge of our lives. That doesn't mean we shouldn't care about anything. But it does mean that when we make plans, it's good to make sure God is behind them; if He's not they won't get anywhere. God has good things in store for us, things we can't even imagine.

PRAY Father God, You know me inside and out. You know what's best for me and You know what makes me happy. I trust that You are in control of my life. Amen.

LOOK OUT

Read: Psalm 96:1-13

KEY VERSE: 'Sing to the LORD a new song' (v1)

Do you like hearing new music, or do you prefer the songs you already know?

This psalm tells us to sing a new song to God. Why? Well, for the same reason that people are always releasing new songs into the charts – partly because old songs get boring after a while, but also because there's always something new that can be said about life. We always need new songs about God because He is so amazing that no one song can say it all!

So what does this psalm focus on about God? The main thing it says is that God is the king of the universe and that He is coming to make everything right: 'he comes to judge the earth' (v13).

Christianity isn't about trying to make ourselves as nice as we can compared to everyone else. Following Jesus is about looking out for God who is on His way to sort the world out. Jesus is coming back! This songs show how the world around us is waiting for God to come. So let's look around us and see what God is doing.

THINK What did you think most about yesterday? Were you concerned with others or were your thoughts mostly about yourself? Today, try to turn your focus to the world around you.

PSALM

DAY
264

DARING TO BELIEVE

Read: Mark 5:25-34

KEY VERSE: 'Daughter, your faith has healed you. Go in peace and be freed from your suffering.' (v34)

Some of the major stars of the New Testament were women! They weren't all goody-goodies – far from it, in fact. But once they'd met Jesus, they could never be the same again. We're about to spend a few days looking at some of these girls and the amazing ways in which God changed them.

The woman in today's reading had been bleeding for 12 years. Imagine how drained, exhausted and miserable she must have felt! She would have spent an absolute fortune on doctors trying to get better. Added to that, she would have felt totally isolated and alone, her type of bleeding classed her as 'unclean' in her culture. But then she heard about Jesus, and dared to believe that he could make her better.

If this woman had been spotted anywhere near Jesus in her 'unclean' state, there'd have been trouble – but that didn't stop her. She was so convinced of God's power in Him that she knew all she had to do was touch the edge of His cloak and she'd be well. How's that for faith?

PRAY Dear Lord, thank You for being totally trustworthy. When I reach out to You, I know that You'll always reach back. Help me to have more faith in You, Jesus. Amen.

WHO'S THAT GIRL?

GIVING YOUR ALL

Read: Mark 12:41-44

KEY VERSE: 'They all gave out of their wealth; but she, out of her poverty, put in everything — all she had to live on.' (v44)

Being a widow in Jerusalem in Jesus' time was no laughing matter. There was no benefits system to help. Finding a job would be an almost impossible task and without a husband to go out and earn the money, many widows had to beg.

With that in mind, the woman in this story must have seemed mad to give away her last couple of coins. But doing so was actually a huge step of faith. She chose to offer her money to God first, knowing that He would provide for her somehow.

Most of us, as we grow up, have lots of choice over the food we eat, the TV shows we watch and the clothes we wear. We choose the things that matter to us the most. This widow put God first, even though it cost her. The rich givers only gave some of their wealth away, but the widow gave everything and was prepared to go without if it meant honouring God.

Priorities matter. God matters. How can you show Him He's first in your life?

THINK What would you do with £10? Can you think of ways you could honour God with it?

DOUBLE MIRACLE

Read: Luke 1:39-45

> **KEY VERSE:** 'As soon as the sound of your greeting
> reached my ears, the baby in my womb leaped for
> joy.' (v44)

Elizabeth and her husband Zechariah couldn't have
children. And now they were getting old, it was even
less likely to happen. So when God sent an angel to tell
Zechariah and Elizabeth that they were going to be parents
in their old age, it must have been quite hard to believe!

But it was true – their son would be called John (John
the Baptist in fact, if you've heard of him) and he would
have a very special job to do. He would prepare people
for the arrival of the Saviour of the world – Jesus!

And John wasn't the only miracle baby on the way.
Elizabeth was actually a relative of Mary, the mother of
Jesus, who was pregnant at the same time. When Mary
came to visit, the unborn baby inside Elizabeth's belly did
a backflip at the sound of her voice! The baby she was
carrying was so special.

What God promises, He does. And He asks us to stick
with Him as He follows through with His Spirit-filled plans.

THINK Promises matter to God. When
was the last time you made a promise to
someone? Did you keep it?

A LIFE WELL LIVED

Read: Luke 2:36-40

> **KEY VERSE:** 'She never left the temple but worshipped night and day, fasting and praying.' (v37)

How often do you go to church? Do you get dragged there, or are you eager to worship God? Anna took devotion to God to a whole new level! She never left the temple, worshipping Him day and night, fasting and praying.

However, as a young woman, Anna had known deep sadness. Her husband died after just a few years of marriage, leaving her on her own.

But Anna didn't get bogged down in her bitterness. Instead, she dedicated the rest of her life to worshipping God. She allowed Him to comfort her, learning that He listens, cares, and brings peace to our hearts. Being a widow was hard in those days, but Anna found that God never left her.

When Anna was very old, God had a special treat in store for her – perhaps as a gift for her devotion to Him all her life. As Mary and Joseph brought the tiny baby Jesus to the temple for a thanksgiving service, Anna was there to meet Him! She knew exactly who Jesus was – she had been waiting for Him.

PRAY Father, thank You for hearing my prayers, never leaving me, and always understanding me. Amen.

WHO'S THAT GIRL?

WELL, WELL, WELL

Read: John 4:7-14

KEY VERSE: 'but whoever drinks the water I give them will never thirst' (v14)

Do you know anyone who has a bit of a bad reputation? Jewish people couldn't stand Samaritans. But when Jesus met a Samaritan woman as He rested by a well, He decided to shake things up a bit.

It wasn't just the Jews who despised this particular woman. Her own community didn't like her either because of the way she lived her life. She looked for love in all the wrong places and ended up in relationships that weren't very good for her. So when she turned up at the well and Jesus asked her for a drink of water, she could hardly believe her ears!

Jesus often did what people weren't expecting. He treated people with love and respect, regardless of how much they'd messed up.

Rather than giving this woman at the well a telling-off, He offered her something so much better: living water. This woman had been trying to fill her life with guys that were no good for her, but Jesus wanted to fill her life properly — forever.

THINK Stuff breaks, people aren't perfect, but Jesus is always good and always there. Having Him at the centre of your life is the best way to live. Is He at the centre of yours?

TOTALLY TRANSFORMED

Read: John 20:11–18

KEY VERSE: 'Jesus said to her, "Mary."' (v16)

Mary (not the mother of Jesus – a different Mary!) had a bit of a wild life, doing some pretty crazy things. She messed with things she should have left alone, and ended up with seven demons living inside her. The demons would have been in charge of her thoughts, feelings, moods and relationships. What a terrible thing for Mary!

But then, in walked Jesus. He commanded the seven demons to leave her and, totally unable to disobey Him, they fled. Totally transformed, Mary became an active follower of Jesus, even giving some of her own money to support Him and the disciples as they travelled around, teaching and healing. So imagine how heartbroken Mary must have been when Jesus was crucified.

But Jesus wasn't finished. When Mary went to visit Jesus' tomb, she became the first person to see Him alive again and find out that death couldn't hold Him. How amazing!

Jesus turned Mary's life around, and He can do the same for You, too. Even if you feel a bit out of control with your feelings or habits, He can transform you. All you have to do is ask.

PRAY Jesus, You are so powerful! You've beaten death and sin. Thank You that Your power is at work in my life too. Amen.

WHO'S THAT GIRL?

JUST AS YOU ARE

Read: Luke 10:38-42

> **KEY VERSE:** 'Martha, Martha... you are worried and upset about many things, but few things are needed — or indeed only one.' (vv41–42)

Martha liked everything to be perfect, and she felt like that was her responsibility. Even when Jesus was at her house, she was frantic that everything be just so. Her sister Mary, on the other hand, simply sat on the floor at Jesus' feet, listening to His every word and learning from Him the way a disciple would.

Martha wasn't too impressed by that — after all, she'd been left to do all the cooking and cleaning by herself! But it was Mary who had things right — all that mattered to her was being with Jesus. And Jesus, kindly but firmly, set Martha straight.

The more time we spend with Jesus — praying, listening and reading the Bible — the more we will get to know Him and the more of a difference He will be able to make in our lives. Martha thought she had to clean everything up before she could spend time with Jesus. Maybe she was trying to make herself 'good enough' for Him. But Mary already understood that Jesus wanted to spend time with her, just as she was.

THINK How could you make more space and time for God without getting distracted?

A MATTER OF
LIFE AND DEATH

Read: John 11:1–7,17–28

> **KEY VERSE:** 'But I know that even now God will give you whatever you ask.' (v22)

Martha and Mary knew all about Jesus' power to heal people. So when their brother became seriously ill, they knew Jesus would be able to make him better. All they had to do was send for Him and He'd come right away, wouldn't He...?

Lazarus, Mary and Martha's brother, was also a good friend of Jesus – so the two sisters couldn't understand why Jesus didn't run round to their house straight away! In fact, Lazarus had been dead for four days by the time Jesus arrived.

But this wasn't a mistake. In delaying a few days, Jesus was able to show that He has power not only in life, but over death, too! He went to the tomb, called out Lazarus' name, and he walked out – alive!

Martha might have felt that Jesus had let her down because He hadn't turned up when she thought He would. But He is able to do anything. When God doesn't answer our prayers when or how we've asked, it doesn't mean He's forgotten or that He's ignoring us. He knows best.

PRAY Lord Jesus, help me to praise You and trust You even when things don't happen in the way I want them to. Amen.

WHO'S THAT GIRL?

FOOLING NO ONE

Read: Acts 4:32–5:11

KEY VERSE: 'You have not lied just to human beings but to God.' (5:4)

When the first Church began, all the followers of Jesus were like one big, happy family. They looked out for each other and shared everything they had. Some people sold their houses and land, and gave the money to the Church. Sapphira and her husband, Ananias, did just that. Only they lied about how much money they had sold it for, and kept most of it for themselves.

If they had been open and honest about how much money they wanted to give to the Church, God wouldn't have been angry with them. But He hates it when we lie and try to cover our tracks. A hypocrite is someone who says one thing and then does the opposite, which is what Sapphira and Ananias did. That's why they paid the price.

This story isn't there to scare us, but to warn us. God knows everything about us – how we think and how we feel. So there's no point in trying to hide things from Him, like Sapphira tried to do. He forgives us when we're truly sorry.

PRAY Father God, I want to be real, open and honest – with You, with my family and with my friends. Please help me. Amen.

A SHINING EXAMPLE

Read: Acts 9:36-42

KEY VERSE: '[Dorcas] was always doing good and helping the poor.' (v36)

Dorcas' mission in life was simply to help others in any way she could. Everyone knew she was a Christian because the generous way she lived was her way of showing God's love.

Dorcas gave herself completely to the community that need her, and they were devastated when she died. Verse 39 says that many of her friends were crying and showing Peter the clothes that Dorcas had made for them when she was alive. She had clearly impacted so many people. So Peter got down on his knees and asked God for a miracle.

There's nothing particularly fancy about what Peter did or how he prayed, but a miracle happened! Dorcas (also known as Tabitha to some of her friends) was raised from the dead!

This was an extraordinary case, but the point is Peter had faith to pray to God and ask Him for the impossible, knowing that He could do it. How brave are your prayers?

THINK Dorcas used her skills to help others, and look how appreciated it was. What skills do you have? Try asking someone who knows you really well to help you think of ways to use your skills to help others.

WHO'S THAT GIRL?

THE COLOUR PURPLE

Read: Acts 16:12–15

KEY VERSE: '"If you consider me a believer in the Lord," she said, "come and stay at my house."' (v15)

Meet Lydia – another woman who gave her life to Jesus, and ended up totally changed! Her job was to sell purple fabric (which cost a lot of money because of the dye they needed), so only the very rich could afford it. Lydia was probably quite a successful businesswoman – some of her customers might even have been royalty.

But as clever and successful as she was, the most important thing about Lydia was the fact that she loved Jesus. When she heard Paul preaching one day, her life changed forever. When she became a Christian, she opened up her home to the apostles and shared everything she had to support Paul and his friends in their work for God.

Lydia responded to the message of Jesus with all that she had. She cared for other Christians and did whatever she could to help them out. Do you think about what other Christians around you might need right now?

PRAY Dear Lord, please change me and shape me and mould me more every day into the person You want me to be. I want to be like Jesus. Amen.

IT STARTS AT HOME

Read: Acts 18:1–4,18–19,24–26

KEY VERSE: 'When Priscilla and Aquila heard him, they invited him to their home and explained to him the way of God more adequately.' (v26)

Some people are amazing when it comes to opening up their homes and making people feel welcome. It almost seems like second nature to them. Maybe you know someone who loves having people round for a cuppa or a good meal so they can talk and spend time together.

Priscilla (and her husband, Aquila) ran a tent-making business, but were also very generous to others. So when they met Paul, who was also a tent-maker, not only did they have lots in common but they were able to offer him somewhere to stay while he was in town preaching.

Because Priscilla and her husband were prepared to make room in their home and business for others, God soon filled that space. They might not have thought that being hospitable was anything special or important, but because they shared, encouraged and gave people a place to stay, people could get on better with the work God had for them to do.

PRAY Thank You, God, for the privilege of serving You. Whatever You ask me to do, please help me to be ready to do it. Amen.

WHO'S THAT GIRL?

EQUALLY LOVED

Read: Matthew 27:55; 28:1-10

KEY VERSE: 'So the women hurried away from the tomb, afraid yet filled with joy, and ran to tell his disciples.' (28:8)

In Jesus' day, women weren't thought of as being as important as men. They were treated as second-class citizens and didn't have the same rights. But Jesus didn't ignore or talk down to women the way some other men did. Instead He included them and valued them the same way He would anyone else.

As far as Jesus was concerned, women were right up there with men in value and importance. In fact, it was women who stood at the cross until Jesus died. It was two women who first saw Jesus after He had risen from the dead, and pass on the good news that He was alive. That was a bold move from Jesus, but He had a point to make.

Jesus doesn't have favourites! He died to save the world and anyone can join His family. Don't ever believe that You have to be excluded just because you're a girl. You are an amazing, created child of God, and He has amazing plans in store for you.

PRAY Lord Jesus, I praise You! There are no second-class tickets to heaven. You love and accept me exactly the same as anyone else. Thank You, Lord. Amen.

RAISE IT UP

Read: Psalm 113:1-9

KEY VERSE: 'He raises the poor from the dust and lifts the needy from the ash heap' (v7)

This psalm was sang during the Passover party time celebrating God setting the Israelites free from Egypt, which means it's likely that Jesus sung this with His disciples the day before He was crucified (Mark 14:26). What do you think these words would have meant to Jesus as He got ready to die?

All through time, God has shown Himself to be the one who brings hope into impossible situations.

1. He breathed life into some dust and created human beings! (Genesis 2)
2. He promised an elderly couple, who weren't able to have kids that they would have more descendants than would be possible to count! (Abraham and Sarah – Genesis 12)
3. He loved a bunch of refugee slaves and made them into a great nation!
4. In His teaching, He is mentioning those who are poor, hurting, sick and those without parents.

Because of these things it shouldn't surprise us that God has power over death. He raised Jesus from the dead. And if God can overcome death, He can overcome anything!

THINK What situations that seem impossible could you raise up to God in prayer today?

PSALM

THE ROCK

Read: Genesis 49:1,22-26

KEY VERSE: 'But his bow remained steady, his strong arms stayed supple... because of the Shepherd, the Rock of Israel' (v24)

Remember Joseph and his dad, Jacob? Jacob had been devastated because he thought that his favourite son, Joseph, had been torn to pieces by a wild animal (not true, but the truth wasn't a whole load better). In his grief, Jacob couldn't see anything good or positive in what he was going through. Have you ever felt like this?

This feeling is totally understandable for anyone going through a really tough time. Often we think God isn't there, or that He doesn't care about us. But the Bible says that God is always with us and He does care.

Years later, when Jacob was reunited with his son, he could see that God had been in control of everything after all. Even though the method might have seemed strange, God had protected Joseph and had saved loads of people through him.

Before he died, Jacob blessed all his children but his blessing for Joseph was extra special. The Lord was Joseph's helper and his rock. No matter what we go though in life, God is always the same – dependable and loving.

PRAY Father God, when things seem tough, remind me to turn to You, not away from You. Amen.

THROUGH IT ALL

ONLY THE BEST

Read: Deuteronomy 32:1-9

KEY VERSE: 'I will proclaim the name of the LORD. Oh, praise the greatness of our God!' (v3)

Moses had messed up and so God told him he couldn't enter the Promised Land. After everything Moses had been through, would he be angry at God for this? No. Moses knew that he had been wrong and so he didn't turn his back on God. He accepted God's decision because it was fair, and because he knew that God's discipline towards him was out of love for him.

Moses even spurred on the Israelite people to praise their great God. He also warned them to stay away from things that God had said 'no' to. Sin might look fun for a while, but don't be fooled into thinking it's good. If we disobey God, then there might be a consequence for our actions. Of course, being corrected by God is never a great experience, but in the long term it's always best for us.

Let's remember to always to turn to Him and say sorry when we have messed up. He loves us so much, He will forgive us and help us get back on track.

THINK Are you always willing to own up to God when you've done something wrong? Do you try to hide it or not think about it? Why not get straight with God now?

GRUMBLERS

Read: Deuteronomy 32:10–18

KEY VERSE: '[God] shielded him and cared for him; he guarded him as the apple of his eye' (v10)

Moses is giving the Israelite people a quick history lesson. He reminds them of how God freed them from slavery, fed them and cared from them. But how did they repay God's kindness? They gave up on Him and worshipped idols instead! This terrible decision resulted in famine, plagues, pain and more. Ignoring God's guidelines is *never* a wise thing to do.

But God did not give up on them. Not once. He looked after them and provided them with water and food. Not just any old boring food; there was honey, fruit, milk, cheese, meat and wine. God cared for and guarded His people 'as the apple of his eye' (v10). He hovered over them like an eagle protecting its young.

Were the Israelites grateful to God? No, they just continued to grumble, quarrel and complain. In spite of everything God had done for them and given them, they didn't even say, 'Thank You'.

Today's reading is a good reminder for us to always focus on the good things in our lives and be grateful rather than always grumbling or complaining.

PRAY Loving God, thank You for all the good things you have done for me and for taking care of me. Amen.

WARRIOR

Read: Judges 5:1-9

KEY VERSE: 'The mountains quaked before the LORD...
the God of Israel.' (v5)

Deborah was a prophetess who had been specially
appointed by God to lead the Israelites back to Him – and
into a battle. Together with Barak, she had to lead them
into battle against the Canaanite army. A very scary task.
The enemy had 900 top-of-the-range chariots, whereas
the Israelites only had wooden make-shift weapons.

But Deborah was one tough cookie and she knew that
God was on her side, so, she faced up to the challenge.
She knew that God would overcome any problem because
even 'the mountains quaked before the LORD' (v5).

The odds were heavily stacked against the Israelite
people, but they had God guiding them and Deborah and
Barak leading the way. So what happened? God sent a
rainstorm to flood the valley where the enemy was based.
Those top-of-range chariots were stuck in the mud. Israel
had triumphed because of their secret weapon – God!

Notice how Deborah straight away gave God the credit?
She didn't claim any praise for being a leader. Her focus
was on God just as it always had been.

THINK Next time you are facing a
difficult situation, think about Deborah.
She relied on God to help her through her
problems and so can you.

THROUGH IT ALL

STRENGTH ON THE INSIDE

Read: 2 Samuel 1:10-27

> **KEY VERSE:** 'A gazelle lies slain on your heights, Israel. How the mighty have fallen!' (v19)

Saul has died, and so David can come out of hiding. Instead of pulling party poppers, he writes a sad song about the death of the former king. David knew that Saul had made mistakes but he wouldn't let anyone criticise Saul. He only sings about Saul's positive points and weeps because things could have been so much better between them. It's this kind of stuff that made David really stand out as someone who lived for God.

Even if people treat us unfairly, it is not right to celebrate if things go badly for them. A good idea is to think about how Jesus would react. When people insulted Jesus, He didn't get angry with them. His response was to 'turn to them the other cheek' (Matt. 5:39). This certainly didn't mean that He was weak, rather that He had amazing inner strength from God. Jesus forgave those who made Him suffer and even prayed for them. He spent no time cheering at the downfall of others.

Let's ask God for His help to react like Jesus did.

PRAY Lord, please help me to see people the way You see them, and to love them the way You love them. Amen.

GOD IN CHARGE

Read: 2 Samuel 7:18–29

KEY VERSE: 'How great you are, Sovereign LORD! There is no one like you, and there is no God but You' (v22)

David really wanted to build a temple in Jerusalem for God. But God thought differently. He wanted Solomon, David's son, to build the Temple instead.

David knew that God didn't think his idea was bad, or even that he was bad. It was just that David wasn't the right person for the job, and now wasn't the right time. Instead of sulking about not getting his way, David talked it over with God.

David praised God for being great and awesome. God knew what was best for him and his family, and had David's best interests at heart. David also knew that if he obeyed God, then all will go well and he would be blessed.

When we've got out heats set on something, it's hard to accept that it might not be the best way of doing things. But it's a good idea to share our plans with God *before* we do them, then we can have His input.

THINK How do you deal with being told 'no'? Would you trust God to know what's best when He says 'no'? Remember, He knows and sees everything — His opinion is the best.

THROUGH IT ALL

FORTRESS

Read: 2 Samuel 22:1–20

> **KEY VERSE:** 'In my distress I called to the LORD; I called out to my God. From his temple he heard my voice; my cry came to his ears.' (v7)

Things were not looking so good for David anymore. Both people of his own nation *and* foreign enemies were after him. David felt like he was drowning in fear under 'waves of death' (v5). So what did he do? Did he just sit there quaking in his boots? No, David prayed and God heard his cry for help.

In today's reading, David talks about how great and powerful God is. David says that 'the LORD thundered from heaven… and scattered the enemy' (vv14–15). When David focuses on God, his fears disappear and he can't help bursting into praise. He sees God as his fortress: someone to go to when he needs help and protection. And God came through!

We can get scared by all kinds of things. But if we look to God and keep loving Him, we can leave our problems with Him. He promises to always help us through our fears.

PRAY Lord, I want You to always be my fortress. Help me to keep remembering that I don't have to face tough situations on my own — I've got You on my side! Amen.

IN HIS HANDS

Read: 2 Kings 19:20,32–37

KEY VERSE: 'I will defend this city and save it' (v34)

Today it is the turn of King Hezekiah to be in big trouble. His enemies, the Assyrians, are marching towards the city of Jerusalem to attack it. The king of Assyria, Sennacherib, had done lots of damage to other cities and he thinks he is invincible. He is even making fun of Hezekiah by saying that God won't bother to rescue him. Hezekiah was terrified.

When things look bleak, it is hard to trust God. Is He really there? Does He care what we are going through?

Thankfully, Hezekiah knew exactly what to do. He went straight to the Temple and talked to God about what was going on. Hezekiah wanted God to help them and also teach the Assyrians that they should respect God.

God replied to Hezekiah and told him that nothing he was worried about would happen! The city was saved and all his worries evaporated into thin air.

Most of us worry about things which actually never happen. Jesus told us that getting stressed about tomorrow won't help one bit. The important thing is to put God first in your life and let Him take care of the future.

THINK Is there something you are worrying about today? Talk to God and ask Him to give you peace about it.

THROUGH IT ALL

YAY FOR NAY

Read: Ruth 1:19–22; 4:13–16

KEY VERSE: 'Then Naomi took the child in her arms and cared for him.' (4:16)

Naomi had been through some really hard times. First she had moved countries because of a famine. Then her husband and grown-up sons had died. Now, it didn't look like she would have any grandchildren.

Naomi was bitter and angry. She blamed God for her poverty, loneliness and suffering. But actually, she wasn't quite alone. She still had one daughter-in-law, Ruth, who refused to leave her. Ruth returned with her to Bethlehem. Then, changing absolutely everything, Ruth ends up marrying a rich landowner called Boaz, and they have a baby. Naomi's life has really turned around.

When really bad things happen, it can make us wonder if God really loves us. And any anger or bitterness we have because of this will affect our relationship with Him, as well as taking a toll on our friendships.

If ever things go really wrong for you, then instead of shutting God out of your life, get closer to Him instead. Sometimes it is only later on that we can clearer see what God was doing in our dark times.

PRAY Father God, thank You for being with me through all the ups and downs. Help me not to turn bitter, but to remember Your goodness. Amen.

HOW TO COMPLAIN

Read: Job 7:11-21

KEY VERSE: 'I will not keep silent, I will speak out in the anguish of my spirit, I will complain in the bitterness of my soul.' (v11)

Job had everything going for him: a lovely wife, big family, money and health. On top of that, he loved the Lord and obeyed Him. Then, all of sudden, tragedy struck! He lost his money, and his family were killed in a terrible accident. However, Job didn't stop believing and trusting in God.

Then more suffering came and Job was very ill. He could understand it. Why had this happened? When couldn't he get some peace? His friends gathered round him but they weren't much comfort. They said that God must be punishing Job for something that he had done wrong. But Job hadn't done anything wrong at all.

Job poured out all his feeling to God and asked many questions. Why has this happened? Why are things not improving? What have I done to deserve this?

We can go to God with all our questions. If you're upset or angry about anything, tell God about it. God want us to talk to him no matter how we are feeling. He takes how we feel seriously.

THINK How are you feeling today? Tell God exactly what's going on with you at the moment. He really wants to know!

THROUGH IT ALL

HE LIVES

Read: Job 19:7–27

KEY VERSE: 'I know that my redeemer lives, and that in the end he will stand on the earth.' (v25)

Satan loves to trick people, and he especially loved making Job feel alone. Job was feeling as though nobody understood or cared about him – especially God. He prayed but felt like none of his prayers were being answered. Things didn't seem to be improving, and Job's hopes felt like they'd been put through the shredder.

Job really wanted people to sympathise with him and notice what he was going through. He said 'Have pity on me, my friends, have pity' (v21). He was alone, at rock bottom. But he still had his faith in God. So, with the last scraps of his faith he shouted, 'I know that my redeemer lives' (v25).

No matter how bad things might be, we need know that God is alive! He has all the answers and the future rests with Him. God is with us in our times of pain and sadness. So don't let Satan try and convince you that you're no good or that no one loves you. God is alive, He's listening and He loves you.

PRAY Lord God, thank You for being with me, in tough times. Help me to use difficult times to get closer to You. Amen.

ANSWERS

Read: Job 23:1-17

KEY VERSE: 'But he knows the way that I take; when he has tested me, I shall come forth as gold.' (v10)

Things don't seem to be improving for poor old Job. His complaints to God grow longer each day. Why has God allowed him to get into this mess without showing him a way out? He wants answers to his questions – now!

However, in this period of waiting Job is learning a few things. First, he'd taken a very close look at his life to see if he was in the wrong. Second, he'd realised that, no matter how he felt, God is always there for him. Third, he understood that if he kept trusting God, he would come through any tough experiences a better person.

The reading uses the picture of gold being melted under intense heat to get rid of all the impurities. That is sort of what is happening to Job; he's facing the pressure in order to get to the pure 'gold' (v10).

Job didn't give up on God, instead he followed Him more closely. He decided to keep on talking to God even if it was sometimes frustrating not getting answers straight away.

THINK How about giving your life a check-up? Is there anything you think, say or do that needs dealing with? God wants to help you put it right!

THROUGH IT ALL

NOT A CLUE

Read: Job 38:1–18

KEY VERSE: 'I will question you, and you shall answer me.' (v3)

Finally God speaks, but not in the way Job was expecting. Job wanted answers from God, not God to ask *him* questions. Sometimes, when God seems quiet, He might be wanting us to think through issues ourselves. He wants us to use our own understanding to figure out where things need dealing with.

Now it was Job's turn to come up with answers. God asked Job, 'Where were you when I laid the earth's foundations?' (v4). He is trying to make Job see that God made the world and everything in it. God knows everything about the whole universe and keeps it all going.

Job suddenly feels very small. He'd been totally focused on his own problems with knowing much about God or His amazing power. He finally realised how limited his own thinking and understanding was. Now he could fully appreciate the greatness of God and His plans. Nothing happens without God knowing all about it. When Job looked at the world from God's point of view, his own problems seemed a lot smaller.

PRAY Dear God, I know that there is always more to learn about You. Help me to grow in my understanding and see things from Your viewpoint. Amen.

EXTRA BLESSING

Read: Job 42:10-17

KEY VERSE: 'After Job had prayed for his friends, the Lord restored his fortunes and gave him twice as much as he had before.' (v10)

Job had suffered a lot but he had learnt *a lot*! He now knew to keep trusting God no matter what happens in his life. Finally, there was light at the end of the tunnel. The bad times are over and God now blesses Job hugely.

Job was sorry for the way he'd directed his anger and frustration at God. And God had something to say to Job's friends for giving him bad advice. They'd told Job he must have done something bad and tried to make him feel guilty. God make it clear that this wasn't the case at all. He told Job to pray for his friends, even though they'd only added to his hurt. This can't have been an easy thing to do, but it helped to deal with things and for Job to move on.

Sometimes it can be hard to forgive people who have hurt us, but when we do, God can heal any pain we may carry in our hearts.

THINK Is there something from Job's story that could help you next time you are going through a bad time? Why not write it down so you don't forget it.

A SAD, SAD SONG

Read: Lamentations 3:22-33

KEY VERSE: 'Though he brings grief, he will show compassion, so great is his unfailing love.' (v32)

Jeremiah was a prophet who spent most of his life encouraging the people of Israel to follow God's commands. Unfortunately, they didn't listen! 'Lament' means sad and the book of Lamentations is mostly poems recording how deeply upset Jeremiah was at the suffering of the people of Israel and what a sad time it was.

But, even so, Jeremiah did not give up hope. He knew that God loved His people and wouldn't abandon them completely. The prophet had another message from God. Jeremiah told them:

- God's love never fails
- Put your trust in Him
- Wait patiently for God to save you
- God doesn't give up on you
- God forgives you when you turn your back on Him

This poem is so encouraging. Even though we may sometimes fail, God's love is unfailing. He can replace our misery with joy and praise. That's so good to know!

Next time you feel upset or worried because you've broken God's rules, remember that He forgives.

PRAY Loving God, thank You for being so amazing. Help me to always remember that You will never give up on me. Amen.

JUST CALL

Read: Psalm 42:1-11

KEY VERSE: 'Put your hope in God, for I will yet praise him, my Saviour and my God.' (v5)

Most of the psalms are positive songs of praise. However, some of them were written while the writer was going through a tough time, and wanted to talk to God about it.

In the past, the psalmist has experienced amazing times of happiness. But now things are different and he's confused. People are asking him, 'Where is your God?' and he is not sure how to reply.

The great thing is that the writer is *still* talking to God. As he pours out his heart to God, he is gently reminded of how to get back on track. These reminders can help us when we are feeling down too.

Firstly, knowing how God loves us can take away hurt from bad experiences. Praying will also help us cope with problems and know how to deal with them God's way. Next, it's helpful to have hope – focusing on the good things both now and to come. Finally, praising God will help us to be thankful rather than gloomy.

THINK When things are tough, do you sometimes wonder, 'Where is God?' Remember, when you do, He is always waiting to talk to you – however you are feeling.

THROUGH IT ALL

OUT OF DISASTER

Read: Psalm 74:4-21

KEY VERSE: 'But God is my King from long ago; he brings salvation on the earth.' (v12)

Uh oh! Things were looking very bad for the people of Israel. Their enemies, the Babylonians, had invaded the city of Israel and destroyed the Temple. The Israelites had been warned: turn back to God or else there would be trouble. But they had ignored the warnings and now they were paying the price. They were feeling hopeless and crushed.

What they needed at this sad time in their history were some words of comfort. They realised they'd messed up and called out to God. They'd gone with the crowd, wanting only to please themselves, but now they wanted God back in control.

They remembered how God had saved them from slavery in Egypt. Now that they were slaves again in Babylon, they believed that one day God would help them.

Today's reading was written by a prophet called Asaph who lived 200 years before the Babylonians invaded Jerusalem. God knew what was coming and prepared this psalm as a comfort to them. The Temple was gone but God was still with them.

PRAY God, I'm so sorry for when I choose to go my way and not Your way. Help me to always follow You every day. Amen.

ROOTED

Read: Psalm 80:1-19

KEY VERSE: 'You transplanted a vine from Egypt; you drove out the nations and planted it.' (v8)

The Israel people are now slaves in Babylon. But God hadn't forgotten them – He had given them a picture to think about.

God's people were like a vine. He had prepared ground for the people to grow and live in when He rescued them out of Egypt and brought them to the Promised Land. He had looked after them so that they grew as a nation. But why had He let them be cut down and destroyed?

The answer is in John 15:1–8 where it says that Jesus is the best vine and His people are the branches. Like pruning branches, God gets rid of things in our lives that don't produce good fruit so that we can produce good fruit like love, joy, peace, kindness, gentleness and self-control. If we're not showing these, then God needs to sort us out so that we grow stronger *in Him*.

The Israelites had been pruned, but their roots in God were still strong, and they would grow again to serve Him.

THINK How do you feel when you are told off at home or school? It's not great, but sometimes it helps us to grow and be better. Remember God cares too much to let us do whatever.

THROUGH IT ALL

RENEWED

Read: Psalm 126:1-6

KEY VERSE: 'The LORD has done great things for us, and we are filled with joy.' (v3)

The time of slavery in Babylon wasn't wasted time for the people of Israel. They were learning how to get back on track with their lives and with God. Things were looking up. They might even be able to go back home to rebuild Jerusalem and the Temple – this was exciting!

Today's reading celebrates God's goodness to them. They had realised that they need some sorting out or 'pruning', and God had turned the lives of His people around. Laughter had replaced tears, songs of joy had replaced cries, and they were filled with happiness rather than misery.

People around them noticed the difference God had made in the attitude of the Israelites too. And the Israelites were keen to talk about the great things God had done for them.

Sometimes we can feel a bit like a desert: empty, lonely and unproductive. But God has sent us a helper, the Holy Spirit, to refresh us – just like a drink of cool water on a hot day.

PRAY Thank You, God, for giving us the Holy Spirit to be with us always. Thank You that You love to see us happy and refreshed. Amen.

MEANINGLESS?

Read: Ecclesiastes 1:1–11

> **KEY VERSE:** 'Meaningless! Meaningless... Everything is meaningless!' (v2)

Solomon was the king of Israel. He was super rich and had the best of everything. Surprisingly, he discovered that having everything didn't necessarily make him happy, and right at the beginning of the book of Ecclesiastes, he says that it's all 'meaningless'. It's boring!

This is not great news for his readers. If Solomon, who had everything and done everything, couldn't find happiness then what hope was there for the rest of them?

But Solomon's book had an important purpose. He wanted to reassure people that they didn't need a lifestyle like his to find meaning and happiness – they needed to style their life on God.

Life can be boring and repetitive sometimes. We get up, we go to school, we go home, and tomorrow we do the same again. One day can seem exactly like the next.

What Solomon learnt though was that when we have God in our lives, life has meaning and a purpose. We start to notice how wonderfully He made us and creation. We begin to listen for Him speaking to us. We are willing to be used to do great things for Him. Life gets exciting!

PRAY Dear Father, You have created a beautiful world with everything I need. Help me to be excited about what I can do for You. Amen.

THROUGH IT ALL

ONLY GOD

Read: Ecclesiastes 2:1-11

KEY VERSE: 'Yet when I surveyed all that my hands had done… everything was meaningless, a chasing after the wind' (v11)

Solomon had it all – the power, the riches, the good looks. So he must have been very happy, right? Well, no, he felt as though his life was empty and meaningless.

Solomon had tried everything to fill his life with purpose and fun. He threw lots of parties, which often meant drinking plenty of alcohol. He kept himself busy with building projects, meeting important people and making lots of money. He tried being creative with art and entertainment. Did any of this help Solomon fill the God-shaped vacuum inside him? Not one bit. Finally, Solomon realised that sin promises to be fun but afterwards left him feeling empty. Only God could give his life purpose.

People today still experiment with alcohol, relationships and forms of entertainment to try to make them happy. Other people are super ambitious and think that an amazing career is the route to happiness. These things might seem good but the Bible tells us that only God can truly give our lives meaning. Solomon wised up to this fact – have you?

THINK What do you think will give you lasting happiness? Ask God to fill you with His joy, which lasts forever.

PIECE OF ADVICE

Read: Ecclesiastes 12:1-8

KEY VERSE: 'Remember your Creator in the days of your youth' (v1)

Who do you go to when you need some advice about something? What sort of advice do they give you? You might have heard pieces of advice like: you only live once, make the most of it while you're young, or enjoy life while you can.

But today, Solomon's got a cracking piece of advice to bring to us. The message he was keen to pass on was: put God first while you are young. Don't wait till you get older to take Him seriously. He's for you now. Right now.

Over the next few years, you'll make choices and decisions, which will affect your life. So why not bring God in on the decision-making process? Rather than putting God on hold, take advantage of being able to ask His opinion. After all, He wants the best for you.

You might also be facing troubles, which can happen at every stage of life. God doesn't promise that life will always be hunky-dory, but He does promise that He will be with us in the good, the bad and the ugly. That might be just the comfort you need right now.

THINK Do you have any big decisions to make? Talk to God about them, then ask Him to help you make the right choices.

THROUGH IT ALL

RESCUER

Read: Psalm 126:1-6

KEY VERSE: 'Restore our fortunes, Lord' (v4)

Do you sometimes see things around you that make it *seem* like your beliefs about God aren't true? The people of Israel believed that God was going to fix things for the whole world and that Israel, particularly Jerusalem, would be the place He would do it. But, even though they believed this, what they actually saw was Israel invaded by a massive army, torn to bits and Jerusalem smashed to ruins! Either they could give up on their faith and forget about God or they could carry on believing. What would you do?

These people didn't go focus what they saw but by what they *believed*. They had faith. They were thrilled because God had brought them back to Zion (another name for Jerusalem) years after terrible invasion. However, they had returned to a pile of rubble! That is why they asked God to 'restore' their 'fortunes'. Even though everything was a mess, they knew that God would do something great, that He was still at work to restore Israel and the world!

God is at work right here, right now, in the world and in His people.

PRAY Lord, I've seen how You restore people and places. Please help me to believe that You are doing the same in my life and the world around me. Amen.

PSALM

BRING IT ON

Read: Ephesians 6:10–20

KEY VERSE: 'Put on the full armour of God, so that you can take your stand against the devil's schemes.' (v11)

Did you know that we're in a battle? It's not a physical battle though. We are fighting the 'spiritual forces of evil'. Following Jesus makes Satan absolutely furious and he *will* pick fights against you to try and stop you living for Jesus. You'll be tempted to do things that God doesn't approve of. But, as Paul reminds us, we can 'be strong in the Lord and in his mighty power' (v1). We can be dressed from head to toe in heaven-made armour and come out on top. Pretty cool, right?

The 'flaming arrows of the evil one' don't always appear on our radars. Our enemy fights dirty, and can be very, very sneaky. But Paul didn't expect us to go down, or give in. He tells us to stand against these forces, stand our ground, and stand strong – and over the next few days we'll see what armour we've got to help us with this. Bring it on!

PRAY Lord, thank You for providing me with spiritual armour to wear through life. Help me to remember there is nothing in the world that You can't defeat. Amen.

DESIGNER OUTFIT

HEADS UP

Read: Isaiah 59:12–20

KEY VERSE: 'and the helmet of salvation on his head' (v17)

So, the first piece of armour that Paul lists in Ephesians: a helmet.

Have you ever heard of the idea that our minds can be like battlefields? Negative thoughts can sometimes seem to pop into our heads out of nowhere. And our thoughts affect us. They can creep into what we believe, and then how we behave.

How will a helmet of salvation sort this out? Well, our 'salvation' means that Jesus has saved us! He has saved us from sin; He has saved us from death! Although Satan tries to get it into our heads that God doesn't care about us or that we're not good enough for Him, if we're wearing that protective head gear, there's no way he'll get through. If we protect our minds by understanding that God has forgiven us, the way we see things can totally change. And if we fill our heads with the truth of how Jesus has saved us, it will spill out into the way we live our lives.

THINK Do you want this helmet? Do you want others to have it? It's free to anyone who believes that Jesus is Lord and asks for His forgiveness! We can't earn it, we just need to receive it.

CHOOSE YOUR ATTITUDE

Read: Philippians 2:1–11

KEY VERSE: 'have the same mindset as Christ Jesus' (v5)

Attitude is so important when taking on the opposition. If you go out there thinking it'll be easy, you could be in for a shock. If you go out there thinking you can do it on your own, you'll most likely be proved wrong.

The helmet of salvation helps us with more than just negative thinking. Some parts of our lives need extra protection. Our attitudes come under constant attack. Moodiness, stubbornness and arrogance are constant threats that can damage our relationships with God and others. Going into action when we're feeling mean, self-centred and moody is the surest way to invite more trouble. It's not the way Jesus went into battle to save us.

Jesus' attitude was not 'me first' but 'God first'. He didn't arrive offering selfies with the crowds, He didn't come to be served but to serve others. His attitudes were controlled by love.

When we put on the helmet of salvation, Paul tells us we are to 'have the same mindset as Christ Jesus' (v5). That's a pretty big challenge! But let's adopt Jesus' way when we're with our friends – and with our enemies.

PRAY Lord, I'm sorry for when my attitude is out of line. Help me to see things the way You do. Amen.

DESIGNER OUTFIT

THE HEART OF IT

Read: Romans 13:8-14

KEY VERSE: 'So let us put aside the deeds of darkness and put on the armour of light.' (v12)

Paul tells us to put on the 'breastplate of righteousness'. Righteousness is being 'right' with God, which is what we are when we accept Jesus. And where does the breastplate go? Right over the heart. And we really do need to protect our hearts in life!

Today's reading introduces us to three ways Satan tries to knock us to the ground. He wants us to:

1. Be out of control
People do this in all sorts of ways, and sure – it might look like great fun. But we're not fit for battle if we're behaving stupidly and not engaging our brain cells!

2. Have wrong desires
The Bible is really clear on how we should behave romantically. When guys and girls start using each other and ignoring God's way, they're in the danger zone.

3. Be jealous
This can ruin relationships, and rust away your armour – leaving you exposed.

So how do we 'wear' our righteousness? Right across the heart. By getting right with God – every day.

PRAY Father God, thank You for saving me. Please protect me from the things that would distract me from following You. Amen.

TOWER ABOVE IT

Read: Proverbs 18:10

> **KEY VERSE:** 'The name of the LORD is a fortified tower; the righteous run to it and are safe.' (v10)

Once again, that word 'righteous' has cropped up — what we are when we're right with God. It's wise guy King Solomon who wrote today's proverb, and he has some advice for us when our minds and hearts feel under attack.

So, why a 'tower'? Cities back then were protected by strong walls (sometimes four metres thick). The city entrances were the weak points, so they built tall towers either side of the gates to fire at the enemy from. The towers that Solomon built contained guard rooms and were a kind of fortress in themselves. If the city was taken, those in the towers could still fight on.

We all have weaknesses that need special protection. Our virtual 'tower' is the name of the Lord Jesus Christ. Jesus towers over the enemy. He is greater and more powerful than anybody and anything.

It is in the name of the Lord Jesus that we are saved, can speak directly to God and ask for help, win our struggles against evil, and receive strength for the spiritual battle.

THINK Is God your first or last thought when you're in trouble? Remember that the name of the Lord is your tower of strength. Get close to Him.

DESIGNER OUTFIT

BELT UP

Read: Ephesians 4:20-32

KEY VERSE: 'put off falsehood and speak truthfully to your neighbour' (v25)

There's a reason that Paul links the belt with the truth: it holds the entire outfit together.

Roman soldiers didn't risk laying into the enemy with their cloaks flapping around in the breeze. They tucked their cloak and tunic into a belt so they didn't trip up. This belt was like a leather apron that protected the lower body and provided a place to put the sword. So, when Paul talks about the 'belt of truth' in the armour of God (Eph. 6:14), we can see it's a pretty important part.

God is truth. Completely genuine and 100% trustworthy. So, what does that make us as children of God? Children of truth, of course! Putting on the belt of truth is more than just knowing the truth, it's living truthfully. Truthful people want to be honest (v28) and put things right in their relationships (v26). They encourage people rather than gossip about them. They forgive rather than stir up trouble (vv29–32). We live in a pretty dishonest world, but people are always looking for the truth. How important is it to you?

PRAY God, thank You that I can trust You completely — and that You will never let me down. Help me to value the truth as You do. Amen.

NO WORD OF A LIE

Read: Isaiah 45:17–19

> **KEY VERSE:** 'I, the LORD, speak the truth; I declare what is right. (v19)

Why is God so powerful? Why is it that God knows best? Why is it that God can be trusted? The answer is that God *is* truth. He never has and never will lie to us.

Our enemy, however, hates truth. The Bible calls Satan the 'father of all lies'. His tactics are to get us to go way off track on the sly without anyone knowing – and if we're not careful, we can begin to believe the lies that he's feeding us: 'No one loves you.' 'You're weird-looking.' 'You're useless.'

But when we put on the belt of truth, we are choosing to believe God when He says, 'You are mine... you are precious... I love you' (Isa. 43:1,4). Knowing who we are in God's eyes is essential. So here's a battle tactic: remind yourself of God's truth.

Know who He is: 'Know therefore that the LORD your God is God: he is the faithful God' (Deut. 7:9).

And know who you are: 'I am fearfully and wonderfully made' (Psa. 139:14).

That's the truth!

THINK What lies do you believe about yourself? Ask God to show you how He sees you. The creator of the universe made you, and He doesn't make mistakes!

DESIGNER OUTFIT

NEW SHOES

Read: Isaiah 26:1-8

KEY VERSE: 'You will keep in perfect peace those whose minds are steadfast' (v3)

What do you think of when it comes to the word 'peace'? Peace and quiet? Your brother leaving you alone? World peace? Hippies?

Paul tells us that we need to get our 'feet fitted with the readiness that comes from the gospel of peace' (Eph. 6:15). You might be wondering, why *peace*? And why *shoes*?

Firstly, God's 'perfect peace' doesn't depend on how we're feeling – we can experience it even in the worst situations. Peace is what we feel when we put our trust totally in God to handle whatever it is we're going through.

A Roman soldier wouldn't have gone on duty in his slippers. Soldiers wore chunky, studded sandals with the thickest soles, complete with shin pads. So, what does God's peace do as footwear? It can keep us standing steady. It takes us where we need to go – down the path God has for us. And it crushes the devil's dirty tactics. If there's anything in your life that's destroying your peace, give it to God. He can handle it!

PRAY Lord Jesus, thank You for Your perfect peace. I trust in You to guide me down the right path, and I give You the situations in my life that are destroying my peace. Amen.

LET IT GO

Read: Philippians 4:1-9

> **KEY VERSE:** 'And the peace of God, which transcends all understanding, will guard your hearts and your minds in Christ Jesus.' (v7)

Euodia and Syntyche were two women in the church at Philippi, and when they fell out it caused problems for the church. We've all been in silly arguments that get out of control. When this happens, we need to ask God to fix our relationships with His peace.

Paul told the two of them to stop fighting each other and team up to carry on telling others about Jesus (v2). Notice that God hadn't stormed off during their disagreements – He was nearby waiting to help them to sort things out (v5).

But what about the other things in life that stress us out and bring us down? It's right here, crystal clear in verse 6: 'Do not be anxious about anything.' Wow! Instead of getting worried or wound up, God wants us to off-load our concerns onto Him. He can deal with our negative thoughts and help us live at peace with Him, ourselves and others.

So, just as you wouldn't go out of the house without your shoes on, don't go out without putting on God's peace.

THINK Do you walk into arguments that can be avoided? How could you make peace instead?

DESIGNER OUTFIT

FLAMING ARROWS

Read: Mark 4:35-41

KEY VERSE: 'Why are you so afraid? Do you still have no faith?' (v40)

Have you ever felt like your faith was under attack? Things go wrong, people insult your beliefs, or you just have doubts? Well, you're not alone.

Paul knew about this and he encouraged Christians to 'take up the shield of faith, with which you can extinguish all the flaming arrows of the evil one' (Eph. 6:16).

Roman shields were state-of the-art. The enemy would often dip their arrows in tar and set them on fire – so the Romans needed protection that would be up to scratch. Their shields were made with wood, leather and either bronze or iron. That's pretty solid!

Our faith in Jesus is always under attack. When the disciples were shaken up by the sudden storm, they were afraid and panicking. But Jesus stepped in. He then had a word with them about their lack of faith. They had seen the problem and convinced themselves they couldn't handle it, while all along Jesus had been there to help them. God's power is way bigger than the things we fear, and our faith in Him is a shield to us.

PRAY Lord God, I have faith that You are in control. Whatever comes at me, help me to remember that You will protect me. Amen.

STAY AWAKE!

Read: 1 Peter 5:5-11

KEY VERSE: 'Resist him, standing firm in the faith' (v9)

We are warned that Satan lurks around looking for our weak points. And let's face it, we all have weak points.

In today's verses, we have three top tips for how to use our shields of faith:

Stay humble! We can't do this all on our own. We need God, and we need each other. 'Humble yourselves, therefore, under God's mighty hand' (v6).

Be alert! Satan tries to distract our attention so he can get round us. He 'prowls around... looking for someone to devour' (v8). Stay sharp!

Resist attacks! We all face pressure and temptation, but we have a 'family of believers' (v9) to help us with this. The Roman army designed their shields so that they could fit together, forming a shell that would protect them on every side, knowing that the enemy would find it difficult to force their way through them. This is what God wants for us as His Church!

We all need a strong defence. Use these tips to get behind your shield of faith today.

THINK Do you share your weaknesses and struggles with others, or keep them to yourself? Try and find a trusted Christian friend who can support you.

DESIGNER OUTFIT

ALIVE AND ACTIVE

Read: Hebrews 4:12-16

KEY VERSE: 'For the word of God is alive and active. Sharper than any double-edged sword' (v12)

Attack can sometimes be the best form of defence. And now that we've got our armour on, God has given us the most powerful weapon EVER! It's this: 'the sword of the Spirit, which is the word of God' (Eph. 6:17).

A sword? We're told to use... a sword? Well, not a literal sword – so don't go getting any funny ideas!

The sword is used to describe the Word of God (the Bible). A double-edged sword was a short sword with a metal blade sharpened on both edges. These weapons were used by the Roman army and could do some serious damage. They were seriously dangerous.

So what does it mean that the Bible is even sharper than that?

We're certainly not meant to use the Bible to do damage, but the Bible is powerful! It can be used to help us in any spiritual battle that might come our way. We're also told that the Bible is alive and active – it's real. Even though it was written a long time ago, it's full of great stuff.

It's relevant, it's real, it's powerful.

PRAY Father, thank You for speaking to me through the Bible. Please help me to love hearing from it. Amen.

WHEN YOU'VE READ THE BOOK

Read: Matthew 4:1–11

KEY VERSE: 'Jesus answered, "It is written"' (v4)

Do you know the feeling of thinking up a really good come-back after the conversation has ended? Well, the Bible is full of come-backs!

Today's reading backs up the fact that the Bible is our weapon, 'sharper than any double-edged sword'. When we are tempted with negative thoughts or a selfish attitude, the Bible helps us to fight back.

When Satan tried to get the better of Jesus, the Son of God answered back with the Word of God. Jesus was starving and exhausted, and the devil took the opportunity to try and tempt Him, but Jesus would not fall for that! He used the Bible to respond to all of Satan's tricks. Knowing our Bible really well is important, as people will often try to twist what it says. In verse 6, Satan misquoted the Bible to try to trick Jesus – but Jesus knew He was being lied to and answered back with the words of Deuteronomy 6:16. Satan is powerless against the Bible. So get to grips with it, memorise verses and spend time in it.

THINK Is there anything you often do that you know is not helpful? Next time you're tempted, look up what the Bible says about it. Use it!

DESIGNER OUTFIT

TAKE IT TO THE CHORUS

Read: 2 Chronicles 20:14-30

KEY VERSE: 'Jehoshaphat appointed men to sing to the LORD and to praise him... as they went out at the head of the army' (v21)

This is probably a first in military strategy: sending in a choir to lead the army into battle. Yep – singing. Psalm 149 tells us to go on the attack with the 'praise of God' and a 'double-edged sword' in our hands. God's Word is powerful whether it is read, spoken or sung.

God's people were about to face off against the combined strength of the Moabites, Ammonites and Meunites. They were totally outnumbered. Wisely, Jehoshaphat asked God to help them. The result wasn't down to them – it was up to God. A secret weapon was unveiled – but not of the stabbing or exploding variety. The attack would be led by people singing the praises of God! Madness? Actually, no. From the moment they belted out praise about the greatness of God's holiness, the enemy was diving for cover and left in bits. The battleground was renamed the 'valley of praise'.

When we praise God, He works in our favour. It doesn't matter if we're tone-deaf – it's what's in our hearts that matters.

PRAY Jesus, You are worthy of all my praise. When times are tough, help me to praise You even more. Amen.

PRAY ON

Read: James 5:13–18

> **KEY VERSE:** 'Is anyone among you in trouble? Let
> them pray.' (v13)

It's one thing to have all you need to complete a task,
but it's another to complete the task well. When Paul
wrote about the armour of God, he also gave us the key
that would allow us to use it to its full potential: 'pray in
the Spirit on all occasions with all kinds of prayers and
requests' (Eph. 6:18).

Prayer is simply talking with and listening to God. We
might pray for a miracle, for an opportunity, for forgiveness
or for a change – and the results can be awesome!

Today's verses give us an idea of how, when and why
we should pray. When we're facing difficulties we can
talk to God. But not just then! It can also simply be
when we're happy. We can talk to God all the time. Why
should we pray? Because it works, and it helps us get
closer to God. We get to know Him more, and so we can
understand ourselves and life more. The question really
is, why shouldn't we pray?!

PRAY Father God, thank You for hearing
my prayers. It's incredible that I can talk
to You about anything. I want to know You
better through prayer. Amen.

DESIGNER OUTFIT

SUITED AND BOOTED

Read: Ephesians 6:13-17

KEY VERSE: 'put on the full armour of God' (v13)

As we wrap up on the armour of God, let's recap what we've found out and hear one final nugget of advice!
Here's what we have so far:

- With the *belt of truth* we resist the devil's lies and replace them with God's truth.
- With the *breastplate of righteousness* we protect the belief in our hearts that we are made right with God through Jesus.
- With the *shoes of peace* we are kept in God's perfect peace no matter our situation.
- With the *shield of faith* we protect ourselves from doubt and attack, so that we can completely trust in God's promises.
- With the *helmet of salvation* we protect our minds by knowing we are saved by Jesus.
- With the *sword of the Spirit (the Word of God)* we can fight back against the devil, with Jesus on our side.

So what's the last bit of advice? Well, notice how today's reading starts with 'put on'. It's no use to us if this designer outfit's left hanging in the wardrobe – we have to *put it on*! The armour of God is available to you – so get dressed!

PRAY Lord, thank You for the armour You give me. Help me to choose to wear it every day. Amen.

WHAT A BOOK!

Read: Psalm 119:145–152

KEY VERSE: 'Yet you are near, LORD, and all your commands are true.' (v151)

One of the main ways that we can get closer to God is by reading the Bible. Do you ever feel guilty about not reading it enough? Well, this psalm has 176 verses about how much the psalmist loves reading the Bible! 'How can I ever be like that?' you may ask...

Well, this psalm was actually written by someone who had messed up – phew, we're not alone! He's 'strayed' from God and wants to find his way back.

When he talks about how much he loves God's Word, what he's saying is that he loves God's character. When he says that he wants to read God's Word, it really means he wants to be near Him.

The Jews believed that when they read their Scriptures, God was there with them. Reading the Bible brings us close to God and invites Him to speak to us, and without the Bible we can't understand much about Jesus. It helps us to get to know Him. Because of that, the Bible is really, really important!

PRAY Lord, thank You for Your Word! Please help me to understand it better so I can come closer to You. Amen.

PSALM

I CAN SEE!

Read: Psalm 73:1-3,22-28

KEY VERSE: 'Yet I am always with you' (v23)

If there's a noise to describe how today's psalm writer felt it would be, 'GRRRRRRR!' He was angry and bitter. He was so mad that he nearly walked out on God.

He had almost made a mistake out of anger, but as he sang he realised that God was helping him all along. God was the one who kept him from making the big mistake! Even when he had been fed up with God, God had been right there with him.

God has an amazing plan for our lives but the devil wants to spoil that. As Christians we can get attacked by invisible forces that will try to make us see things the wrong way.

The singer of this psalm got close to God and then saw everything clearly. God is with us no matter how bad we feel, and even if we forget it, He is still with us. Even when we ignore God, He still looks after us. But when we ditch our pride and pray to Him, He opens our eyes to see things how He does — and that can make all the difference!

THINK In what ways do you think God has looked after you behind the scenes? Give Him some credit for it!

PSALM

WHEN IT'S ALL GONE WRONG

Read: Ruth 1:1-5,20-21

KEY VERSE: 'Mahlon and Kilion also died, and Naomi was left without her two sons and her husband' (v5)

Early on in the year we read the amazing story of Queen Esther, who showed amazing bravery and courage, and ended up saving her people from death! Over the next few days we'll read about another amazing woman called Ruth, who also showed extraordinary courage and loyalty.

Before we meet Ruth, we meet her mother-in-law, Naomi. She was having a terrible year, having lost her husband and both her sons. She was deeply hurting and very angry with God. She was also aware that her daughters-in-law, Ruth and another woman called Orpah, might not stay with her for long.

Sometimes it can feel like God doesn't care when things go wrong for us, and that we are left to face our fears alone. But that just isn't true. He cares so much more than we know, and He's always at work behind the scenes. So next time you feel like this, chat to Him about it.

PRAY Lord Jesus, help me to remember just how much You care about me. When things go wrong in my life, help me to run towards You, not blame You. Amen.

RUTH

THREE WIDOWS

Read: Ruth 1:6–18

KEY VERSE: 'Where you go I will go, and where you stay I will stay.' (v16)

So the story begins with three widows: Naomi, and her daughters-in-law, Orpah and Ruth. Widows in those days would often have to beg in order to survive without a husband to provide for them. What would these three widows do now?

There had been a famine in Bethlehem, Naomi's hometown, but now that was over she planned to return. She gave Orpah and Ruth a choice as to whether or not to stay with her. Orpah decided to return to her own people in Moab, where she might find another husband.

Ruth, however, flatly insisted that she would stay with Naomi. She was serious about worshipping God and trusting her future to Him. She would put God first and leave the rest up to Him.

We often face hard choices in life, which can be even harder when we're sad or scared. The good news is we have a loving God who will never leave us, and blesses us when we honour Him with our choices.

THINK Do you have a hard choice to make at the moment? Talk it through with God and ask Him to help you put Him first.

STICKING IT OUT

Read: Ruth 1:19–2:3

KEY VERSE: 'So she went out... and began to glean behind the harvesters.' (2:3)

Ruth and Naomi arrived in Bethlehem as beggars. Neither of them had a husband or any sons to provide for them. Poor Ruth – had she made the right decision in sticking with Naomi?

In those days, thanks to the law of the land, farmers had to make sure that the poor would be taken care of. So when they were harvesting, they would deliberately leave some behind on the ground so that people like Ruth could pick it up and have enough to eat. They called this gleaning.

Ruth was able to glean from the barley fields belonging to a man named Boaz. It was hard work but she stuck at it, and never complained.

Our attitude towards our problems makes a huge difference to how we handle them. Ruth didn't blame God for how poor she was, or give up and head home to Moab. Instead she worked hard, kept her promises, and tried to make the best of the situation. She was loyal and loving, and trusted that God would work things out for her good.

PRAY Father God, help me not to complain when things don't go my way. Show me where You're working behind the scenes, even when I'm having a hard time. Amen.

RUTH

A TOTAL GENTLEMAN

Read: Ruth 2:4-18

KEY VERSE: 'pull out some stalks for her from the bundles and leave them for her to pick up' (v16)

Ruth carried on working in Boaz's field. It turns out he was actually a relative of Naomi's, and he wanted to help however he could. So he decided to help Ruth by praying for her and giving her some special treatment.

First of all, Boaz made sure his workers deliberately dropped extra grain for her. Ruth would also be allowed to drink from the workers' water supply so that she wouldn't get too thirsty, working hard out in the sun. He also made sure she had a good lunch every day, and that the other workers would treat her with respect. A little kindness goes a very long way!

Ruth had caught Boaz's attention because of her loyalty to Naomi, and by how hard she was working to provide for her. Remember, Ruth wasn't forced to be there – she was choosing to stick with her mother-in-law, even after her husband had died. God loves it when we keep our promises and honour Him in the process.

THINK Ruth's good character turned heads. Who inspires you with their kindness and good attitude? Why not tell them you've noticed?

KEEPING IT IN THE FAMILY

Read: Ruth 2:19-23

KEY VERSE: 'That man is our close relative; he is one of our guardian-redeemers.' (v20)

When Naomi realised that the field Ruth had been working in belonged to Boaz, one of her relatives, she was delighted that there was someone who would be able to take care of them. Suddenly there was real hope!

Under Jewish law, a widow was cared for by her sons, and if she did not have sons then one of her husband's brothers had to marry her. In Naomi and Ruth's situation, where all these relatives were dead, it was the next closest relative who had to support them. There was one man in the family before Boaz who should have done this, but he made no effort to help them, leaving Boaz next in line. Would he step up and be their guardian-redeemer?

Jesus is our redeemer! He settled our account with God by dying on the cross for us and paid a debt we never could on our own. He has swooped in to save us and give us hope – amazing!

PRAY Lord Jesus, thank You for paying my debt. Not only that, but You continue to provide for me every day. Help me to be generous and bless others with all that You have given me. Amen.

RUTH

WAITING FOR THE RIGHT TIME

Read: Ruth 3:1-18

KEY VERSE: 'don't be afraid. I will do for you all you ask' (v11)

If there's a romantic love story in the Bible, this is it!

Boaz was already interested in Ruth. She'd caught his attention with her goodness and kindness, and they'd probably got to know each other while she worked in his field. Boaz had respected the rights of the other relative to step up and marry Ruth as her guardian-redeemer, but now that the other man had bowed out of the race, why wasn't Boaz swooping in and proposing?

The timing had to be right. It's always a good idea to think carefully about romantic relationships. Marriage is a big deal, and anyone considering it needs to know it's the right thing before they run up the aisle.

Naomi told Ruth to be patient and not rush ahead of God's plans for her life. When we allow God to take control, rather than our feelings, things will work out much better.

PRAY Dear God, thank You for always having my best interests at heart. Help me to ask You what You think of something before I go rushing into it. Amen.

WORTH EVERY PENNY

Read: Ruth 4:1-12

KEY VERSE: 'I have also acquired Ruth the Moabite, Mahlon's widow, as my wife' (v10)

They say the course of true love never did run smooth! But for Ruth and Boaz, all the funny legal bits and pieces were about to be sorted out so that they could get married and skip off into the sunset to live happily ever after.

It was a strange old custom, but instead of signing a contract, Boaz handed over his sandal. This was a sign that the deal was on – he and Ruth were engaged! (If this story were taking place nowadays, we're sure he'd have got her a nice sparkly ring – but perhaps the sandal gesture was just as romantic!)

So many people love the book of Ruth in the Bible because they love a good love story! But there's so much more to it than that. The story is kind of like what Jesus did for us. Boaz gave Ruth his sandal to show his love for her as he saved her from the difficulties she'd been facing. Jesus went to the cross to show His love for us as he saved us from our sin.

PRAY Thank You, Jesus, for redeeming me. Because of the price You paid for me, I can be part of Your family forever. That's so amazing! I worship You, Jesus. Amen.

RUTH

HAPPILY EVER AFTER

Read: Ruth 4:13-17

KEY VERSE: 'The LORD enabled her to conceive, and she gave birth to a son.' (v13)

Because she had been so faithful and kind, Ruth got a happy ending she would never even have dreamed of at the beginning of her story. She never turned her back on God, and she never took the easy way out – and God rewarded her for keeping her promise to Naomi.

Ruth and Boaz got married and had a family of their own. Even after all the pain and loss she had been through earlier on in her life, Ruth had another chance at happiness, and Naomi had another chance to be a grandmother. When they first set out for Bethlehem, they had no idea that things would end in this happy way, but they trusted God anyway.

Our attitude is so important. When we are sucked into a whirlwind of feeling sorry for ourselves, life gets in such a spin that we can easily think it's the end of the world. It can seem easier to shut God out rather than carry on following Him. But even when you're finding faith quite hard, stick with it! God will never let you down.

THINK Are you worried about what will happen in the future? Why? Talk to God about your concerns and ask Him to help you trust Him.

AN EPIC FAMILY TREE

Read: Ruth 4:18-22

KEY VERSE: 'Obed the father of Jesse, and Jesse the father of David.' (v22)

Boaz and Ruth were delighted when God gave them a baby boy. But Boaz, the guardian-redeemer, and Ruth, the foreigner who had trusted God, had no idea what part they were playing in God's greater plans.

Today's Bible verses might look like just a boring list of names, but look closer. One of Ruth's great-grandsons, David, would become king of Israel – the greatest ever king of Israel! He would be king who would lead the nation to love, obey and praise God. But wait – there's more! Two of David's descendants would be Mary and Joseph. Yes, Ruth and Boaz were great, great (and lots more greats) grandparents to Jesus!

What an honour for Naomi, the woman who thought God had given up on her. What an honour for Ruth, who thought all hope was lost. What an honour for Boaz the guardian-redeemer to be in the same family line as the greatest redeemer!

PRAY Lord God, thank You for
everything You've taught me through the story of Ruth. Please change me because of it, and help me to follow You the way she did. Amen.

RUTH

BE CLOSE

Read: Psalm 84:1-12

KEY VERSE: 'How lovely is your dwelling-place, LORD Almighty!' (v1)

Is there anyone you know who really gets on your nerves when you've been around them for a long time? Something amazing about God is that He actually chooses to be close to us. Why does He love us? Maybe we will never know, but we do know that He does love us enough to want to spend *forever* with us!

This psalm is by an Israelite looking at the Temple in Jerusalem. He knows that the Temple is God's home on earth, and that is the reason he loves the sight of it so much. He and the rest of God's people (and even the birds!) love being close to God – there's nothing like it!

Here's the incredible news for us: everything the Temple was to the Israelites – God's home and the place where people had their sins forgiven – is found in Jesus Christ. Because of Him, our sins are forgiven, and with Him, God is with us!

If we belong to Jesus, then God the Holy Spirit is living in us. We all need God to be close – it's what we're made for.

THINK Is spending time with God something that you enjoy, or something that feels like more of a chore? Talk to another Christian about this.

PSALM

ME, HOLY?

Read: Ephesians 1:1-2

KEY VERSE: 'To God's holy people in Ephesus, the faithful in Christ Jesus' (v1)

The book of Ephesians is a letter written by Paul to the Christians living in Ephesus. So what relevance does it have for today? We can so often think negatively about ourselves, but actually there's a whole bunch of great things that we need to know! Get ready to dive into Ephesians and hear the truth about who you are in Christ.

Right at the beginning, Paul addresses Ephesians as 'God's holy people' – God's clean and blameless people. So who were they? People who never did anything wrong? Nope! These were just ordinary people who had become followers of Jesus. All Christians are God's holy people, you included!

We all mess up. That's a fact. So how could God call us holy? Well, when we believe and accept that Jesus died to wipe our slate clean, the slate is well and truly bleached! We don't have to work for it; we don't have to prove ourselves. That's amazing news!

When Paul calls the Ephesians holy, he 100% believes it. Not because of anything they've done but because of what Jesus did.

PRAY Lord Jesus, You are the reason that I am right with God – forgiven and holy! Help me to always believe this. Amen.

KNOW WHO YOU ARE

PART OF THE FAMILY

Read: Ephesians 1:3-10

KEY VERSE: 'All praise to God, the Father... who... decided in advance to adopt us into his own family by bringing us to himself through Jesus Christ' (vv3–5, NLT)

When Paul wrote this letter, adoption meant something very different to how we see it today.

Picture this: a Roman emperor needs an heir to the throne. None of his sons fit the bill, so he goes in search of a man who does tick all the boxes and then adopts him. The law stated that the adopted son:

- Gained all the rights of his new family.
- Became his father's heir. He was equal in every way to any of the father's birth sons.
- Had a brand-new life. All his debts and records were cleared. It was as if he was born the day he was adopted.
- Was absolutely and permanently the son of his new father.

As this letter is also for today, we can know that through Jesus we gain all the rights that He has, we are new people, all our mistakes are washed away, and we are God's children and always will be. NOTHING can change that!

THINK Do you ever feel let down by your family? Whatever happens, you are a daughter of God. That's pretty special!

GUARANTEED

Read: Ephesians 1:11–14

KEY VERSE: 'When you believed, you were marked in him with a seal, the promised Holy Spirit, who is a deposit guaranteeing our inheritance' (vv13–14)

Have you ever received a message that said, 'Congratulations! You've been selected, claim your prize now!'? On the whole, we know that these are scams. But when Paul wrote something similar to the Christians in Ephesus, it was 100% genuine and went something like this...

Dear _____(your name),

Congratulations! You have been personally selected by God to receive eternal life. Yes, and there's no charge – it's absolutely free! The cost has been paid by the Lord Jesus Christ. Just look at the benefits:

You are a child of God, you are part of God's family.
You have a new life, all your mistakes are forgiven.
A place in heaven has your name on it.

So what's the catch? The one and only condition is that you believe that Jesus died and rose from the dead to make all this available to you, and choose to turn to Him.

Yours sincerely, Paul.

PRAY Father, thank You for promising these amazing things to me and sending the Holy Spirit as a sign that You will never break Your promises. Help me to be more aware of the Holy Spirit today. Amen.

KNOW WHO YOU ARE

CHEERLEADING

Read: Ephesians 1:15-23

KEY VERSE: 'I have not stopped giving thanks for you, remembering you in my prayers' (v16)

Some people see life as being one big competition. When that happens, it can stop them being happy about what's going on in the lives of others.

Paul was the opposite of this. He had spent two years with the Christians in Ephesus, teaching and helping them. He wasn't around them anymore, but he still couldn't stop thanking God for them!

Paul was committed to thanking God for all the Christians he knew. He kept them in his thoughts and prayed for them, desperately wanting them to know what amazing hope they now had because of Jesus, realise the incredible power that He has, and ultimately know God better.

When a person becomes a Christian, that's something to be thankful for! But let's also remember how important it is to pray for other Christians to grow closer to God.

We don't need to compete with other people, we can be secure in the fact that God loves us. So when we see others getting to know God more, let's be their biggest cheerleaders.

THINK Do you find it hard to pray and be thankful for other Christians? List some of the Christians you know and talk to God about them now.

I'M ALIVE!

Read: Ephesians 2:1-5

> **KEY VERSE:** 'God, who is rich in mercy, made us alive with Christ even when we were dead in transgressions' (vv4–5)

Are you dead or alive? What a weird question! But Paul said that we can be fighting fit yet still be 'lifeless' as far as God is concerned. Let's get to grips with this idea.

How can we be both dead and alive? The answer is to do with the fact that we have a body and a soul. Our body, our physical home for our soul, can be super healthy. We can eat the right things and exercise regularly – and that's great – but that's only half of who we are.

So when we read that we were 'dead in our transgressions' (transgressions is a fancy word for sin and wrongdoing) it means that our souls were dead. Before Jesus set us free by paying for our sin once and for all on the cross, our souls were dead because we were disconnected from God. But Jesus did go to the cross, He did set us free and we can now be connected to God!

PRAY Lord, thank You for loving me so much! Thank You for setting me free and bringing my soul to life through Your work on the cross. Amen.

KNOW WHO YOU ARE

SAVED BY GRACE

Read: Ephesians 2:6-10

KEY VERSE: 'For it is by grace you have been saved, through faith – and this is not from yourselves, it is the gift of God' (v8)

How do we earn God's acceptance and a place in heaven? Do we need to put in overtime on prayer and good deeds? Thankfully, God does not work in this way.

So how are we saved? What is it that gets us VIP access to God? Quite simply, we need to accept a gift. That's all! And that gift is grace. Grace means not repaying wrong with wrong. It means we get far better than we deserve. Jesus *is* grace. So being saved isn't about what you do but who you know – Jesus! He paid the price of our VIP ticket by dying for us, we just need to turn to Him.

But what does this mean for us? It means that not only are we certain of where we will one day be – heaven – but we can know God with us now. And (read verse 10 again) God has prepared good things for YOU to do on earth! He has a jobs list with your name at the top.

THINK Do you believe that God has good things planned out for you? All He wants is for you to get in line with His plans and His way of life.

EQUAL

Read: Ephesians 2:11-22

KEY VERSE: 'you are no longer foreigners and strangers, but fellow citizens with God's people and also members of his household' (v19)

Before Jesus came to earth, people had to follow a certain set of rules to be able to connect with God. If you followed these rules you were called a Jew, and if you didn't, a Gentile. Jesus changed all that – but it took a while for the message to sink in...

Many of the Christians in Ephesus were Greeks, Turks or Italians. They didn't follow the Jewish traditions, and so many Christians looked down on these people as second-class believers.

Paul himself had once been a proud Pharisee and fan of all things Jewish. He had been brought up to eat, dress and think like a Jew, not a Gentile. And then he met Jesus.

Paul learnt that Jesus died for the sins of the *whole* world, not just a select few. Paul told the Ephesians that the only way to have peace with God was through Jesus, and that *anyone* who called on His name would be saved.

THINK Do you ever look down on other Christians? It's not our traditions, our cross necklaces or our fish car stickers that make us Christians. If we call on Jesus' name, we're all God's family.

KNOW WHO YOU ARE

LET ME SHARE
WITH YOU...

Read: Ephesians 3:1-6

KEY VERSE: 'Gentiles are heirs together with Israel, members together of one body, and sharers together in the promise in Christ Jesus' (v6)

An eerie darkness cast its shadow over Jerusalem. A lone voice from outside the city could be heard crying out, 'It is finished.' A little while later His dead body was carried to a small garden tomb.

Who was the lone voice? What had He finished? The lone voice was Jesus – everyone knew that. But the rest was a mystery. It was the Holy Spirit who let Paul and the other apostles in on the secret. Jesus had finished His great plan to save us, and He rose from the dead to show He had the power to carry it through.

This was pretty radical news for non-Jewish people (Gentiles), because Jesus had thrown open the door for them to have eternal life. The barrier dividing Jews and Gentiles was smashed. Anyone – yes anyone – could share in the great promises of Jesus. And Paul wanted the foreigners in the great city of Ephesus to know what Jesus had done for them.

PRAY Jesus, help me to understand what you did for me and be ready to tell the people around me about You. Amen.

RICH

Read: Ephesians 3:7-17

KEY VERSE: 'I pray that out of his glorious riches he may strengthen you with power' (v16)

What comes to mind when you hear the word 'wealthy'? Do you picture mansions, cars and millionaires? Well, today we're not talking dollar bills. We're on about a different kind of treasure...

A few days ago we thought about how we can be both dead and alive. Well, here's another crazy idea to get your head around: we can be both rich *and* poor. And again, it's all to do with the fact that we are both physical and spiritual beings. So we can be physically poor, yet spiritually rich! That's why Paul, writing in poverty from prison, was able to celebrate the riches of Christ in his life.

Never mind winning the lottery, when you encounter Jesus, you are rich beyond measure. Rich with what though? Peace, security, acceptance, belonging, love, joy – just to name a few! Wow!

Sometimes we try to satisfy a longing to be rich with physical things (money, belongings, achievements) when the truth is, they will never really fulfil us. God's riches are the only real riches.

THINK Think about the things you really want at the moment. Are these physical things or spiritual things? Ask God for His peace and joy – they're what you really need!

KNOW WHO YOU ARE

HOW MUCH?

Read: Ephesians 3:17–21

KEY VERSE: 'how wide and long and high and deep is the love of Christ' (v18)

Everyone wants to be loved, and everyone *loves* love. Films, songs and books often have love as the central theme. It's almost impossible to appreciate God's love. It's so huge and our minds can't take it in. Which is why Paul prayed that the Christian in Ephesus would understand how much God really, really, really, cares for them.

The trouble is we all tend to limit God's love. Sometimes we can think that because we have done something dreadful God won't forgive us. Or because things are working out badly, we think He doesn't care about us.

But God's love doesn't have borders you can cross. You can't escape from it wherever you go, whoever you are or whatever you do. It's a waste of time running away from God, or thinking He won't forgive you, or that He doesn't care. The truth is that he loves you more than you can even imagine.

The more you get to know God, the more you'll appreciate His huge, never-ending, unconditional love – and the more you'll share some of that love with others.

PRAY Father God, thank You for loving me no matter what. I always want my life to show how much I love You. Amen.

UNITED

Read: Ephesians 4:1-6

KEY VERSE: 'Make every effort to keep the unity of the Spirit through the bond of peace.' (v3)

Part of who we are as Christians is that we are a part of something – the Church! We are in a family, a diverse group full of different life experiences, opinions, outlooks and personalities. So what does it mean to be *united* with each other, especially with those who are very different to us?

ONE BODY – The Church is known as the body of Christ. Just like a human body, different parts need to work together as one.

ONE SPIRIT – The same Holy Spirit lives inside each Christian to make us more like Jesus.

ONE HOPE – Our hope is in Jesus, now and for eternity.

ONE LORD – What do all Christians have in common? The Lord Jesus as Saviour!

ONE FAITH – We all believe and trust in Jesus, and follow His teachings.

ONE BAPTISM – All Christians are baptised in the same Holy Spirit.

ONE GOD AND FATHER – Remember we are all members of God's family.

THINK How do you think that we as Christians can stay united? Do you think of yourself as being united with other Christians?

KNOW WHO YOU ARE

BUILDING UP

Read: Ephesians 4:7–13

KEY VERSE: 'equip his people for works of service, so that the body of Christ may be built up' (v12)

Why does God give us talents? Today, let's find out about the most important reason for our gifts...

Military conquerors would return from battle in triumph and share anything that they had looted among the soldiers. Paul uses this image to describe Jesus, the ultimate winner, celebrating victory in heaven and sharing out gifts to His followers. These gifts enable us to serve God and help others. Yes, believe it or not, you have the ability to stand out for God in at least one way.

Some are able to explain God's words clearly. Others are great at talking about Jesus. Then there are those good at organising. Those with abilities to lead awe-inspiring worship. Those great at making people feel welcome. Those who are known by their kind actions. The list goes on and on. (See 1 Cor. 12:4–11,27–31 and Rom. 12:3–8.)

God-given abilities aren't for our benefit but to encourage and help others. They aren't given to make us feel good but to *do* good. They are God's way of giving all of us a fantastic role in His family.

PRAY Lord Jesus, please show me the things that I can do for You and for others. Amen.

GROWING UP

Read: Ephesians 4:14-16

KEY VERSE: 'we will grow to become in every respect the mature body of him who is the head, that is, Christ' (v15)

We're always changing, growing up. Think about what your life was like a year ago today and you might be surprised by the difference to how it is now. So how do we 'grow up' as Christians? We could take three bits of advice from Paul today:

1. Let your Bible be your anchor (v14)

The waves that Paul speaks of are the lies we hear every day about who we are, where we came from, who God is, what we need etc. Our weapon against these things is the Bible. God's Word is the truth, so let's listen to it more than we listen to the world.

2. Speak the truth to each other (vv15-16)

When our friends are going through a tricky time, or we can see that they're believing in a lie, we have a responsibility to gently help them and tell them the truth! Let's look out for each other.

3. Make Jesus number one (v15)

Jesus is the head, not the tail! He needs to come first – before our friends, before our goals, before ourselves. It will cost us, but it will be totally worth it.

THINK Which bit of advice most speaks to you today?

KNOW WHO YOU ARE

NO MORE RAGS

Read: Ephesians 4:17-24

KEY VERSE: 'put off your old self... put on the new self' (vv22,24)

Imagine everything that makes you who you are is a coat. (Just go with it!) Now imagine that every mistake you've ever made, every nasty thing that happened to you, every time someone hurt you, has torn or stained that coat. Some of us think that becoming a Christian will be like sewing up a few of the rips and adding some patches over the stains. Well, it's not...

Becoming a Christian is like being handed a brand-new coat! You can throw that old, smelly, tatty thing away! Like Paul says, we should 'put off' the old and 'put on the new'. What do they both look like? Here's a little glimpse:

Old self
- You don't care what is right and wrong
- You don't care what God thinks about the way you live
- You believe: if It feels good – do it

New self
- You let the Holy Spirit teach you right from wrong
- You care about what God thinks
- You believe: if God says so – go for it!

THINK Are there some bits of the old that you know you still need to let go of in order to take on the new?

STEER CLEAR

Read: Ephesians 4:25-32

KEY VERSE: 'do not give the devil a foothold' (v27)

Do not give the devil a foothold. What does that mean?!
It's really important for us to understand, so let's find out...

The devil is not on our side. He wants to ruin our
lives. Heavy stuff, we know, but it's true. A foothold is
something used during climbing to help the climber get
higher and higher. In a similar way, we might do things in
life that make the devil's job easier. This is not something
to be scared about as God is ultimately in control and He
protects us, but we do need to be aware of it. And if we
are aware of the things we do that create 'footholds' we
can prevent them in the first place. So what are some of
these things? Paul lets us know:

- Stealing
- Not controlling a bad temper
- Gossiping
- Saying hurtful words
- Being bitter
- Arguing

Let's do our best to stay well away from these things
and 'not give the devil a foothold.'

PRAY Dear God, I don't want to make
the devil's job easier. Help me to keep my
life in check and give me strength to resist
temptations. Amen.

KNOW WHO YOU ARE

LIGHT THE WAY

Read: Ephesians 5:1-20

KEY VERSE: 'For you were once darkness, but now you are light in the Lord. Live as children of light' (v8)

Light and dark. Completely opposite and completely separate. So what exactly is Paul saying when he calls us 'children of light'? How should that change things?

There is a lot of 'darkness' in the world and the root cause of all the darkness is sin (disobeying God) – and we are all capable of this. But we were not created by God to add to the darkness – no! We were created for light.

Look at it like this. When you walk into a room that's in pitch-black darkness, you're going to walk into things, fall over furniture and make a mess. That's kind of how we live when we don't know Jesus. We stumble through life, messing up and getting bruised. Now imagine someone comes along and turns on the light – you can see! You can tidy up, put things back in order and avoid anything that might harm you. When we meet Jesus, and get to know Him more, we realise that we have a meaning for life, a purpose, because we can finally see it.

THINK When people look at you, do you think they see something different about you?

YOU FIRST

Read: Ephesians 5:21

KEY VERSE: 'Submit to one another out of reverence for Christ.' (v21)

Just one verse today, and it's a biggie. But what does 'submit' mean? Doesn't that sound a bit... old fashioned?

Well, it might help to take a quick peek at something Jesus said in Matthew 22:34–40. He had been asked by the religious leaders at that time what the most important commandment was. His answer was this: first, we must love God with our whole heart, and second, we must love others as much as we would like to be loved. You see, God's kingdom is unlike any other kingdom. It's a kingdom where people put God first and others before themselves, where people are more concerned about the needs of others than their own.

Jesus is our greatest example of this. He didn't deserve death. He could have run away. But He was obedient to God and went through with it because of His love for us.

To submit to others means getting rid of our 'me first' attitude and changing it to 'you first'. It means loving people because God has told us to, not because we might get something out of it.

PRAY Jesus, please be with me today. Help me to be kind in the way that I treat other people every day. Amen.

KNOW WHO YOU ARE

HONOUR

Read: Ephesians 6:1-4

> **KEY VERSE:** 'Children, obey your parents... "Honour your father and mother"' (vv1–2)

Remember yesterday we were talking about submitting to each other? Well, God wants us to honour our parents or whoever looks after us too...

We can do this by respecting them and allowing them to guide us, as they do their best to lovingly raise us in the right way. But the problem is that most of us hate being told what to do – especially when it seems to spoil our fun!

The good news is that God wants to help us obey our parents. He knows it's not an easy thing for us to do. And, to encourage us, He's told us that the reason to do this is so that *we* will have good, long lives.

Does that mean that parents are allowed to treat us however they like? No way! The reading goes on to say that parents shouldn't treat their children badly. They are there to protect us. They've got a big responsibility given to them by God.

It might be hard, but let's do our best to listen to what our parents say and let them know that we value them.

THINK How have things been with your parents or those looking after you recently? Have you listened to them and been respectful to them?

AT YOUR SERVICE

Read: Ephesians 6:5–9

> **KEY VERSE:** 'Serve wholeheartedly, as if you were serving the Lord, not people' (v7)

Picture the queen of England and now picture one of her guards. Who is more important? In our culture we'd say the queen is, wouldn't we? But in God's kingdom the culture is a bit different...

Jesus is both king and servant, and He wants to teach us something very key that goes against what the world teaches us. It's this: serving others does not make us more or less important, but it pleases God greatly.

In John 13:1–17, Jesus did something that completely shocked His disciples. He did the servant's job and He washed their feet. He was setting an example for us all. We are not less important than anyone else when we serve – when we mop the floor, serve tea at church or empty the bins.

When Paul wrote this letter to the Ephesians, slavery was very common and Paul knew some of the readers would have been slaves. But he wanted to show them that it was possible to serve God by obeying their masters. He encouraged them to see it not as serving their masters but God! Because, really, serving is all about Him.

PRAY Father, please help me to follow Jesus' example and seek to serve others. I want to understand this more today. Amen.

KITTED OUT

Read: Ephesians 6:10-24

KEY VERSE: 'Put on the full armour of God, so that you can take your stand against the devil's schemes.' (v11)

For our last look at Ephesians, we're back with the armour of God! It wasn't too long ago that we looked at this, so how have you been doing with it?

Remember, we are at war. Not a physical war, a spiritual one against evil. But God's got us covered – literally. The only thing is, we have to continue to choose to wear our armour. Have a look below and see if you can remember what each part does. Turn back to day 316 if you need reminding!

- Belt of truth
- Breastplate of righteousness
- Shoes of peace
- Shield of faith
- Helmet of salvation
- Sword of the Spirit

If we want to grow as Christians and make a difference in the world, wearing the armour is essential. So it's helpful to have a check-up and see if we've left some of it in our wardrobes without realising – then we can get back on track.

THINK Think about some ways to help yourself remember to put this armour on every day.

DON'T HOLD BACK

Read: Psalm 62:1-12

KEY VERSE: 'pour out your heart before him; God is a refuge for us' (v8, ESVUK)

There are loads of great songs in the world that are actually about some really deep topics. You can tell a lot about a musician by the music they produce. Sometimes their song lyrics even tell you exactly what's going on their lives right now. The psalms can be a bit like that — the writers are telling God exactly how they feel.

Look at how this psalm tells us to share what's going on in our hearts with God. There's no filter needed, He can handle it all. In fact, just one verse earlier the psalmist tells us to trust God, so it really does mean to share *everything* with Him.

Sometimes we believe that we have to always be polite to God, answering with an 'I'm fine, thanks'. But the truth is, God already knows how we feel and it's so much better for us to be completely honest with Him. When we talk to Him, it's like we're opening the door for Him to come in and help with what we're facing. Remember, He has the ability to take away anything weighing us down and instead fill us with peace.

PRAY Lord, I want to be honest and open with You, no matter what kind of emotions I'm feeling. Thank You for always being there to talk to. Amen.

PSALM

HE IS!

Read: Psalm 100:1-5

KEY VERSE: 'Know that the LORD is God.' (v3)

How do you do in quizzes? Are you good with your facts? The questions that get asked in quizzes can be on absolutely anything. But it's when we're challenged that we realise we know quite a lot more than we thought we did – including quite a lot of random stuff!

Here's a fact that isn't random at all – it's really important for us to know: 'The LORD is God.' He's the one who made us, and so 'we are his' (v3). Wow! We *belong* to God. Have you ever thought about it like that?

There is no one higher than God. Not one person. No one can measure up to Him. He's over everything, and we belong to Him! God is king, you are His daughter. That changes everything.

When you go through a difficult time, knowing who God is and who you are because of that makes such a difference. He's in charge, He's the highest, greatest, most powerful, and He absolutely adores YOU! With that in mind, bad times don't seem as overwhelming – we've got God on our side!

So be confident in who God is and what that means for you today.

PRAY Father, I praise You and recognise You as my God. Thank You for making me Your daughter – it is such a privilege. Amen.

PSALM

I'LL BE BACK!

Read: Acts 1:1-11

KEY VERSE: 'This same Jesus, who has been taken from you into heaven, will come back in the same way you have seen him go into heaven.' (v11)

Have you ever had to say goodbye to a friend or family member, knowing you won't see them again for a very long time? It can be really tough to do this, and we might wonder if we will still have a close relationship with that person.

Forty days after Jesus had risen from the dead, He left the disciples to return to heaven. The disciples were keen to know what was going to happen next. Was He leaving for good? What would they do without Him?

As the disciples watched Jesus lift off to heaven, they were told by two angels that Jesus would come back one day. Wow! The angels couldn't say when (they didn't know), but a date and time had been set. And in the meantime, the Holy Spirit was going to be with them, actually living in them. They were not alone.

THINK Did you know that Jesus will come back to earth one day? Every day we get one day closer to His return. What would your reaction be like if Jesus came back today?

FAST FORWARD

WHAT A DIFFERENCE

Read: Revelation 1:12-18

KEY VERSE: 'Do not be afraid. I am the First and the Last. I am the Living One; I was dead, and now look, I am alive for ever and ever!' (vv17–18)

John was the only disciple who stuck around to see Jesus being crucified. Years later, God gave him an amazing glimpse of Jesus in heaven. Just look at the difference between Jesus our crucified Saviour, and Jesus our risen Lord...

At the cross, Jesus' face was bruised, He wore a crown of thorns on top of His bloodstained hair, His eyes were swollen, He was silent. His clothes were taken and shared among the soldiers, He was stabbed in His side with a spear, He was given a staff so that people would laugh at Him, His feet were nailed to the cross.

Now in heaven His face is shining like the sun, His hair is white like wool and snow, His eyes are like blazing fire, He speaks loudly, He wears a royal robe and a gold sash worn by high priests. He is the King of power and is pictured with a sword coming out of His mouth, He holds stars in His hands, His feet are now like bronze.

Our future is safe with Him.

PRAY Jesus, You really are amazing. I put my trust and my future in Your hands. Amen.

ON THE THRONE

Read: Revelation 4:1–11

KEY VERSE: 'You are worthy, our Lord and God, to receive glory and honour and power' (v11)

What's the nicest house you've ever been in? Maybe it has a pool? A massive TV? A fridge filled to the brim? Well, it's got nothing on what we're about to see...

Let's look into the future with another of John's visions. This time it's a guided tour of God's headquarters.

This is some throne room. There's every colour you've ever seen. Then – thunder! Lightning! This is awesome! As we look in more, we see someone there – Almighty God! He appears to sparkle light like a diamond. Wow! Just wow. This whole scene is fantastically majestic.

Around the throne, representatives from the 12 ancient tribes of Israel, and the 12 apostles take off their golden crowns and worship God. They've been awarded crowns because of how they've stuck by God, but when it comes to being worshipped, they know who that should be given to. No one other than God.

One thing's for sure, God reigns and always will do! He sits on the throne of heaven and is absolutely glorious.

THINK Imagine there's a throne in your heart. Does God have the top spot? Or do you need to knock something or someone else off that seat so God can sit in His rightful place?

FAST FORWARD

LION AND LAMB

Read: Revelation 5:1-14

KEY VERSE: 'Worthy is the Lamb, who was slain, to receive power and wealth and wisdom and strength and honour and glory and praise!'

So why all this fuss about a scroll? We're not told what it is — but John was crying because there didn't appear to be anyone in heaven worthy enough to open it. And that wasn't good.

It's right then that Jesus breaks into the scene. As a lion, powerful and strong, He has won and is able to carry out the task. How is this possible?

The clue was right before John's eyes. Jesus had been introduced as a lion, but appeared as a lamb. In Old Testament times, God's agreement with humans was that a lamb could be sacrificed to take the punishment for their sin. Jesus came to earth as 'the Lamb of God' (John 1:29) to offer Himself as a once-and-for-all-time sacrifice. No one else could do that.

The 24 elders then got the harps out and started singing about Jesus. Then a ginormous choir of angels burst in to join the praise party. Following that, they were joined by every creature in heaven and on earth. Who's worthy of such worship? Only Jesus!

PRAY Jesus, lion and lamb, thank You so much for making me part of God's family. You are worthy of my worship — forever. Amen.

LOUD

Read: 1 Thessalonians 4:13-18

KEY VERSE: 'the Lord himself will come down from heaven… and the dead in Christ will rise' (v16)

Let's fast forward to a great event still to take place — Jesus returning to earth. A secret date and time is set. You might have heard people say they know when this will happen but the truth is that no one knows when Jesus will arrive.

Here's what we do know: it won't be a small event, it's going to be massive. We'll hear Him first. There'll be a loud sound. Loud enough to raise the dead. Which is just what will happen!

That was great news for the people this letter was being written to. They'd been wondering what happened to Christians who died before Jesus had come back. Paul reminded them that God has the power over death. And when Jesus returns, God's people who are dead will be the first to go and join Him. No, we're not going to be running away from real-life zombies, the people will be made alive and given new bodies — instantly!

Even the Christians living when Jesus returns will also be transformed with new bodies. And they will join the others with Jesus, forever.

THINK Are you a loud Christian? Loud doesn't need to mean that you're a shouter, but that you're happy to let people know what you believe.

FAST FORWARD

SURPRISE

Read: Matthew 24:36-44

> **KEY VERSE:** 'So you also must be ready, because the Son of Man will come at an hour when you do not expect him.' (v44)

How mad is it that Jesus could return at any time? Technically, he could come back before you even finish reading this! So it's best we get prepared for it.

When God said that He would be sending a flood, bad enough to drown the entire earth, no one listened. They carried on with their ways of ignoring God. Noah, however, spent his life getting ready for the flood, and managed to escape it in the ark.

Although Jesus has promised to return and is giving the world time to turn to Him and ask for His forgiveness, most people live their lives not caring about God. As Christians, we have the exciting, scary, brilliant and important task of telling people about Jesus. People will be shocked when He returns and it may be too late for them to join Him. So let's make it our job to 'ruin the surprise' and give people a chance to get to know Jesus and be saved.

THINK Think of one person you know
who doesn't know Jesus. Pray for them, asking God to show Himself to them. Then try and talk about Jesus with them this week. Go for it!

TIME

Read: 2 Peter 3:3-10

> **KEY VERSE:** 'The Lord is not slow in keeping his promise... Instead he is patient with you, not wanting anyone to perish, but everyone to come to repentance.' (v9)

Peter says that our planet has a sell-by date. It won't last forever, it's on its way out. And Peter wasn't the first to learn this. Gold told Isaiah, 700 years earlier, that He would create new heavens and a new earth. The new earth will be so absolutely incredible that we won't even think about our current earth. You might be thinking about all the unlimited ice-cream there may be, but on this new earth, there's an even better feature: no tears or sadness, only joy.

God's plan is to put an end to death. Yes — death itself will be destroyed. God will raise us from the dead and we will live with Him on a new and wonderful earth forever.

But Jesus is taking His time returning to earth for a very good reason (v9). He wants to give people the chance to turn to Him for forgiveness. The seconds are ticking away, and in every moment we have before the big event, Jesus is desperate for people to meet Him.

PRAY God, thank You for being patient with us. Please help me to tell the people around me about You and Your forgiveness. Amen.

FAST FORWARD

WRITTEN IN THE BOOK

Read: Revelation 20:11-15

KEY VERSE: 'Another book was opened, which is the book of life.' (v12)

Do 'good' people go to heaven, and 'bad' people go to hell? Lots of people think that. But the truth is it's all down to Jesus and His book.

You see, there are two books that we're told about. Daniel had a vision of the Book of Judgment (Dan. 7:10). This books records all the things that anyone who has ever lived has done, and is the 'guilty' book. That's a scary thought, isn't it? The incredible news is that anyone who trusts in Jesus has their record rubbed out! But those who haven't trusted Jesus still have their records and face spending eternity without Him.

So what happens to those who trust and follow Jesus and so have had their records rubbed out of the Book of Judgment? They end up in the Book of Life. Anyone listed in this is seen as 'not guilty' and will spend eternity with their Saviour, Jesus. Have you decided to follow Jesus? If you want to, pray the prayer below:

PRAY Lord Jesus, I'm sorry for the things I've done wrong. I choose to turn away from living selfishly and follow You instead. Thank You for dying for me and rising again. Be welcome in my heart. Amen.

STAMP OUT

Read: 1 Corinthians 15:24–28

KEY VERSE: 'For he "has put everything under his feet".' (v27)

Have you ever supported or been a part of a team that's losing? It's rubbish, isn't it? Some people seem to react OK to this, while some throw tantrums that could rival a toddler's!

Here's a fact: Jesus will have the ultimate victory in the end, and we are on His team. To show how Jesus is 'on top' of everything, we hear of a picture of Jesus having everything 'under His feet'. Jesus will stamp out His enemies. They will be squashed. But who are they?

Enemy number one is the devil. He's the main one. He tempts us, lies to us and tries to get us to ignore God. He's a defeated evil loser who's still causing trouble. But he'll be put to an end completely one day, and all the evil that he's caused will be squashed to pulp then too. The second and last enemy to be flattened is death. Jesus will do away with death, pain, sadness and grief – that's amazing news!

Jesus is the ultimate winner. Isn't it great to know you're on the ultimate winning side forever?

THINK Do you sometimes let things get on top of you? Remember whose side you're on. With Jesus you're on top! There's nothing too big for Him to handle.

FAST FORWARD

NEW EVERYTHING

Read: Revelation 21:1-7

KEY VERSE: 'He who was seated on the throne said, "I am making everything new!"' (v5)

Heaven. What will it be like? Well... new, new and more new. As sin damaged and diseased all of God's creation, it will be binned and replaced with a new creation. Just listen to this: if anyone is in Christ, the new creation has come: the old has gone, the new is here!' (2 Cor. 5:17).

Jesus became a real human being – the kind of human being that God wants us to be. We can't be like that by just working hard, but by allowing God to work in us. And one day, if we believe and trust in Jesus as King, God will completely recreate us to be like Him.

In God's new heaven, we will be His people and He will be our God. He'll care for us in every way. All the hurt and pain of our old lives will be history. We'll never experience sadness, pain, fear, anger or death again. And the great thing is that God isn't offering us this five-star accommodation for a weekend getaway. We'll enjoy it forever!

THINK Write down a list of things you think might be included in the new creation, both for you personally and for the world, eg no more arguments, everyone has enough to eat...

WHEN?

Read: Mark 13:1-8

KEY VERSE: 'Tell us, when will these things happen? And what will be the sign that they are all about to be fulfilled?' (v4)

No one but God knows the date and time when Jesus will return. If anyone ever claims to know the date, they're lying. But Jesus did give some clues.

There have been wars throughout history, but from what Jesus said it appears that the world He surprises will be a very unfriendly place. Because of greed, wars and natural disasters, many will starve or become ill.

Jesus also warned that people would pretend to be Him and that many would believe them. Today, there have already been con men trying to fool people into believing they are Jesus, persuading people to become their followers.

Things on earth will get tough before Jesus returns, but remember, there's new life on the way! In fact, Jesus describes it as a woman being in labour – the pain is because something amazing is about to happen. Difficulties won't last forever. God is in control and our future is safe with Him.

PRAY God, however tough things get, I believe that You're still in charge. Thank You for having the future planned out. Please help me with the tough situations I face today. Amen.

FAST FORWARD

POPULARITY

Read: Mark 13:9–13

KEY VERSE: 'Everyone will hate you because of me, but the one who stands firm to the end will be saved.' (v13)

Do you ever feel like you put on a bit of an act to make people like you more? We all need to be loved, and sometimes we can see being popular as a way of getting a kind of love. No one wants to be hated, and no one wants to be hated by everyone!

The problem is that following Jesus won't always make us popular. That's because we do what God wants. Sometimes that makes people like us – eg helping people or being kind – and that's great. But other times it could make us very unpopular – eg standing up for people who are being made fun of, or refusing to lie about something.

Jesus became so unpopular that He was crucified. He knows what it's like for the crowd to turn against someone. But here's the thing: you will only need popularity if you don't know you are loved. If we know we're loved by God, the creator of the entire world, then other people's opinions don't matter as much. God loves you more than you can imagine and He thinks you're brilliant!

THINK Do you need some help from God to not let the opinions of others get to you? Talk with Him today about this.

SPRING CLEAN

Read: 2 Peter 3:10–18

KEY VERSE: 'make every effort to be found spotless, blameless and at peace with him' (v14)

Does your family like to make sure that the house is spotless when visitors are coming around? That's what Jesus wants our lives to be like when He suddenly shows up. That's why it's important to have a catch-up with God every day for a little spring cleaning.

It's so important to be good friends with God. What He values the most is for us to live in the way that He says is right, and part of that means saying sorry if we go off on the wrong track. 'Hiding' from God because we know we've done something He wouldn't be pleased with doesn't do any good – and actually means we'll miss out on loads of fun with Him. Instead, let's own up to our mistakes, ask for His forgiveness and move on. That way, if Jesus does surprise the world in our lifetimes, we won't be embarrassed – we'll be over the moon!

PRAY Jesus, thank You that You are the way to God and heaven, and You forgive me. Help me to come to You, not hide from You, when I mess up. I want to always be open with You. Amen.

FAST FORWARD

COMING SOON

Read: Revelation 22:12–21

KEY VERSE: 'Yes, I am coming soon.' (v20)

Coming soon to a cloud near you – Jesus! He's coming back to earth and it could be any moment now...! Or now! Or... even now!

What we do today is important. Our choices affect our future in one way or another. If we choose to put things off like going to bed on time, we might feel very tired the next day.

So how do we live the best life we can? With Jesus, of course! As we read today, Jesus offers us 'the free gift of the water of life' (v17). The Holy Spirit living in us gives us all we need. Without God, we are 'thirsty'. That's not to say that our friends who aren't Christians are all at risk of dying from dehydration. What it means is that something is missing. People try to quench that thirst for God with things like friends, fame, money, popularity – but nothing works. Because we need God, who is the 'living water', to quench that thirst forever.

True, life-changing happiness is being made clean by Jesus and having Him in our lives now and forever.

THINK Are you excited about the day that Jesus comes back to earth? If you are a follower of Jesus, this is something to look forward to.

EVERYBODY NOW!

Read: Psalm 150:1-6

KEY VERSE: 'Let everything that has breath praise the LORD.' (v6)

We've reached our last day of *One You, One Year*! What an incredible time it's been. Well done for sticking it out. It's time to celebrate all that God's done in your life, and today's psalm is a party starter!

It's good to be quiet to listen to God. It's very good to read the Bible and find out about Him. It's also great to talk directly to God about your life.

BUT... sometimes the very best thing we can do – and the thing we need to do the most – is join in with the rest of the universe and praise God with everything we've got.

You can jump around, shout your head off, laugh, sing like nobody's listening, dance across the room, wave your arms around, rip up a guitar solo or even blow a trumpet! God will be praised, and if we don't do it, someone else will.

It's a MASSIVE privilege to praise God. It brings us closer to Him, and it makes the problems we face seem tiny compared to Him!

God's the greatest! Make the most of every opportunity to praise Him.

THINK Think about what you are grateful to God for doing in your journey through *One You, One Year*. Now give Him all the praise!

FAST FORWARD

GET EXCITED ABOUT THE BIBLE, EVERY DAY!

Want to understand the Bible more?

The reading curriculum for *One You, One Year* is adapted from various issues of *YP's*, daily Bible reading notes for ages 11–14.

YP's is packed full of amazing insights into what the Bible actually says, and what it means to live every day for God. Stay in the daily rhythm you're in and order your *YP's* today. It couldn't be easier!

Published every two months.
Available as individual copies or a one-year subscription.

Check it out and buy at cwr.org.uk/youth
Also available from Christian bookshops.

YOUR FRIENDS AND FAMILY ARE UNIQUE AND IMPORTANT TOO!

The Bible has got so much to say about who God is and who we are, and this is the stuff we all really need to hear. To help your friends and family, we've picked out a year's worth of great topics for both boys and girls your age.

Check them out and buy at cwr.org.uk/youth
Also available from Christian bookshops.

MORE GREAT STUFF TO READ...

YP's Guide to the Bible

Want to get stuck into the Bible but don't know where to start? Well, this one's for you! Helpful definitions, timelines, guides to every book in the Bible, and much more.

Guide to Knowing God

See how what you believe about God really does affect your life. This guide will help you to think bigger than ever before – and you'll have fun along the way!

YP's Guide to Starting Secondary School

Starting secondary school can be a bit overwhelming... but help is at hand. This little book is full of useful advice, puzzles, questionnaires and reminders that God is always with you.

YP's for New Christians

Being a Christian sounds great, but what exactly does it involve? In just 30 days you can find out how completely mind-blowing life with God can be.

Check these all out and buy at **cwr.org.uk/youth**
Also available from Christian bookshops.